522-7727 - 8frè
C.a. Boyd
ARI

MW00975493

The KPMG Peat Marwick
1991–92 Business Adviser for Growing Companies

The KPMG Peat Marwick

1991-92 Business Adviser
for
Growing Companies

Mark Stevens and KPMG Peat Marwick

Collier Books

Macmillan Publishing Company

New York

Maxwell Macmillan Canada

Toronto

Maxwell Macmillan International

New York   Oxford   Singapore   Sydney

Copyright © 1991 by Peat Marwick Main & Co. and
Mark Stevens

All rights reserved. No part of this book may be reproduced or
transmitted in any form or by any means, electronic or mechanical,
including photocopying, recording, or by any information storage and
retrieval system, without permission in writing from the Publisher.

Collier Books
Macmillan Publishing Company
866 Third Avenue, New York, NY 10022

Maxwell Macmillan Canada, Inc.
1200 Eglinton Avenue East, Suite 200
Don Mills, Ontario M3C 3N1

Macmillan Publishing Company is part of the
Maxwell Communication Group of Companies.

Library of Congress Cataloging-in-Publication Data
Stevens, Mark, 1947–
    The KPMG Peat Marwick 1991–92 business adviser for
growing companies/Mark Stevens and KPMG Peat Marwick.
        p.   cm.
    ISBN 0-02-034500-3
    1. Small business—Management. I. KPMG Peat Marwick. II.
Title.
HD62.7.S818 1991
658.02′2—dc20   89-24025   CIP

Macmillan books are available at special discounts for bulk purchases
for sales promotions, premiums, fund-raising, or educational use.
For details, contact:

Special Sales Director
Macmillan Publishing Company
866 Third Avenue
New York, NY 10022

10 9 8 7 6 5 4 3 2 1

PRINTED IN THE UNITED STATES OF AMERICA

Contents

Contents

The KPMG Peat Marwick Business Adviser for Growing Companies is not intended to provide a complete discussion of each subject. Consult a professional adviser for assistance with your own situation.

The KPMG Peat Marwick
1991–92 Business Adviser for Growing Companies

Managing a Growing Company

Dynamic Strategic Planning

Planning is for you, for your company, and for success. Never be lulled into thinking you're doing it for somebody else, even if it is prospective investors, your board of directors, or internal pressure that sparks you into it. By taking responsibility for planning, you can get out of the process what you want from it and make it an activity around which company synergy is built. By instilling your company culture with a dynamic planning process, you integrate one of the critical success factors for sustainable growth.

Henry David Thoreau said: "In the long run, men hit only what they aim at." Planning includes aiming and much more. It involves the development of a thorough understanding of your target, your competition, and your own resources. The quality of assessment will determine whether you have the necessary resources to "make a killing" and whether your competition will take away your prize before you fully claim it.

Why Plan?

The competitiveness of industry and the tremendous increase in companies seeking venture capital have made business plans and the business planning process more important than ever before. Today, you wouldn't *think* of trying to raise money from professional investors without a detailed business plan.

However, mention business planning and many an entrepreneur will conjure up memories of long, tedious hours spent writing a document intended to raise capital. To some, formal planning may seem like an expendable activity and "dynamic" business planning may even sound like a contradiction in terms.

"Ironically, because good business planning is rare and seems hard to find time for, its absence or inadequacy is often the underlying cause of business failure—especially in high growth industries," says Gurudev S. Khalsa, a senior manager in KPMG Peat Marwick's Seattle office, who is responsible for strategic management and business planning services. "Because dynamic planning is results-oriented, it translates information into immediate action on the company's true strategic priorities." This approach to planning can be the factor that differentiates one company's success from its competitors' lack thereof.

Khalsa often describes dynamic planning for his clients by explaining what it is not. "Dynamic planning is not primarily about raising money. It is not budgeting. It is not an event nor is it a shelf-dwelling document," he says. "Dynamic planning is a process that inspires strategic thinking, builds consensus, inspires action, and ultimately becomes part of a company's culture. Picture the documentation of a dynamic business plan as a loose-leaf notebook

that is frequently used and easily updated as new information emerges and company strategy evolves."

According to Khalsa, the dynamic planning process:

Starts with commitment and leadership from top management

Creates a shared vision of the company's direction

Uses consensus-building and decentralized participation to bring the plan to life in the minds of those responsible for implementing it

Assesses critically the external factors (including competition) and the internal resources (both strengths and weaknesses) to frame the company's strategic alternatives

Identifies and focuses on the most important strategic issues, which may include market evaluation, product development, marketing strategy, distribution, financing, management, and human resources

Emphasizes strategies and action plans as the "guts" of the process

Establishes time lines and responsibilities for implementation

Solicits feedback from implementation experience to confirm or reconsider goals and strategies

Builds synergy and a dynamic planning mindset that is incorporated into the way the company operates

2

"The last step is particularly important in our concept of this process and our role as its facilitator," says Khalsa. "By bringing strategic issues to the surface and guiding our clients through a process to address them, we help them effect change and make the dynamic planning process their own."

Choosing Members for a Board of Directors

Middle market companies often face significant problems when recruiting board members these days, but a systematic approach to identifying and selecting new directors can improve the process.

The issue of personal liability remains a pertinent factor contributing to this situation, but it is not the only one. Directors must address ever more complicated issues affecting company operations and, in the bargain, make greater time commitments to the board. When a company needs to recruit a new director, management must assess these factors and develop a recruiting strategy that demonstrates to the prospective board member the company's understanding of the specific qualifications and responsibilities required of a new director and how the candidate fulfills these requirements.

Recruiting Format for Directors

Companies should develop and implement formal, systematic approaches to recruiting qualified board members. A company that shows its stockholders it is aggressively seeking the best person to fill a directorship inspires their confidence.

Before beginning a search for a new member, a company should examine its current board to determine its strengths and weaknesses. Rather than tapping a network of personal friends or business acquaintances, management should examine its board committees' needs and responsibilities to determine what specific expertise is required of a new director. Then the organization may implement a formal recruiting program.

Approach

Either the company's directors or an executive search firm may recruit a new board member, but it is important to note that recruiting to fill a directorship requires a different approach than that used to fill a senior management position. Recruiters in search of a director must gather and evaluate all information on potential candidates before approaching them about the position, as opposed to interviewing candidates to determine their qualifications.

The formal approach a company should take to identify and choose a new board member includes these steps:

3

Develop background requirements. The CEO and the board's nominating committee determine the specific experience and duties required of a new director, basing their judgments, in part, on the expertise required by the board's various committees.

Identify qualified individuals. The board or its search firm contacts individuals who are qualified to recommend candidates for the position.

Evaluate potential candidates. Once the research is complete, the nominating committee reviews the candidates' backgrounds to determine which individuals they wish to approach.

Anticipate questions. The directors' and officers' (D&O) liability issue has brought directorships into the limelight, so management should be prepared to discuss candidates' specific questions. What are the company's inherent problems? Is it expanding, maintaining, or losing its market share? Is the company involved in any lawsuits or under investigation by the IRS? Could it be vulnerable to a takeover? Both the board and the potential directors will benefit from the discussion of such pertinent issues.

Meet the potential director. The CEO usually makes the initial contact with the targeted individual. If the candidate is interested in learning more about the opportunity, a meeting with the nominating committee or the full board is arranged. During this meeting, both the directors and the candidate ask questions and decide if they can work together effectively.

Conclusion

A board of directors accomplishes a number of objectives by implementing such a formal selection process. It identifies qualified individuals before those candidates know of the vacancy. More important, by determining the background experience required of a new director, the board is able to give the potential candidate a clear picture of how his or her expertise will be useful to the board. This understanding allows the directors to make an educated, objective choice.

Directors' Advice and Counsel Help Management Grow a Company

"A good board of directors is the cheapest form of consultancy," says John Nash, president of the National Association of Corporate Directors (NACD). But a limited understanding of the board's role can prevent corporate management from capitalizing on that bargain. In the following interview Nash comments on the relationship between boards and management and describes the role directors should play in the governance of middle market companies.

Question: What is the biggest misconception middle market companies have about the role of the board of directors?

Nash: The biggest misconception is that the board is involved in managing the company. Boards do not manage. They are strictly advisory and consulting bodies. Many middle market companies are owned or controlled by their founders. An owner holding 70 percent of the stock may be apt to say, "This is my company. I own it, I can do what I want with it, and I don't need anyone to tell me how to run it." This type of owner needs to understand that boards do not run companies.

In the same vein, middle market owners often feel that directors, by virtue of their position, challenge the power of the CEO and top management. Directors challenge management's assumptions—not its authority.

Question: Isn't there a fine line between challenging assumptions and challenging authority, particularly for the smaller company?

Nash: No, it's not a fine line at all. Take, for example, a company's long-range or strategic planning process. Management draws up the strategic plan. The board's role is to analyze it. In so doing, the board may point out weaknesses in the plan or request more verification that the strategy is the best one for the company. This is not an authority challenge. It is an effort to look out for the best interests of *all* the shareholders, which boards of public companies are legally required to do.

Question: Do boards of smaller companies have more flexibility than boards of larger companies to turn their advisory role into more active participation in the business?

Nash: No. While it is up to the board to know what is going on in the business, it does not immerse itself in the day-to-day operations of the business. Directors do not do management's work.

Question: Do you see any differences between the function of a midsize company's board and that of a larger company's board?

Nash: In a Fortune 100 company the board concentrates more on monitoring management. In a midsize company, however, directors play the larger role of advisers and consultants to management. The middle market CEO usually taps outside directors for their expertise, the caliber of which he or she may not be able to afford in-house on a full-time basis.

Question: You were quoted in a recent issue of *Inc.* magazine as saying that only 5 percent of middle market companies have boards with a majority of outside directors. Should midsize companies be using outside directors more often than they do?

Nash: Depending on the size of the company, the average middle market board has five to seven directors. On a five-member board I'd like to see three outsiders. I have no problem with insiders on the board because, after all, who knows a business better than its management? But, generally, I'd like to see a majority of independent outside directors. They can give more balance, bring valuable expertise to bear, and give the benefit of objectivity rather than emotion. When a board consists of only insiders, it thinks like management. Insiders deal with the day-to-day affairs of the business and may not be thinking about the broader picture. Outsiders bring a good outside view.

Question: What qualifications should a CEO look for in outside directors?

Nash: That depends. Before putting anyone on the board, a CEO should define the company's goals and the board's role in achieving them. For instance, does the company want to broaden its horizons in the international market? If so, maybe the board needs an international marketing expert. Is management planning to take a privately held company public? In that case, someone who has successfully taken a company public may be a valuable addition to the board. Perhaps a $25 million company has plans to become a $50 million company. Well, wouldn't it be great to have as a director a CEO who increased a company's sales from $25 million to $50 million annually in a two- or three-year period?

Question: What is the best way to identify potential board members?

Nash: First, by soliciting recommendations of board candidates from resources who deal with management and boards all the time, such as a company's external accountants. They know who the successful people are and how well a company is run. Outside corporate counsel are also good information sources because they represent other highly successful companies. And bankers loan money to successful companies and know which ones are located in a company's backyard.

Management can also use executive search firms or professional associations. The NACD, for instance, maintains a register of talented people who serve on boards. Business clubs and nonprofit organizations are also great places to meet highly successful businesspeople who might make good corporate directors.

Question: Who shouldn't be considered for board membership?

Nash: Never put customers or suppliers on your board. They will expect favored treatment. You shouldn't put your own attorney, accountant, investment banker, or commercial banker on your board either. That's not to say that these individuals don't make good directors, but you already pay for advice and counsel from them, so why waste a board seat?

Question: Changing corporate circumstances will often dictate a change in board membership. Rather than wait for circumstances to prompt a change, should management simply limit a director's term?

Nash: I run contrary to what a lot of people believe on this point. I personally don't sit on a board for more than five years. I feel that by that time I've made my contribution. If someone is making a major contribution, I suppose there is no reason not to keep that person on the board. But I believe that if a company starts out with a staggered board and rotates one third of its directors every year, it has the opportunity to get rid of dead wood or a director who, for reasons of chemistry, does not get along with management or other board members. It also gives the company the chance to bring in new expertise without increasing board size.

Question: What are the significant issues that the board of a midsize company should be addressing?

Nash: One of the key issues facing the board is to help management determine what business the company is in—its product or service line, customer base, competitive position, and so on—and whether it should be in that business as the company and the industry change over time. Once those parameters are set and a long-range strategic plan is in place, the board serves in an advisory capacity to help the CEO and top management grow the company.

For midsize companies trouble often comes with growth. If a company expands too fast, it can experience financial and possibly legal problems. In this regard, a good board of directors can help a company protect itself from itself. The board is there to make sure the company does not engage in any illegal activity, to see that the proper controls are in place for ensuring orderly growth, to protect shareholders' interests, and to see that the company maintains financial stability in line with its goals and objectives.

To do so, the board must ask tough questions of management and reassure itself that it is getting valid information on which to base decisions. After all, directors can be held legally accountable if they don't.

Question: How important is directors' and officers' liability insurance in the event a shareholder suit is brought?

Nash: Historically, D&O liability insurance has been very costly and difficult for smaller companies to obtain. But today, because of intensified marketplace competition, insurance companies are looking for business wherever they can get it. Now there is broader coverage, rates have started to decline, and D&O is more readily available than it was even a year or two ago. This is advantageous to the director because in today's litigious environment, anyone serving on the board of a closely held company would want D&O coverage. Directors of a privately held company, however, might consider whether they need liability insurance or whether a letter of indemnification from the company would provide sufficient protection, given that the risk of shareholder suit is minimal in a privately held company.

7

Question: Some companies have informal boards of advisers as opposed to a more formal board of directors. When is this a good idea?

Nash: If a company has never had outside directors, it's not a bad idea for the CEO to put one or two outside advisers on the board for six months to a year. In fact, it may be the best way for a company to get its feet wet because, unencumbered by legal liability, either party can simply walk away if he or she feels the arrangement isn't working. One thing to consider as a potential adviser, however, is that a CEO doesn't *have to* heed the suggestions of an advisory director. Some CEOs may want advisers on the board simply to use their names and to give the appearance that all governance requirements are being met.

Question: Finally, what's in all of this for the board member?

Nash: Once you become a president, a CEO, or a highly successful businessperson, you are always looking for new challenges. That's what keeps you young. That's what keeps you going. Through board membership, you get that challenge along with the ego boost of being recognized for your accomplishments by your peers. Serving on a board is also exciting because of the caliber of people you meet, the learning experience it provides, and the satisfaction you feel in helping a company achieve its goals. And it's fun! My advice to prospective directors: If it's not fun, don't do it.

Managing Your Working Capital

Cash Management

Not very many years ago a company measured its total success by how much of its product it was able to sell. Today, that same company may find that its success is heavily influenced by cash flow management. Volatile interest rates, shrinking profit margins, and increasing operating costs have caused most companies to reassess their cash management methods and goals.

The rapid pace of change in today's financial environment requires that control over cash collection and disbursements be maintained. The increasing importance of strict cash con-trol and the development of technology that facilitates the efficient margin of cash movement information have drastically altered the financial environment. Today, cash management is not just a tool to improve profits in the short term but a key to the liquidity necessary for many firms to continue their operations.

Cash Management Overview

Cash management is the systematic integration of the collection, cash concentration and mobilization, disbursement, and information reporting and cash position procedures as defined below:

Collections and accounts receivable management: receiving cash from customers as soon as possible and gaining access to these funds.

Cash concentration and mobilization: bringing cash into one central bank as inexpensively and quickly as possible.

Disbursements, accounts payable, and inventory management: paying suppliers in the proper form, on the specified date, and in the correct amount, and optimizing the investment in inventories, if applicable.

Information reporting and cash position: collecting and transmitting information concerning cash movements to facilitate informed, timely decisions about the daily distribution of the company's cash; measuring current short-term assets and projecting needed levels of liquidity to match nonsynchronized cash flows in order to maximize investment revenues or to minimize financing expense.

These procedures involve credit policies, order entry, shipping, invoicing, accounts receivable management, collection systems, inventory management, payables management, short-term investment and financing, cash forecasting, and bank relationship management. Taken together, they will allow you either to invest additional funds at a reasonable market rate or to lower your borrowing needs.

The primary goals of an efficient, integrated cash management system are:

To reduce the operating costs of the cash flow system so that cash benefits exceed costs

To minimize investment in noncash assets to increase cash or reduce borrowing requirements

To maximize non-interest-bearing or low-interest liabilities to increase cash or reduce borrowing requirements

To "work" cash funds as hard as possible to gain the greatest interest benefits or reduce borrowing costs

To reduce management's involvement in day-to-day cash management operations

To compensate banks fairly, but not excessively, for products used

To pay bills on time and take all discounts

To create invoices and to ship goods as soon as reasonably possible

Collections and Accounts Receivable Management

The objectives of collections and accounts receivable management are to accelerate cash receipts, increase profits through increased sales, minimize the cost of carrying receivables, and minimize bad debts. Some of the questions that should be asked include the following:

Order Entry

How quickly are sales orders turned into invoices?

Are there follow-up procedures for order mistakes/adjustments?

Does the order entry system interface with billing, inventory, and accounts receivable?

Shipping/Freight

How are products shipped?

What are the average monthly freight charges as a percentage of sales?

Billing

How often are bills generated?

Is billing a centralized function?

How does the billing system interface with other related systems?

Remittance Patterns

Who are your major customers?

Are your sales seasonal?

Are discounts taken by customers monitored to determine whether they have been earned?

Remittance Processing

Are remittances received and posted on a centralized basis?

Are payments received in your office?

When and how are remittances deposited at your bank?

Do you have a lockbox?

Are any payments received electronically?

Do you ever receive cash?

Accounts Receivable Management

What are your written credit policies?

Do you age your receivables on a regular basis?

What are your typical trade terms?

Cash Concentration and Mobilization

The objectives of cash concentration and mobilization are to minimize idle cash and to ensure adequate cash or cash equivalents to meet transaction demands, precautionary demands, and speculative demands.

Transaction demands are cash requirements necessary to conduct the "ordinary course" of business, such as purchasing merchandise and paying employees. Precautionary demands are cash requirements for contingent use. Speculative demands are cash requirements to take advantage of any opportunities to earn an abnormal return, such as the opportunity to buy a large quantity of merchandise at a low price. The following questions should be considered:

Cash Transfer

Do you have a central payables account?

Do you have field locations, divisions, or lockboxes making deposits to outlying accounts?

How is cash moved from outlying accounts into the central account?

What criteria are used to judge the optimum transfer mechanism?

Deposit Reporting

How do you capture information about remote deposits?

Do you use a concentration reporting service?

Do you know when you have excess balances in your bank accounts?

Bank Products and Services

What types of bank accounts do you have?

Are you taking advantage of automated investment accounts being offered by banks?

Do you use zero balance accounts to enhance your concentration system?

Are you familiar with account tiering?

Lockboxes, zero balance accounts, and controlled disbursement are three bank products that help in the collection and disbursement process:

Lockbox. A lockbox is a collection service for check payments remitted through the mail to corporations. The service reduces mail time, eliminates processing delays, and improves funds availability. Typically, your company authorizes a bank to act as your agent to receive and process mailed payments. You instruct your customers to remit to your bank's lockbox address, where the bank picks up the mail, transports it back to its processing center, processes the items according to your instructions, and deposits the items into your account.

How do you know if your company needs a lockbox? If you can answer "yes" to any of the following questions, a lockbox could bring you substantial benefits:

Are clerical costs high? Do your clerks spend a large part of their time handling and processing payments? If your clerks had more time, could you delegate some of your daily tasks to them, thereby freeing yourself for more important tasks?

Is theft a problem in your receivables area? Could it become a problem?

Is tracing lost receivable payments a common or time-consuming problem?

Do you currently invest overnight?

Does your bank grant you access to your funds in what you consider a reasonable amount of time?

Zero balance accounts (ZBAs). ZBAs are corporate checking accounts maintained by the bank at zero balance levels for customers who require centralized control of cash while maintaining decentralized disbursement and depository functions. You authorize your bank to open two or more demand deposit accounts. Funds are concentrated in the master account, and at the end of the day, the ZBA activity is posted to the master account and the ZBA's balance is adjusted to zero. In this manner, a ZBA allows the company to keep funds working and reduces the need for forecasting.

When used in concert with controlled disbursing, the ZBA becomes a very powerful disbursement tool, providing control information very early in the day.

Controlled disbursement. Controlled disbursement provides notification, usually prior to noon, of today's presentments against your account. This early notification allows you to fix your daily cash position in time to meet investment market deadlines. Controlled disbursement effectively eliminates the need for daily cash forecasting on transaction accounts and increases fund control.

Are these products right for your company? Once again, a "yes" to any of these questions means that they can bring you some benefits:

Do you write checks? Are you looking for ways to reduce idle balances?

Is your controller spending too much time attempting to forecast disbursements and missing the mark on the forecast too often?

Is your firm moving toward decentralized disbursing but maintaining centralized control?

Managing the float. In addition to the generally well understood accounting elements of the cash flow system, float is an important concept that should be taken into account. Float is the delay built into the normal processing or handling of checks. More specifically, in cash management we deal with several types of float:

Mail float represents the time during which funds are unavailable to a firm because they are moving through the U.S. postal system.

Processing float represents the time during which funds are mired in accounting departments prior to deposit at your bank or while they sit in a bank's lockbox department before they are deposited to your account.

Availability float represents the promise made by your bank defining exactly when your deposited funds will be available to you. The availability offered varies from bank to bank.

Clearing float represents the time it takes an item to move from the deposit bank back to the drawee bank. This process is alternately referred to as presentation float or back float.

Float is always a cost to the corporation. On the collection side, it slows access to funds. On the disbursement side, if not managed properly, funds flow out faster than necessary.

Disbursements, Accounts Payable, and Inventory Management

The objectives of managing disbursements, payables, and inventory are to optimize financing through trade credit, optimize availability of products and services, keep creditors happy and yet not disburse funds before they need to be disbursed, optimize total inventory costs and losses from obsolescence, and reduce the probability of production shutdown due to a shortage of parts or supplies. You should ask these questions:

Disbursements

What types of disbursements do you make?

Is a centralized disbursement bank account used?

How do you fund your disbursing accounts?

Do you make a conscious effort to decelerate the bill payment system?

Supplier Characteristics

Who are your major suppliers and where are they located?

Do you maintain a list of alternative suppliers?

Is there a clearly defined policy for dealing with trade creditors?

Accounts Payable

Is the accounts payable system centralized?

Is selective use of cash discounts made?

Is an aging schedule of payables compiled regularly?

Purchasing

Are capital outlays based on return-on-investment hurdles?

Are lease/purchase alternatives evaluated?

Are the purchasing policies and procedures functioning effectively?

Inventories

Is inventory management centralized?

What percent of assets does each type of inventory represent?

How are order quantities or lot sizes determined?

What are the average carrying costs?

How are safety stock levels evaluated?

Is there a quality control system?

Information Reporting and Cash Position

The objectives of information reporting and determining your cash position are to identify the size and probable timing of borrowings and repayments and to provide meaningful information enabling management to make optimal decisions regarding operating levels, capital expenditures, asset management, and funding.

In addition, the current systems should be monitored so that timely changes may be made as business needs change. You should ask these questions:

Budgeting

On what levels are budgets developed?

Are comparisons made between planned and actual expenses?

Is the budget ever revised during the fiscal year?

Management Reporting

What kinds of management reports are produced?

To whom are these reports distributed?

What is each report's purpose?

Cash Forecasting

Are cash position worksheets prepared?

Are short- and long-term forecasts prepared?

Are actual cash flows compared to forecasts?

Bank Balance Reporting

Are bank account balances monitored regularly?

How is balance information received?

Banking Relationships

Is an account analysis received monthly from each bank?

Are banking charges monitored?

Are banks compensated in fees or balances?

Short-term Investment

Are there investment policies and procedures?

What are your investment objectives?

Are investments made overnight?

Financing and Credit Management

What are your sources of credit?

What are your borrowing limits and guidelines?

Is your borrowing seasonal?

Bank Relationships

Bank Selection

Banks are selected for a variety of reasons ranging from a historical relationship basis to the pricing of certain services. You should select a bank based on types of criteria such as pricing, location, transaction accuracy, availability of credit, and noncredit services. Frequently, more qualitative criteria such as the overall quality of service or innovation is important in the selection of a bank, but these criteria should be well documented. Services offered by banks are becoming increasingly varied and complicated. Many companies are submitting requests for proposal (RFPs) to banks before selecting banks and services. The chart presented opposite lists various criteria to consider in opening accounts.

Bank Service Agreements

With each new bank relationship many banks require a service agreement. It should be negotiated both by the company and by the bank. The agreement must be retained and reviewed on a regular basis to ensure that it is current and requires no modifications. If modifications are required, authorized persons must approve and sign the new agreement. Generally, each agreement should contain the following items:

Service descriptions and pricing

Termination clause

Bank Selection Criteria	
Type of Bank Account	*Criteria*
Local Depository	Location
	Payroll check cashing
	Community involvement
	Financial adequacy
	Competitive pricing
Concentration	Competitive pricing
	Better clearing schedule
	Innovative ways to improve cash management
	Provide major credit needs
	Long-term relationship
	Few operating errors
	Willingness to customize services
	Officer knowledge and expertise
Lockbox	Operational capability
	Responsiveness
	Timely information
	Availability
	Competitive pricing
	Accuracy
	Reporting flexibility
Disbursement	Timely notification
	Operating capability
	Funding requirements
	Competitive pricing
	Float gain
	Early notification
	Reporting flexibility

Warranties

Security agreements

Waivers

Bank Compensation

Bank services are an expensive commodity so the cash manager needs to monitor how the company compensates its banks. Banks can be

16

compensated with fees, compensating balances, or a combination of both. Your company must determine which method is the most cost beneficial.

The account analysis statement provided by the bank is the key source of information necessary to effectively monitor the cost of bank services. From a cash management perspective, it is the most important document a cash manager can receive. The analysis is a detailed statement defining charges for all activities occurring in the account: the associated volumes, the ledger and collected balances, the float, the reserve requirement, the earnings credit rate, and the profit/loss on the account. Typical charges assessed for services may include, but are not limited to, the following:

Checks deposited

Deposits made

Checks paid

Coin and currency deposited

Account maintenance

Automated clearinghouse (ACH) tape deposit
and item charge

Wire transfers initiated/received

Return-item processing

Monitoring Bank Performance

A successful banking relationship requires constant monitoring of a bank's performance. It is critical for keeping the bank attentive to your needs and maximizing the efficient use of your relationship. Performance should be measured in the following areas:

Financial condition

Operational capability

Quality of service

Staff expertise

Pricing

With the increase in the number of bank failures, it has become good corporate policy to monitor the financial condition of the company's banks. Failure to regularly monitor the financial condition of banks increases the potential for losses that can result from relationships with financially unstable banks. There are a number of services a company can subscribe to in order to monitor bank financial and management performance.

When evaluating overall bank performance, the measurement process should attempt to quantify subjective and objective areas. Developing a numerical scale to prioritize issues may be helpful. This would be developed by each individual company. The Bank Report Card on page 18 illustrates one measurement process.

Monitoring bank performance also permits you to continually assess the necessity for each account. Often, companies maintain unnecessary bank accounts either because of a long-term relationship with the bank or because the cash manager is unaware of the superfluous account. Identifying and eliminating such accounts can help to reduce banking costs.

Category Description	Maximum Point Value	Bank A	Bank B
	Bank Report Card		
Financial condition	22		
Comparative cost	18		
Clearing schedule	11		
Long-term relationship	10		
Operation errors	4		
Office knowledge and expertise	6		
Office responsiveness	10		
Account analysis timeliness/accuracy	15		
Innovative ways to improve cash management	4		
	100	—	—

Bank Relationship Management

Communicating expectations to the bank is the key to a successful bank relationship. Expectations are derived from clear performance objectives established by your company as well as the bank's. There should be ongoing conversations with the bank so both parties have a clear understanding of the relationship. If your company is growing, the bank should be willing to cultivate that growth with financial support and counseling.

Loss Prevention in the 1990s: A Look at Inventory Shrinkage

Shoplifters, dishonest employees, and errors in paperwork cause retailers to lose up to $30 billion a year in inventory shrinkage. As a result, shrinkage is being recognized as a major drain on profits throughout the retail industry and is demanding attention from the industry's top executives.

"For many retailers, inventory shrinkage is an elusive problem," says Toby Horowitz, senior manager of loss prevention for Peat Marwick's merchandising practice in New York City. "Unlike profit margins, which can be reported regularly, shrinkage is reported based on a physical inventory taken on an annual or semiannual basis."

Shrinkage represents the difference between inventory indicated in the retailer's books and what is actually found when a physical count of the merchandise is taken. A recent survey conducted by Peat Marwick's national merchandising practice reveals that most retailers attribute their shrinkage to employee theft, followed by shoplifting and paperwork error. Moreover, they believe that 40 percent of their losses occur at the point of sale. For the majority of retailers, shrinkage averages 2 to 3 percent of sales, which is a large percentage of their pretax earnings.

18

In the past, internal loss prevention involved making sure dishonest employees didn't walk out of the store with merchandise under their arms. Today, retailers must also deal with employees participating in sophisticated credit card scams involving thousands of dollars.

Employees don't have to be dishonest to contribute to a shrinkage problem. A major cause of shrinkage is poor inventory management such as mistakes in accounting, unrecorded markdowns or price changes, poor physical inventories, employee discount abuse, and errors in coupon processing. "Inadequate shipping and receiving procedures, system programming errors, and incorrect reporting and/or return of damaged goods to vendors are areas frequently identified as causes for shrinkage," says James J. Tuchi, a principal in management consulting for the wholesale distribution and manufacturing practice in Peat Marwick's Short Hills, New Jersey, office.

The retail environment has changed from the days when a store's profit margin was so high that shrinkage didn't matter. Because inventory shrinkage is a major profit drain, its effective control represents a significant profit opportunity. Inventory shrinkage should be thought of as a controllable expense and not as a cost of doing business. "Today, shrinkage is affected by a host of industrywide, even nationwide, trends," says Horowitz. "Chronic labor shortages around the country are making it increasingly difficult for retailers to find and retain a suitable, stable, work force." Retailers are being forced to lower their hiring standards or rely on part-time help to staff their stores. The result has been a marked decline in service and growing inventory shortfalls. While retailers cannot solve the labor crisis, they can respond to it by strengthening employee training and education and tailoring it to fit the needs of a more mobile work force. Making employees aware of the company's loss prevention efforts and the severity of the issue are also key factors in preventing theft and errors.

A second major trend affecting retailers is the drug abuse problem and its presence in the work force. "There is a real concern in the industry regarding vulnerability to theft to support drug habits," explains Wendy Farina, senior consultant in Peat Marwick's loss prevention practice in New York City. "The correlation between drug use and the rise in both internal and external theft is easy to see. Not so obvious are the affects drugs have on the existing employee base."

Increased absenteeism, deteriorating productivity and performance, and emotional problems have an indirect impact on the employer's profitability. To combat this problem, many companies have instituted substance abuse testing programs. Typically these programs consist of "pre-hire" testing, "for cause" testing, and/or employee assistance programs. One retailer's pre-hire testing of 1,881 applicants found that 294 (15.6 percent) tested positive.

Finally, retailers who have undergone a merger, acquisition, or restructuring have an additional reason to take a strategic approach to loss prevention. Pressure to lower expenses and raise margins, coupled with reduced levels of supervision, make shrinkage control a top priority. Changes in organizational structure, for example, can often dramatically reduce shrinkage in a newly structured or merged company.

Many retailers are taking new approaches in their loss prevention programs. For example, recent changes in the law have all but eliminated the use of the polygraph, once considered a critical loss prevention tool. New restrictions have also been placed on its use in investigations, further limiting a retailer's course of action. Monitoring of sales transactions using personal computers and closed-circuit television has proved effective in reducing employee theft. "Paying special attention to your everyday transactions—checks, coupons, rebates, gift certificates, and merchandise credits—can uncover hidden sources of shrinkage," says Horowitz.

A strategic approach to a loss prevention program seeks to identify the underlying causes of shrinkage and employs a combination of techniques and technologies uniquely suited to the retailer. "The one common thread between inventory shrinkage and the solution is management's understanding of the problem and the commitment it makes to fix it," says Horowitz.

3

Financing Your Company

3-29-93

Every middle market company shares at least one concern: They need to raise capital on the best possible terms. Yet many owners and executives, while expert at managing their businesses, approach the subject of financing with uncertainty and sometimes even apprehension. This is understandable given today's tough lending environment and the complexity of the credit and equity markets. The purpose of this section is to ease this uncertainty and apprehension by providing an accurate and convenient source of current information on financing alternatives.

The Middle Market Challenge

Smaller companies are the backbone of the American economy, accounting for a disproportionate number of new jobs and new products. Yet middle market companies often find it difficult to raise capital on any terms.

There's an old joke among bankers that it takes a week to authorize a $2 million loan but a month or longer to approve a $500,000 loan. This is certainly an exaggeration, but the humor does illustrate a very real dilemma: Middle market companies seeking to raise capital in the $500,000 to $2 million range often have more difficulty than companies seeking to raise more or less funds. The reason? Loans under $500,000 can often be guaranteed by the borrower's personal assets, eliminating the need for a lengthy—and expensive—collateral investigation by the bank. Loans over $2 million adequately compensate the lender for the administrative costs of making the loan. But loans falling between these amounts tend to be the least profitable for a lender and can therefore be harder to obtain and carry higher rates.

Ironically, it is fast-growing companies that often have the most difficult time securing financing. Lenders and investors are sometimes afraid that these high-flying companies will grow out of control. That's why many lenders and investors prefer a company with a solid track record and moderate, predictable, and, above all, manageable growth.

The current economic environment makes raising capital even more difficult for middle market companies. Interest rates remain stubbornly high and credit availability has been constricted due to well-publicized failures in the savings and loan industry. Also, the collapse of the junk bond market in 1990 has at least temporarily dried up this once abundant source of financing.

Little wonder, given this environment, that many middle market executives are more concerned with the *availability* of capital than with the terms of the financing.

Despite these challenges, your company *can* secure the financing it needs to continue to flourish. The small-business owner today

has a wider range of financing alternatives than ever before. The key to securing financing is understanding the advantages and disadvantages of each financing source, the typical financing terms offered by each source, and the qualities that the sources are seeking in borrowers.

Outlined below are the pros and cons of each major financing alternative, describing the usual terms and briefly assessing when and why the alternative could be appropriate for your company.

Internal Capital

One of the most readily available sources of financing is also the most overlooked—generating cash through the improved management of cash inflows and outflows.

Before turning to outside sources for cash, including banks and the equity markets, a growing business should always carefully review its internal policies and procedures to determine if it is maximizing the amount of cash generated by its operations. In most instances, the ability to generate or earmark needed capital from within an organization will produce a lower cost of capital than going outside of the company. Even well-managed companies are often surprised to discover that internal financing can eliminate the need for additional external funds.

Accounts Receivables Management

Proper management of accounts receivable can accelerate cash receipts, boost profits through increased sales, minimize the cost of carrying receivables, and minimize bad debts. Even for a small company, improved receivables management can represent a potentially large source of new funds.

A proper receivables management enhancement program looks at every phase of the order cycle from order entry through remittance processing.

Order entry. How quickly are sales orders turned into invoices? Are there follow-up procedures for order mistakes? Does the order entry system interface with billing, inventory, and accounts receivable?

Shipping/freight. How often are bills generated? Is billing a centralized function? How does the billing system interface with other related systems?

Credit policies. Credit terms should always be structured to accelerate payment to the extent that industry practices allow. Credit strategies that can expedite payment include requiring deposits upon order and progress billings for custom items. Favorable credit terms for individual customers should be moni-

tored on an ongoing basis to ensure that they are justified by current activity.

Remittance processing. The manner in which customer payments are processed can greatly increase cash flow. Strategies for improved remittance processing include using a lockbox system and establishing electronic funds transfer between your company and its customers.

Billing and collection. Aggressive follow-up can often improve receivables collection, although the cost of such procedures must be carefully weighed against the expected benefits. Big-ticket items should be billed as soon as possible after shipment. However, for continuous purchases by customers, cycle billing, in which a certain number of customers are billed on a specified day every month, may even out cash flow while minimizing the expense of billing.

Supplier/Trade Credit

Supplier or trade credit should be used whenever possible. This type of credit can be one of the easiest sources of capital to obtain and is certainly one of the least costly sources of financing.

While there is no explicit cost of supplier credit, failure to take advantage of discounts offered by suppliers can often translate to substantial annual costs.

Inventory Turnover

A company's inventory represents an investment of cash, and for many companies, inventory is the largest asset on the balance sheet. Effective management of the inventory investment must balance the costs of holding inventory with the company's customer service objectives.

The costs associated with excess inventory include acquisition costs such as materials, purchasing, and shipping expenses; assembly costs such as direct labor; and holding costs such as rent, warehousing, interest, insurance, damage, and obsolescence costs.

These costs must be carefully evaluated against the benefits of maintaining a high level of inventory. These include customer satisfaction through the immediate availability of products and the reduced probability of a production shutdown due to shortages of parts or supplies.

The optimum inventory level minimizes carrying costs while ensuring the appropriate safety stock levels. Achieving this level will free up cash for operating needs and long-term investment.

Fixed Assets

The need to acquire new property and equipment is often the reason a company seeks new financing. The initial investment in fixed assets can be significant while the benefits, including anticipated cash flows, are usually realized over several years. Because of this, fixed assets usually require long-term financing. Many companies, in their eagerness to expand, succumb to the temptation of acquiring fixed assets through short-term financing. Remember, borrowing short term to finance long term is usually unwise since fixed assets rarely generate adequate cash, in the short run, to pay the interest expense and principal on short-term debt.

Fixed assets can be a source as well as a use of cash. In evaluating internal financing possibilities, be alert for opportunities to turn fixed assets into cash. An obvious example is selling excess or unused equipment. Sale and lease-back arrangements can also be used to generate cash while retaining the benefit of a piece of equipment or other asset.

Disbursements and Accounts Payable Management

The longer a company can hold onto its money before paying vendors, the greater the return it can earn on its cash. The objective is, therefore, to disburse funds to vendors only when required while maintaining productive relations with those creditors.

Many companies underestimate the value of this source of capital, but consider this example:

A company with $2 million in revenues buys $1.2 million in goods and services a year. If this company pays its bills every thirty days, it has effectively obtained $100,000 of steady financing at no cost. If this company were to pay its vendors every sixty days instead of every thirty days, it would effectively "borrow" another $100,000—again at no cost.

Obviously, the amount of funds available from simply delaying payment is limited, probably to a maximum of ninety days. Common credit terms in your industry affect both the amount you can get from this source and the rate you will pay for the funds. Within these restrictions, however, companies still have a broad array of vendor strategies that can maximize their cash position:

Invoices should be dated upon receipt and payment made based on when the purchased material is received or on the invoice date, if later.

Invoices offering early-payment discounts should be paid quickly, but only if the discount makes economic sense. Invoices without discounts should be paid at the latest possible date.

Employing an aging schedule of payments, if it is compiled regularly, can free up cash for additional purchases and sometimes eliminate the need to seek outside financing.

Debt Capital

Debt is the most prevalent form of external financing for middle market companies. Debt provides opportunities for financial leverage (in the form of increased earnings) to current owners' benefit. As long as the company can invest the proceeds of its borrowings at a rate of return higher than the cost of the borrowed funds, the difference will always flow to the bottom line.

A prime reason for the popularity of debt is that, unlike equity, it enables the shareholders to retain ownership and control. Debt is also easier to obtain than equity owing to the greater number of debt sources, including banks, insurance companies, savings and loans, and leasing companies.

Debt is a highly flexible form of capital. It can be secured or unsecured. It can be short, intermediate, or long term, enabling a business to match its capital needs with the appropriate capital sources. Finally, the interest cost of servicing debt is tax deductible.

Debt is not without its disadvantages, however. Unlike equity, debt is not permanent capital and it must be repaid. Interest and principal must be repaid regardless of the operating performance of the business, reducing operating flexibility. And because debt has a prior claim on a company's assets, it can reduce the company's attractiveness to other financing sources, thereby reducing access to future capital.

Given these advantages and disadvantages, debt should be considered an appropriate alternative under the following conditions:

Your company is able to repay. The financial risk associated with debt is minimized when

25

the business has a demonstrated ability to repay on a timely basis.

Assets are available as collateral. Debt is an attractive financing tool when a company has available assets to serve as collateral; this means that less stockholder money is needed to finance working capital and/or acquire additional assets.

Cost is less than equity. This will depend on the prevailing interest rates, the overall structure of the financing transaction, and the creditworthiness of the company.

Commercial Banks

Commercial banks are the most widely used, best known, and most flexible source of capital. Banks will finance equipment, make equipment leasing loans, make working-capital loans, take facility mortgages, and meet a host of other needs.

When to use. Commercial bank loans are most often used to meet a company's working-capital needs. Such loans are also used to provide capital for the general expansion of the business such as moving into new markets or expansion of the product line or sales force. Commercial bank loans can also finance machinery purchases and the acquisition of real estate.

Advantages. Commercial banks aim to be "full service" institutions, meeting virtually all the banking and financial service needs of a company. For middle market companies, this makes commercial banks a single, convenient, and flexible source of capital. Commercial banks are also usually the low-cost provider of capital to middle market companies.

Disadvantages. Commercial banks prefer to lend to stable businesses with an established track record and a management that has demonstrated its ability to successfully run the company. This means that commercial banks generally avoid start-ups and troubled companies. Commercial banks will usually require personal collateral as guarantee for the debt.

Cost. Today, most commercial bank loans involve a floating rate that varies in relation to an established benchmark, usually the prime lending rate. Occasionally, a bank will allow a company to negotiate a fixed rate position. In addition, there are often various interest rate protection arrangements that can be purchased to protect a company in a floating rate financing situation from dramatically increasing rates.

The cost of a loan could range from the prime lending rate to prime plus four or five percentage points. This will depend on the strength of your company's operations, balance sheets, and collateral position.

Deal structure. Maturities of commercial bank loans vary widely. Commercial banks, in order to compete with other debt financing sources, have become much more flexible in this area than they have been in the past. Maturities can range from ninety days for a demand (or short-term) note to ten to twelve years for long-term loans. Mortgage loans on real estate may have longer terms, sometimes extending to between fifteen and twenty-five years.

Commercial banks may also make available committed lines of credit for a period of time up to several years. Maturities of these loan commitments generally fall between demand notes and term loans.

Depending on the financial history of the company and its prospects for the future, commercial bank loans can be unsecured. Blanket liens or general floating liens covering all of the company's assets or specific liens on specific assets may be required. Commercial bank loans usually require personal guarantees to ensure the commitment of the individual business owner and to provide a collateral or backstop position for the lender.

Asset-based Lenders

Asset-based lenders include commercial finance companies and factors. In asset-based lending, a company uses its current assets and occasionally its fixed assets as collateral to obtain a revolving loan. Current assets include accounts receivable and inventory.

Factoring is a centuries-old method of asset-based financing appropriate for any manufacturer or distributor to mass merchandise outlets. Typically, a factor purchases the borrower's receivables and extends funds prior to collection of those receivables, charging a commission that varies with the factor's perceived risk.

When to use. Asset-based financing is most often used to provide working capital as well as to provide capital for the purchase of equipment, machinery, and real estate. Asset-based lending is also commonly used in financing acquisitions, especially leveraged buyouts.

Advantages. Unlike commercial banks, asset-based lenders will often consider lending to troubled or equity-poor companies. Since asset-based lenders require inventory and/or receivables as collateral, they are particularly receptive to companies with high inventory and/or receivables turnover. While some asset-based lenders will write a loan for six months to a year, the payback on an asset-based loan is often open, provided the borrower's collateral remains fresh. The revolving nature of such loans permits flexibility since the asset-based collateralizing loan grows with a company's expanding operations.

Disadvantages. While the strength of a borrower required by asset-based lenders is low, the cost of funds is often inversely high, making asset-based loans one of the most costly types of debt financing. If the borrower's collateral base contracts (even for valid business reasons), the company may suddenly have to repay part of the loan. Since asset-based loans usually start off as demand notes, if the company runs into problems the lender can move quickly to take control and liquidate the collateral.

Cost. Asset-based loans virtually always use a floating rate based on the prime lending rate or another established benchmark. The cost typically ranges from prime plus 1 percent to prime plus 6 percent.

Deal structure. Most asset-based loans are revolving credit agreements ("revolver" or "evergreen" loans), but some finance companies will write loans with terms ranging from one to ten years. Asset-based lenders require first liens on the specific assets financed and most will require personal guarantees.

Savings and Loans

Over the past decade, savings and loans have become much more aggressive lenders to middle market companies. Their original business (savings accounts for attracting money and mortgages for the generation of income) has become extremely competitive and regulatory bodies, which once barred S&Ls from commercial lending, now permit them to enter this area. The much-publicized S&L crisis of the late 1980s and early 1990s will undoubtedly affect these institutions and their lending arrangements for many years to come.

When to use. S&Ls most often make loans for real estate acquisition or refinancing. However, S&Ls will also lend for the purchase of machinery and equipment and at times they have loaned to companies for working-capital needs.

Advantages. S&Ls are usually the most experienced real estate lenders. They are frequently able to offer attractive rates, thanks in part to their relatively low and oftentimes fixed cost of money. And S&Ls generally offer attractive loan-to-asset-value ratios, which means that they will sometimes lend more to a company on a given property than will a commercial bank.

Disadvantages. S&Ls usually prefer to lend to strongly capitalized and well-established businesses. In the wake of the S&L crisis, these institutions are resuming their traditionally conservative attitude toward commercial loans. This means that they are being very careful when considering working-capital loan requests, preferring to lend for real estate, machinery, and equipment purchases, where the collateral position is stronger.

Cost. S&L loans are usually priced competitively with commercial banks. Real estate and machinery/equipment loans often carry a variable rate, although fixed rates are sometimes available. Working-capital loan pricing usually floats with the prime rate; again, competitive with commercial banks.

Deal structure. Real estate loans usually have maturities of ten to twenty-five years, although there is some opportunity for a longer amortization with a mid-term balloon. Machinery and equipment loans generally have maturities of no longer than ten years.

Loans from S&Ls are virtually always fully secured by the specific assets to be financed by the loan or by a backup of liquid assets (such as marketable securities). S&Ls will generally loan up to 70 percent of the fair market value of real estate. For machinery and equipment, the loan-to-value ratio is generally 60 percent of the quick liquidation value, sometimes called the "hammer value."

Leasing Companies

Leasing companies can be an excellent way to finance machinery and equipment. Often overlooked as a financing source, a lease is really just another form of financing.

When to use. Leasing is most often used to acquire machinery and equipment, although real estate can also be leased. Leases can be used as part of a financing package to fund an acquisition.

Advantages. The principal benefit of leasing is that you may be able to finance 100 percent of an asset's cost with little or no down payment. The lessee also may have little or no risk of ownership—such as obsolescence—and leases are usually relatively easy to enter into.

Leasing companies generally require at least an average credit rating.

Disadvantages. Leases may carry a higher cost than other types of debt. The benefits of ownership—such as appreciation of the leased asset—are usually retained by the lessor. Leasing calls for "collateral give-up," even though you may have the leased equipment appearing on your books, it is, in fact, collateral for the lease agreement and therefore it is not available to support another loan.

Cost. The cost of a lease ranges from prime (although it will rarely be that low) to prime plus 6 percent. The cost of the lease may be reduced if it is structured to provide tax advantages to the leasing company; the cost of the lease will be increased if the tax advantages are structured to benefit the lessee.

Deal structure. The length of payback will vary depending on the nature of the asset being leased and the type of lease. An operating lease is generally short term while a financing lease usually approximates the useful life of the asset being leased.

Since the lessor retains title to the asset during the lease term, leasing is generally a form of secured lending.

Life Insurance Companies and Pension Funds

Life insurance companies and pension funds may be appropriate financing sources if you are seeking a large amount of capital. However, keep in mind that generalizations are risky since each will have its own investment preferences, differing amounts of capital to loan, individual cost factors, and target rates of return.

When to use. Insurance companies will lend for long-term working-capital or growth-capital needs. They will also finance the purchase of real estate, machinery, and equipment.

Advantages. The principal benefit of insurance company and pension fund loans is the possibility of a fixed interest rate commensurate with your credit rating. This makes them good sources of long-term debt capital.

Disadvantages. The minimum loan amounts may be too high for many middle market companies. While some insurance companies and pension funds will be interested in loan requests as low as $500,000, others may not lend below $2 million. Insurance company and pension fund loans often contain restrictive covenants, many of which will be standardized and nonnegotiable by the lender.

Cost. In the past, insurance companies and pension funds offered fixed-rate loans tied to long-term market rates; this is because of the fixed-cost nature of their own investments. Recently, many insurers and pension funds have moved to variable rates.

Deal structure. Maturities will vary depending on the use of the proceeds of the loan, typically between five and ten years with longer maturities sometimes available on real estate financing transactions.

When borrowers are financially strong and have a good track record and solid management, debt from life insurance companies and pension funds may be in the form of unsecured debentures or straight unsecured debt. When the loans are for the purchase of assets, they are usually secured by those assets.

Small Business Administration

Small Business Administration (SBA) loans are available to independently owned businesses that are not dominant in their industry. There are special programs to assist women, minorities, the handicapped, and veterans in business.

There are two basic SBA loan programs: guaranty loans and direct loans.

Guaranty loans are made by a private lending source, most often a bank. Up to 90 percent of the loan is guaranteed by the SBA with a maximum guarantee of $500,000. Loans exceeding $155,000 can carry a maximum guarantee by the SBA of 85 percent. In return for these guarantees, the lender must pay a fee (a small portion of the interest charged the borrower) to the SBA. The original lender must still make a separate credit decision on making the loan, but may be more understanding in evaluating loan applications that will be protected by an 85 percent or 90 percent government guarantee in the event of default.

Direct loans up to a maximum of $150,000 may be available to small businesses unable to qualify for an SBA guaranteed loan. Funds for direct loans are allocated geographically and are extremely limited: They are generally available only to businesses that fall into certain categories such as companies owned by Vietnam veterans or the handicapped or businesses located in high-unemployment areas.

When to use. SBA loan programs are designed to assist companies whose debt-to-equity ratios or credit ratings disqualify them for conventional financing. SBA loans can be used to finance working-capital requirements, purchase machinery and equipment, or to acquire and/or renovate real estate that is owned by the company and used in the operation of its business.

Advantages. The SBA is the lender of last resort for companies with high debt-to-equity ratios or poor credit ratings. The cost of these loans does not necessarily reflect their higher credit risk. They can be used to finance a wide variety of assets.

Disadvantages. SBA loans can be difficult to obtain due to the scarcity of direct loan funds and to the red tape and paperwork involved in arranging a guaranteed loan. There are often high closing costs involved, particularly legal fees, and the collateral and personal guarantee requirements are stringent.

Cost. SBA loans may be structured with variable or fixed interest rates, although there are government/SBA maximums. Interest rates for guaranteed loans are negotiated between the borrower and the lender within the imposed maximums.

Interest rates on loans with maturities of less than seven years cannot exceed 2.25 percent over the prime rate.

Interest rates on loans with maturities of seven years or more cannot exceed 2.75 percent over the prime rate.

Interest rates on direct loans are structured around the federal government's cost of money.

Deal structure. The maturities of SBA loans depend on the use of the proceeds, ranging from short-term loans to those up to twenty-five years. The typical term is between seven and fifteen years.

SBA loans are always secured with liens on business assets. Personal guarantees by owners and chief executive officers (even if they don't own the business) are always required. Liens on personal assets of company principals may also be required when there is a shortfall in business assets.

Equity Capital

Raising equity capital involves transferring a portion of an owner's interest in a business to an investor or group of investors in return for an infusion of funds. The chief advantage of equity over debt is that equity is a permanent form of capital; no repayment is required. The cash flow cost of equity (in the form of dividends) is determined by the company rather than the lender.

The principal disadvantage of equity is its dilution of the ownership of the current owner or stockholders. Equity can be an extremely expensive form of capital, especially for a rapidly growing business. And dividends on equity, unlike interest payments on debt, are not tax deductible.

If you are not averse to sharing ownership of your business with an investor or investors, equity can be an appropriate financing alternative. Raising capital through equity spreads the risk of loss across a broader base of investors—but remember, it also spreads any potential gain. If your company already has a high level of debt, equity may be your only alternative for raising additional capital.

Private Placements

Individual investors and corporations are perhaps the most abundant source of equity capital for small and medium-sized companies. Family members and friends may believe in your business—or in you personally—and might therefore be more willing than a professional lender or venture capital firm to risk their money in return for a stake in your business. Your suppliers may also be interested in investing in your business to maintain a productive relationship, as might current or prospective customers who need your product or service.

Wealthy individuals with no prior connection to your business are another source of equity capital. These "angels" are often eager to take an equity position in middle market companies with solid growth prospects. The "angel network" is usually informal, although your company's attorneys or accountants may be able to introduce you to interested investors. In some areas, the network has become more formalized. For example, the New Hampshire Venture Capital Network, a not-for-profit corporation managed by the University of New Hampshire, connects high-net-worth individuals with entrepreneurs seeking start-up or expansion capital.

When to use. Private placements are most appropriate in start-up situations. Wealthy individuals and corporations frequently provide seed capital in the early stages of a company. Investments range from as little as $25,000 to $500,000 and up.

Advantages. Individual investors usually have more flexibility than institutions, permitting a bit more latitude in negotiations. While prudent investors will always carefully evaluate potential risks, they may have more leeway in determining return-on-investment hurdles and can frequently take a longer-term approach than more conventional investors.

Disadvantages. As with most types of equity, private placements are an expensive way to raise capital and require that the owner give up equity—often a substantial amount of it—to the investor.

Cost. The cost of the equity give-up has to be calculated within a number of assumed parameters such as the current value of the company and its projected growth in earnings. The interest cost on any loan or subordinated loan position that accompanies this form of capital has to be added to this cost.

Deal structure. The structure of the investment is flexible, depending on the investor's preference and tax and investment objectives. The most common form of investment is common stock and/or a subordinated loan.

Professional Venture Capitalists

Venture capitalists provide capital to start-up or growing companies in return for a portion of equity. Venture capital firms spread their risk over a number of companies, expecting potentially huge returns from a handful of investments to compensate for the inevitable losses in others.

When to use. Venture capital firms are interested in companies with extremely high growth rates. They prefer businesses that are projected to grow to substantial annual sales levels ($50 million and up) within three to five years. They are looking to invest in companies that might go public at some point, and prefer businesses that have proprietary products with a large potential market. Venture capitalists generally invest a minimum of $250,000 to $500,000.

Advantages. Although the amount of funds available through venture capitalists fluctuates, there is usually abundant capital for promising companies. Leading venture capitalists often bring to the companies in which they invest their own business expertise and, in some cases, their invaluable contacts.

Disadvantages. Venture capital firms often expect companies they invest in to go public in order to maximize the liquid value of their investment. This means that pressure from them for sales and profit growth can be intense.

Cost. For owners, the value of the equity they give up is the major cost of venture capital. Venture capitalists usually prefer a four- to seven-year investment horizon. They target a range of four to fifteen times the money they have invested over the investment horizon, generally translating into a 30 to 40 percent annual return.

33

Deal structure. Although the structure of a venture capital deal varies from company to company, common stock is the most frequently used form of equity. Recently, some venture capitalists have been offsetting their risk by including put-options in their agreements that would require the company to buy back its stock at a point in time in the future at a specified price in the event the company does not go public. In these cases, owners often insist on calls that give them the right to force the venture capitalist to sell the stock back, usually at a specified price.

Public Equity Markets

The term "going public" refers to a closely held company's first sale of securities to the general public. In deciding whether or not to go public, it is helpful to evaluate a company from an underwriter's or investor's perspective.

Underwriters and the investing public look first to the quality, integrity, and experience of management as a key indicator that an investment will be protected and enhanced. They prefer steady earnings growth in excess of 20 percent a year. They look for companies with revenues of at least $20 million and net earnings of at least $1 million.

When to use. The public equity markets are best for companies that need large amounts of equity capital. Companies should consider going public when their operations, prospects, and market conditions combine to place a high potential value on their common stock. A public offering may also be recommended when owners wish to liquidate a portion of their current holdings.

Advantages. Going public gives a company access to large amounts of capital without restrictions on the use of the funds other than those stated as part of the offering. The sale of equity securities will increase the company's net worth and generally improve the company's borrowing capability. The ability to offer stock-based compensation plans to key employees can help attract and retain managerial talent.

Disadvantages. A company loses some flexibility when it goes public, becoming subject to a host of regulatory constraints. The company's goals and energies must be directed toward increasing the price of its stock. There is also the possibility of the original owners losing control of the company.

Cost. The cost of a public offering can be substantial when taking into account underwriter's commissions and legal and accounting fees. In addition, the ongoing expense of being a public company can be significant.

Deal structure. Public offerings almost always involve common stock. Warrants are sometimes coupled with the stock in order to form a "unit."

SBICs and SSBICs

Small Business Investment Companies (SBICs) and Specialized Small Business Investment Companies (SSBICs—operated for the economically and socially disadvantaged) support start-up and young companies through a combination of debt and equity financing. There are approximately three hundred to four hundred SBICs and SSBICs operating around the country. They are regulated but not owned by the Small Business Administration.

When to use. Like venture capitalists, SBICs prefer fast-growth companies that are likely to go public within five years. SBIC and SSBIC capital can be used for expansion, working capital, and start-up capital. These funds can also be used in acquisition and leveraged-buyout financing. The typical range of investment is between $100,000 and $1 million.

Advantages. SBICs and SSBICs provide risk/equity capital that may not be available elsewhere. They offer opportunity to augment a company's equity base through subordinated debt, which opens up other possible borrowing situations.

Disadvantages. SBICs usually require some equity and could insist upon control or significant influence over the business. SBIC debt is usually convertible to stock, which means that if your company's value skyrockets, you may give up more than you initially intended. SBIC

agreements also frequently contain restrictive covenants limiting salaries, capital expenditures, and dividends.

Cost. The cost of SBIC and SSBIC capital relates to an interest rate on the debt or a dividend on stock investments, plus equity participation in the company.

Deal structure. The structure of an SBIC or SSBIC investment can be either straight debt or straight equity. However, most investments involve some form of hybrid security to provide the SBIC with the potential for ownership in the business. This may mean convertible debt or subordinated debt with attached warrants to purchase common stock.

For a directory of SBICs send $5.00 to the National Association of SBICs, Suite 1101, 1156 15th Street, N.W., Washington, D.C. 20005.

Merchant Bankers

Merchant bankers invest in companies that need to recapitalize. They provide senior or subordinated debt and/or equity with the expectation that the company will redeem the obligation within three to five years. At that point, management would once again own the entire company. Unlike a venture capitalist, the merchant banker is *not* looking for the company to redeem its investment by going public.

When to use. Merchant banks are excellent capital sources for companies going through a restructuring. These companies should have stable earnings, consistent cash flow, and a strong asset base capable of supporting other financing, if necessary. Merchant bankers usually invest in companies with sales over $10 million and/or capitalization over $5 million. They look for strong management with a substantial portion of their net worth at stake in the company.

Advantages. Most merchant banks help recapitalize a company and then have the company "take out" the bank with funds from operations. This leaves management with 100 percent ownership. Merchant bankers rarely insist on exercising control of the company.

Disadvantages. This is a somewhat limited source of capital as there are currently relatively few merchant banks. Merchant bankers only invest their capital in financially stable companies—which may be the ones who need it least!

Cost. For subordinated debt, merchant bankers look for a return of 20 to 25 percent, which may include some current return in the form of interest to compensate them for the cost of money as well as warrants, options, or outright equity, based on the cost of money. For equity investments, merchant bankers may seek a 35 to 40 percent annual return.

Deal structure. Merchant banking deals can be straight equity investments, may involve senior or subordinated debt, or could be a combination of the two.

Small Business Innovation Research Program

The Small Business Innovation Research (SBIR) program is designed to stimulate technological innovation by allocating a portion of federal research and development funds for direct awards to small, innovative companies. These represent a form of "equity" financing in that they provide funds to pursue research without a repayment requirement. Phase I SBIR awards provide up to $50,000 for a preliminary feasibility study. Phase II awards provide up to $500,000 to continue research of promising projects. In Phase III, companies must arrange for private-sector capital (or regular government contracts) to commercialize the new technologies.

When to use. The SBIR program is a unique source of seed capital for funding high-risk feasibility-related research. SBIR funds can also serve as expansion capital, allowing companies to explore new technology areas with funds not available internally.

Advantages. SBIR awards are a low-cost funding source with no ownership dilution. They provide experience and credibility in the government contract arena, which can be a significant market opportunity.

Disadvantages. Funds provided by SBIR awards are usually limited to $550,000 per project, assuming maximum funding under Phases I and II. In addition, a funding lag between Phase I and Phase II, which averages eight months, can create financial and continuity problems for smaller companies.

Cost. A commitment of personnel and resources to SBIR proposal preparation represents the only "cost" of the program.

Deal structure. The majority of SBIR awards take the form of contracts. Grants and cooperative agreements may also be used. Rights to technology developed under the program remain with the company. However, the government receives a royalty-free license for internal use of the technology by the government.

Employee Stock Ownership Plans

An Employee Stock Ownership Plan (ESOP) is essentially a form of internal financing in that it amounts to selling a piece of your company to your employees.

An ESOP works like this: The company helps to finance or guarantee a bank loan, enabling the ESOP to use the proceeds to buy company stock, thus producing cash for the company. The company makes annual contributions to the ESOP in the form of employee benefit contributions and gets a tax deduction in return. The ESOP in turn uses the contributions to repay the bank loan.

Though a form of employee benefit plan such as a pension or profit-sharing plan, an ESOP differs from traditional benefit plans in two important ways. First, an ESOP invests primarily in the securities of the sponsoring corporation while a pension or profit-sharing plan invests proceeds in a diversified portfolio of securities. Second, because an ESOP may borrow money on employer credit, it is an important corporate financing tool. ESOP indebtedness must be reflected on the balance sheet of the employer as debt, which is offset by a reduction of shareholders' equity.

When to use. ESOPs are appropriate for raising capital for a wide range of needs including the purchase of a plant or equipment as well as working capital. However, some companies are more suited to ESOPs than others. If top management runs the company mostly to support its lifestyle, the company is probably not the best candidate for an ESOP. Once employees are shareholders, they may have rights under state or federal laws to receive annual financial reports and to question executive perks, among other things. If your goal is to build a business by retaining profits, however, your company is a better prospect for an ESOP.

Advantages. ESOPs can be an extremely attractive form of financing for a growing middle market company. Contributions to an ESOP that are used to repay bank debt are fully tax deductible (within limits), making repayment of both the principal and the interest on debt tax deductible. (In traditional debt financing, only the interest portion of the debt is deductible.) An ESOP can build morale and productivity because it gives employees a financial stake in the company's future. When employees cash in their shares, they receive very favorable tax treatment on any gain they may have made. An ESOP allows the owner to determine how big a piece of the company to give up and restricts company stock from getting into public hands.

Disadvantages. Unlike traditional debt financing, an ESOP requires that the owner give up some degree of control in the company. Further, if the company's stock is not readily tradable on an established market, the employees must have the right to require the company to repurchase that stock under a fair valuation formula when they die, retire, or terminate, thus exposing the company to a "repurchase liability." Finally, ESOPs are closely regulated by the government, which can place an onerous bookkeeping burden on a small company.

Cost. The cost of an ESOP will vary from company to company. A feasibility study

should be undertaken to determine your individual cost, taking into account such factors as the size of your projected annual contribution, the tax savings your contribution will generate, the return on investment you can expect from that saving, and the dilution of share ownership.

ESOPs also should be evaluated in light of your current employee benefits. If your company is already providing its employees with a well-funded pension plan, the ESOP may be viewed as additional compensation expense. However, if your company has no deferred compensation plan and you establish an ESOP rather than a traditional pension or profit-sharing plan, the financial analysis is likely to weigh heavily in favor of an ESOP over traditional tools of corporate finance.

Deal structure. ESOPs are usually structured as follows: Say your corporation wishes to finance a new plant at a cost of $5 million. An ESOP is formed to borrow this amount. The ESOP then takes the $5 million and purchases new stock from its corporate sponsor, your company, at fair market value (as determined by an appraisal). The lender holds the corporate shares as collateral and usually also gets a corporate guarantee of the indebtedness. Each year, your company makes a tax-deductible contribution to the ESOP. The ESOP then uses this contribution to repay the bank debt. As the bank is repaid, shares that had been held as collateral are freed up, and allocated to employees' accounts.

Hybrid Securities

Hybrid securities combine the elements of both debt and equity capital such as convertible debt and convertible preferred stock.

When to use. Hybrid securities may be appropriate for companies whose balance sheets aren't strong enough to support additional "straight" (nonconvertible) debt. It is best used when current owners of companies in this position want to raise capital while minimizing the dilution of their ownership interest.

Advantages. For investors, hybrids offer the potential of additional compensation through the conversion (or equity) feature. Because of this, the cash flow cost of hybrids (interest or dividend) is often lower than with straight debt, since investors may trade off current cash flow for the potential of gaining additional return available through the equity feature. Dilution to the existing stockholders is likely to be less than if a straight equity instrument were offered.

Disadvantages. If the conversion option is exercised, the current owners will experience some dilution, in addition to having paid out interest or dividends. Hybrids are typically a more expensive form of financing than straight debt, yet they don't provide the advantages of a true equity financing.

Cost. The company's cost is generally the interest and/or dividends paid currently on the hybrid securities as well as the ultimate potential cost of the conversion feature if, and when, it is exercised.

Deal structure. Hybrid securities are generally structured as debt with an option to convert to equity, preferred stock with an option to convert to common stock, or in some other creative form combining debt and equity features.

Other Forms of Financing

Mergers and Acquisitions Financing

For many middle market companies, a merger or acquisition is the fastest and most economical way to foster rapid growth. However, obtaining M&A financing today can be difficult given recent junk bond problems and troubled mergers. M&A financing is still available, although it may be less plentiful and more expensive than in the past.

Leveraged buyouts (LBO). Virtually all acquisition financing transactions completed in the current marketplace, whether they involve large or small companies, are leveraged in some fashion. Because of this, the financing technique known as a *leveraged buyout* has become extremely popular.

An LBO can be an attractive method to purchase a business from both the buyer's and seller's points of view. LBOs are also used by public companies to buy out existing shareholders and "go private." An LBO enables the buyer to offer an attractive, all-cash price to the seller. It can cut the buyer's up-front investment and offers the opportunity to generate a high rate of return to the equity investors.

What type of company is appropriate for an LBO? Earnings must be substantial and consistent. Cash flow must be healthy. The company should have hard assets, good liquidity, and little existing leverage on its balance sheet. What's more, the typical LBO candidate is often a mature company with a dominant market position in a low-growth business. Strong management is another prerequisite.

Leveraged recapitalizations. The leveraged recapitalization, or leveraged recap, is a financially less risky offshoot of an LBO. A leveraged recap enables an owner to cash in while retaining control of the company and adds less debt than an LBO. With a leveraged recap, the company retains some of its borrowing power for future growth and acquisitions.

There are three types of leveraged recaps. In a "limited" recap, the company borrows a modest amount from a traditional lending institution and uses the loan proceeds to pay a dividend or to buy back shares. A "high-leveraged" recap (with debt/equity ratios of 8:1 and higher) leaves the owner with less-than-complete control since lenders will receive warrants entitling them to a sizable minority interest. A "low-leveraged" recap balances the need for liquidity and continuing control against the risks of added debt.

Various financial groups and institutions specialize in leveraged recaps including LBO groups, some commercial banks, equity funds, and merchant and investment banks.

Acquisition financing. In acquisition financing, unlike other sources of capital, your company's entire balance sheet must be financed, rather than a single asset or collateral. This means that the deal structure may be complex, involving both debt and equity securities.

Senior debt can be provided by commercial banks, asset-based lenders, insurance companies, and, in some cases, sellers. The financing provided by these sources is at the senior level, can be secured or unsecured, and can be either short term or long term.

Subordinated debt may be provided by insurance companies, pension funds, venture capital funds, and sellers. Securities are either in the form of senior or junior subordinate notes, which, by definition, are subordinate to senior debt. This means that senior debt sources regard subordinated debt as part of a company's equity base for borrowing purposes.

Equity in acquisition funding can be provided by insurance companies, venture capital funds, private investors, management, and sellers. Equity securities can be either preferred or common stock.

Export Financing

Even relatively small companies are increasingly selling their products and services abroad. But the costs associated with exporting can require financing beyond the capacity of your working capital. Fortunately, middle market companies have several good sources of export financing.

Commercial banks. If you already have a relationship with a commercial bank, begin your search for export financing there. Even if your lender doesn't provide adequate international services, it may be able to refer you to a correspondent bank in the country to which you want to export.

Commercial banks provide both short- and medium-term export financing. In addition, they can advise on export regulations; collect foreign invoices, drafts, letters of credit, and other foreign receivables; transfer funds internationally; provide letters of introduction and letters of credit; and supply credit information on potential buyers overseas.

Export-import bank (Eximbank). Over the past fifty years, the Eximbank has financed more than $190 billion in export sales of American goods and services through a variety of loan, guarantee, and insurance programs for U.S. exporters and their overseas customers. To encourage small businesses to sell overseas, Eximbank maintains a special telephone hotline to provide information on the availability and use of its export credit insurance, guarantees, and direct and intermediary loans. Call (800) 424-5201. The Eximbank also offers small-business briefings for individual companies and groups nationwide.

Small business administration (SBA). The SBA offers export counseling, training, financial assistance, and legal advice. Several of its financial assistance programs are similar to those offered by the Eximbank. An agreement between the two agencies allows them to join their resources to make more credit available to a single borrower—up to $1,000,000 per borrower. Applications are made by a U.S. exporter through a commercial bank that submits the application to an SBA field office for processing. The SBA also provides a revolving line of credit for financing pre-export production; purchasing labor, supplies, materials, and inventory; and for funding market development. Contact the nearest SBA field office for more information.

Overseas private investment corporation (OPIC). Through OPIC, the federal government facilitates U.S. private investments in less developed nations. OPIC is an independent, financially self-supporting corporation, fully owned by the U.S. government with offices in Washington, D.C.

41

OPIC provides political-risk insurance and medium- to long-range financing for U.S. companies seeking joint venture opportunities with foreign project sponsors. For more information, call (800) 424-6742 or, in the Washington, D.C., metropolitan area, (202) 457-7010.

Obtaining Financing for Your Company

The Financing Plan

Each financing source will have its own specific requirements as to the information it requires, the type of collateral it is looking for, and the terms of the deal. However, all financing sources, whether lending institutions, venture capitalists, or public investors, will require a financing plan or package. The plan is similar to a business plan but with several key differences.

Financing plan versus business plan. A financing plan focuses on the cash needs of a business or venture. A business plan focuses on the company's marketing and product strategies as well as the operating tactics the business intends to use to achieve its goals.

In a financing plan there may be an overview of the business, its products, and its management. However, the prospective financing source is usually expected to understand these details in advance. The primary emphasis, therefore, is on the company's cash needs, cash sources, and the use to which the cash will be put.

Since the cash-needs forecast in a financing plan is really a by-product of the business plan, the financing plan must be analyzed in conjunction with the business plan. Therefore, the development of a business plan is a critical step in determining the financing need.

The Financing Package

The financing package is prepared after completing the financing plan. It comprises aspects of both the business and the financing plan. Its purpose is to present to a prospective capital source the financing request that was determined as part of the financing plan. It provides the capital source with sufficient information to make a *preliminary* determination as to whether it is interested in pursuing the investment or loan. The financing package also provides the background information to enable the capital source to perform the additional "due diligence" work necessary to make a final credit or investment decision.

Elements of a financing package. There is no "right" or "wrong" way to format a financing package. However, most financing packages contain the following items:

Description of the assets being acquired or the project to be financed

- Proposed offering of securities or loan request—a discussion of the form of capital requested

- Company or project overview including brief descriptions of products or services; customer base; marketplace; competition; production process; facilities, furniture, and equipment; and management/ownership

- Narrative financial summary including key ratios

- Historical financial statements covering, if possible, the past five years

- Forecasted financial statements for three years into the future including a source and use of funds (or cash) statement

- Details of collateral assets incorporating fair market value of fixed assets, receivables, and inventory

- Resumes of key management

Negotiating with Capital Sources

The decision to lend to or invest in your company will inevitably hinge on the capital source's estimation of your company's business, financial history, and prospects. However, there are some guidelines to keep in mind when negotiating with a lender or investor that will put your proposal in the best possible light.

The importance of personal contact. It is always preferable to contact financial sources

that you already know. Growing companies should continuously strive to expand and reinforce financing contacts *before* a specific capital need arises. This will establish your credibility with the capital source and foster a more comfortable, productive relationship.

Even if you have no previous contact with a financing source, it is always desirable to approach a source in person. This may be done with a short introductory meeting after which your financing package may be submitted. If a face-to-face introductory meeting is not possible, always begin with a telephone call to introduce yourself, your company, and the financing opportunity.

Know your sources. Debt source contacts are usually employees of financing institutions overseeing the deployment of someone else's funds. Equity contacts, on the other hand, are often principals in the investor organization and thus oversee the development of their own capital. Debt capital is also inherently less risky and more liquid than equity and can thus involve an easier credit decision. Given all this, it is not surprising that there is more competition by lending sources than by equity sources to get into financing opportunities. Debt sources may therefore be generally more receptive to your financing needs than equity sources, which may already be deluged with venture capital requests and business plans.

Keep in mind that no matter how scarce or available capital may be at a given point in time, no lender or investor wants to miss out on considering an opportunity. Therefore, you should always approach capital sources from a position of strength. If your financing opportunity is legitimate and not merely an attempt to disguise a weak financial situation, you have something of value to capital sources and should present yourself accordingly.

Understand the source's criteria. The best way to ensure a positive outcome in your search for capital is to understand how you will be assessed. Banks have traditionally used the "Six C's" to evaluate borrowers. These criteria are valid for virtually any financing situation.

Capital. Financing sources want to know if the owner has committed a significant amount of his or her own money to the business.

Coverage. Financing sources want to be sure that cash flow covers debt service.

Capacity. Financing sources want assurances that the company will continue to grow in the future.

Circumstances. Is the company dependent on a handful of major customers? How is the company positioned to withstand a downturn in its business? Financing sources will look at the financing package to determine the market circumstances that govern a company.

Collateral. Financing sources will want a recent appraisal of the assets that are to be used as collateral.

Character. The honesty, integrity, and dedication of an owner can be as important to a lender or investor as the company's financial reports.

Approaching Your Banker in a Tight Financing Market

The availability of financing is always a primary concern for middle market companies and this is especially so now when many lenders have been compelled by a variety of circumstances to be more cautious in extending credit.

"It's not inappropriate that banks have become more cautious in the current economic environment," says Jeffrey S. Hurwitz, partner in charge of middle market services in Peat Marwick's Cincinnati, Ohio, office. "However, they have to assume some degree of risk, or they'll have a tough time being successful. Borrowers need to convince their banks that they are worthy customers. Even now, the money is out there if a company knows how to ask for it and has a credible business and financing plan."

Hurwitz suggests following these strategies when negotiating with your banker or seeking a new lender:

Your business plan must justify as well as clarify your financing needs. Spend time fine-tuning it and be prepared to defend it.

2 "You don't want to appear timid or unsure in asserting your goals," notes Hurwitz. "A borrower who anticipates difficulty in obtaining financing communicates that uncertainty to the banker, who then may become less likely to assume the risks involved with a loan."

II Prepare the business plan with credible financial projections. Offer best-, standard-, and worst-case scenarios demonstrating your ability to generate positive cash flow to adequately service the debt.

3 "You need to know your business plan and financial projections inside and out and to be committed to them," adds Hurwitz. "The better able you are to demonstrate your needs, the more comfortable the bank will be to assume risk."

III Ask for enough money to meet your needs or you may not get the financing.

"You may damage your credibility with your banker by asking for less than what your business plan calls for," says Hurwitz. "The banker will know that with less money

you won't be able to accomplish your goals, and you may be putting the business unnecessarily at risk. In those circumstances, the smaller loan may be a bigger risk for the banker. Also, remember that generally you'll get only one opportunity to ask, so make sure you get what you need the first time."

IV Get to know the internal goals of various banks to find one that wants to develop its portfolio by working with businesses in your industry.

V Choose a lender who is willing to invest the time required to understand your business and who wants to grow with it.

"Remember, too, that in any financing arrangement, the object is to obtain as much capital as possible, for as long as possible, at the best terms, and at the lowest cost," notes Hurwitz. "Too often people focus only on the cost of capital, but the other three elements are equally, and sometimes more, important."

Nonpublic Financing: Sources of Debt Capital

(1) Commercial Banks

Cost:	Almost always a floating rate based on the prime rate plus up to 4 additional percentage points
Maturity:	Varies across the board from demand (or ninety-day notes) to committed lines of credit (one to three years) to intermediate-term loans (three to five years) and long-term mortgages
Collateral:	Unsecured, general floating liens or specific liens on specific assets Personal guarantees
Generally used for:	Working capital needs General expansion Purchase of machinery and equipment
Advantages:	Universal source "Cradle-to-grave" relationships Usually low-cost provider of capital
Disadvantages:	Preference given to stable, established businesses Start-up companies are avoided May require personal collateral or personal guarantees

(2) Commercial Finance Companies

Cost:	Almost always a floating rate based upon the prime rate plus up to six additional percentage points
Maturity:	One- to eight-year (usually depending on loan size—the larger the loan, the longer the commitment) revolving credit agreements; term loans of up to ten years
Collateral:	Always required; first liens on assets to be financed; personal guarantees usually required
Generally used for:	Financing increased working-capital needs Acquisitions Purchase of machinery, equipment, and real estate
Advantages:	Aggressive lenders against balance sheet collateral Will lend to troubled situations Revolving credit arrangement allows availability to expand as asset base expands
Disadvantages:	High-rate lenders If asset base contracts, borrower has to repay appropriate part of advance quickly Structured initially as demand obligations, will usually move quickly to liquidate if trouble occurs

(3) Leasing Companies

Cost:	Usually a cost (implicit in the lease) equal to prime plus up to six percentage points; tax-advantaged leases (to the lessor) may be less expensive

Maturity:	Varies with type of asset leased; *operating* leases are short term (as short as a few months); *financing* leases approximate the useful life of the asset
Collateral:	Leasing is a form of secured lending since lessor retains title to the asset
Generally used for:	Machinery and equipment
	Real estate
	Acquisition financing
Advantages:	Easy to deal with
	100 percent of cost of asset can be financed
	Risk of ownership with lessor
Disadvantages:	Usually high cost
	Benefits of ownership, such as appreciation, are generally retained by lessor (However, various tax benefits may be passed through to the lessee; these benefits are usually associated with additional cost to the lessee in the form of higher lease payments.)

(4) Savings and Loan Associations

Cost:	Fixed or variable rate, usually tied to long-term market rates; on working-capital loans, floating, tied to the prime rate, priced competitively with local commercial banks
Maturity:	Usually long-term (fifteen years); occasionally lines of credit
Collateral:	Almost always secured
Generally used for:	Real estate
	Occasionally working capital and purchase of machinery and equipment
Advantages:	Familiar, experienced lenders in real estate area
	Attractive rates
	Attractive loan to asset ratios
Disadvantages:	Usually prefer strongly capitalized and established businesses
	Careful lenders to commercial businesses for working-capital needs

(5) Life Insurance Companies/Pension Funds

Cost:	Usually fixed rate tied to long-term market rates
Maturity:	Varying between five to ten years and twenty-five years depending on use of proceeds
Collateral:	Unsecured debentures for established financially strong borrowers
	Secured for asset acquisition purposes
Generally used for:	Machinery and equipment
	Real estate
	Long-term working capital support needs
Advantages:	Provides long-term capital
	Market rates of interest
Disadvantages:	Minimum loan amounts are usually high (for example, $1 million or more)
	Restrictive loan agreements usually required

(6) The Small Business Administration

Cost:	Can be floating or fixed but subject to a government-imposed ceiling
Maturity:	Seven to twenty-five years, depending on use of proceeds

Continued

Collateral:	Almost always secured by general floating liens on specific collateral; personal guarantees of owner required
Generally used for:	Business ineligible for conventional financing
	Working capital
	Machinery and equipment
	Real estate
Advantages:	"Lender of last resort"
	Cost not commensurate with risk
	Financing available for all types of assets
Disadvantages:	All-inclusive liens usually required
	Guarantees of major stockholders required
	Financing available only to businesses that qualify

(7) Industrial Revenue Bonds

Cost:	Can be floating or fixed, but at "tax-exempt" rate, which is usually 70 percent to 85 percent of prevailing prime rate
Maturity:	Usually five to fifteen years
Collateral:	Almost always secured by fixed assets
Generally used for:	Machinery and equipment
	Real estate
	Rehabilitation of existing fixed assets
	Limited working-capital financing
	Acquisition financing
Advantages:	Low rate
	Acceptable maturities
	Usually funded by the company's commercial bank
Disadvantages:	Can be hard to obtain, subject to market availability
	Government can change rules
	Higher closing costs, particularly higher legal fees

(8) Leveraged Buyouts (LBOs)

Definition:	The acquisition of a business or a group of assets using a high level of debt and little equity
Purpose:	To increase the return of investors' committed capital by leveraging a small equity infusion with a large amount of debt
When a leveraged buyout is used:	To purchase an established business where there is a strong asset base and existing cash flow. The existing cash flow is used to retire the purchase money debt, and the strong asset base is used to further cushion the lender.
Participating debt sources:	Commercial banks, particularly where there is an existing strong cash flow
	Asset-based lenders, where cash flow may be weak but the asset (collateral) base is strong
	Industrial revenue bonds to finance with an attractive rate and maturity basis the purchase of machinery and equipment and real property

Nonpublic Financing: Sources of Equity Capital

(1) Small Business Innovation Research Grants (SBIR Grants)

Amount available:	Initially $50,000 with later commitment of up to $500,000
Deal structure:	Grant by agency or department of federal government
Cost:	Well-researched, documented proposal must be constructed and offered for review
Generally used for:	Seed capital
Advantages:	Low cost, no equity give-up
Disadvantages:	Limited initial commitment of only $50,000

(2) R & D Partnerships

Amount available:	Varying from quite small to hundreds of millions of dollars for publicly sponsored issues
Deal structure:	Tax-oriented limited partnership offering early tax write-offs and, later, capital gains to investors
Cost:	Varies depending on market conditions and success of project; structured, however, to be less expensive than debt but more expensive than equity
Generally used:	When funds for new product research are needed, tax advantages cannot be immediately used by company, and company wishes to share risk with outside investors
Advantages:	High-risk funds come from outside the business
Disadvantages:	Can be very high cost if project is very successful

(3) Professional Venture Capitalists

Amount available:	Usually $500,000 and above
Deal structure:	Varies across the board; in many instances, convertible preferred stock
Cost:	Long-term capital gain sought in area of three to ten times money invested over four- to seven-year investment horizon.
Generally used:	When business has extremely high growth potential ($50 million to $100 million sales in five years) and company plans to go public rather than remain private
Advantages:	Large amounts of risk capital available, much more than in case of wealthy individuals
	Investors bring contacts and business experience
Disadvantages:	Company must follow planned high sales growth path expected by investors
	Company must become public, usually as soon as possible

(4) Small Business Investment Companies (SBICs)

Amount available:	Varies by SBIC but usual range is from $100,000 to $1 million
Deal structure:	Varies from straight debt to straight equity; most common form of deal is hybrid security, either convertible debt or subordinated debt instrument with warrants to buy common stock attached
Cost:	Costs include both a rate of interest or dividend and equity participation in the business.

Continued

Generally used for:	Expansion capital
	Working capital
	Acquisition financing
	Leveraged buyouts
Advantages:	Provides subordinated capital, augmenting the equity base for borrowing purposes
	By regulation, maturity on debt instruments must be at least five years
	Interest rates are usually fixed
Disadvantages:	Equity give-up required; investors may seek influence over business (for example, board of directors' seat)
	Usually must be fast-growth company with plans for going public within three to five years

(5) Specialized Small Business Investment Companies (MESBICs)

Amount available:	Varies by SSBIC but usual range is from $100,000 to $1 million; SSBIC capital is available only to businesses operated by economically and socially disadvantaged owners
Deal structure:	Similar to deals structured with SBICs
Cost:	Similar to costs of SBIC capital
Generally used for:	Startup capital
	Working capital
	Expansion capital
	Acquisition financing
	Leveraged buyouts
Advantages:	Source of risk/equity capital for businesses operated by economically and socially disadvantaged owners
	Provides subordinated capital augmenting the equity base for borrowing purposes
	Interest rates are usually fixed
Disadvantages:	By law can be used only to fund businesses operated by economically and socially disadvantaged owners
	Equity give-up required
	Investors may seek influence over business
	Usually must be fast-growth company with plans for going public within three to five years

4

Dealing with Mergers and Acquisitions

Dealing with Intermediaries

The 1980s saw approximately twenty thousand merger and acquisition (M&A) announcements. It's a safe bet that a lot more deals actually took place. Many, perhaps most of them, were helped along by M&A intermediaries who in some instances will even conduct auctions in order to get the very best price on the sale of a company.

If you've decided to sell or to purchase, you face the question of whether and how to deal with intermediaries. Many sellers and buyers go it alone. Some mistrust intermediaries, some don't want to pay a transaction fee, and others assume that no intermediary would want to work with them—but deciding to do without intermediaries can be risky. For example, most owners need help to set a reasonable selling price, one that reflects the M&A marketplace and sustains the owner's living standards after the deal is done.

Dealing with intermediaries confronts you with important business issues. Knowing these issues helps you get the deal done. Not knowing can create unpleasant surprises—and M&A deals have plenty of surprises already.

Who Are the Players?

Investment bankers, business brokers, and accounting/consulting firms have long served as M&A intermediaries. Others such as banks and attorneys are also active.

Investment banks have advised clients on corporate finance matters (including M&As) for close to a century. They tend to represent buyers and sellers on larger M&A deals (transactions in excess of $50 million). The relationships that investment banks develop with their clients tend to be more transaction oriented since the transactions themselves are the prime source of M&A revenue for investment banks.

Business brokers have also assisted sellers in M&A transactions for many years. The broker community is highly fragmented and varied. Brokers most often assist owners of privately held companies in finding and contacting potential bidders, much as a real estate broker might assist with the sale of a home. Business brokers tend to represent businesses that sell for between $500,000 and $10 million.

Commercial banks have become more active in the M&A arena as a result of diversification and deregulation within the financial industry. Banks rely largely on their networks of lending customers as a source of M&A referrals on both the buy and sell sides. Commercial banks, like investment banks, can assemble pools of debt and equity capital to help their clients complete transactions. For larger transactions the ability to raise debt and equity capi-

tal gives bankers and investment bankers an extra dimension as M&A intermediaries.

Attorneys' client contacts are usually top-quality and can generate good leads. Attorneys tend to specialize in certain technical—and crucial—aspects of each deal. They rarely act as matchmaker, although the larger firms are heading in that direction.

Accounting/consulting firms have been in the M&A business for most of this century, providing "traditional services" such as due diligence and tax planning. In the past twenty-five years, several accounting/consulting firms have diversified their M&A efforts. These firms now represent sellers and divesters, find and contact potential bidders, perform acquisition searches and business valuations, suggest deal structures, build financial models, and advise during negotiations—in addition to providing traditional services.

The more aggressive accounting/consulting firms capitalize on their worldwide networks of partners, offices, and clients not only to find the right "marriage" but also to inject the industry and technical expertise that any M&A transaction requires. This expertise, developed by serving clients throughout the economy, can be a distinct advantage if the right team is assembled.

How Do Fee Arrangements Work?

The fees charged to sellers and purchasers by M&A intermediaries vary greatly. Fees tend to average 2 percent to 3 percent on deals worth less than $20 million and less than 1 percent on deals worth more than $100 million. Clearly, the services to be rendered will affect the fee arrangement.

Most of the fee, however it is calculated, is payable at closing. The intermediary usually receives a nonrefundable retainer ranging between $25,000 and $100,000. Intermediaries consider the retainer to be insurance that the seller or purchaser is serious. The retainer also serves to defray—only partially—the substantial time and costs needed to do a good job.

Transaction fees that depend on the purchase price must be carefully defined. Purchasers and sellers should consider the various ways in which the transaction may eventually be structured. For example, a transaction may be structured as a sale of stock or as a sale of assets. Furthermore, certain assets may be excluded and/or some of the purchase price may depend on future results. On which amount(s) will the intermediary's fee be based?

Yet another issue is how the fee will or won't link the seller's or purchaser's goals with the goals of the intermediary. If the purchaser offers to pay an M&A adviser 1 percent of the purchase price, what will ensure that the adviser works toward the minimum successful bid? Conversely, will a 1 percent fee offered by the seller to an intermediary be adequate to ensure that the adviser obtains the very best bid? Or should the seller offer a special incentive such as 5 percent of the amount by which the winning bid exceeds an agreed-upon level?

Regardless of the fee structure, most intermediaries representing sellers require an exclusive arrangement for a year or so. Exclusivity means that the intermediary is entitled to a fee no matter who introduces the eventual purchaser—as long as the transaction closes within a specified time period.

Exclusivity protects intermediaries from investing a year of time and money only to be deprived of compensation due to someone else's actions. Exclusivity protects the purchaser or seller by increasing the energy their intermediary devotes to getting the deal done. The intermediary works harder because the odds of a fee are higher. Sellers usually agree to exclusive arrangements; buyers rarely do.

Another part of most M&A fee arrangements is the "break-up" fee. The break-up fee entitles the intermediary, upon termination under specified circumstances, to a fee that is substantially less than the expected transaction fee. Break-up fees protect both intermediaries and their clients from unforeseen changes in plans.

How Can a Good Intermediary Help You?

Whatever the proposed fee arrangements, they should be compared beforehand with the M&A services expected. Intermediaries can assist sellers in a number of ways:

- Proposing asking price strategies
- Assembling information

- Saving management time
- Drawing upon past experiences
- Finding and accrediting potential bidders
- Acting as a buffer between the principals
- Structuring the deal
- Offering advice on negotiating
- Maintaining confidentiality

When intermediaries do nothing more than suggest a buyer or seller the fee should be highly negotiable, especially if the intermediary can't provide meaningful introductions at a senior level. Ideas are useful, but closing the deal requires a lot more.

What Should You Look For in an Intermediary?

The key issue in deciding whom to retain as an intermediary is which people will actually work with you. People matter most. One frequent problem here is lack of experience—all too often senior M&A advisers vanish after Day One, replaced by first- or second-year staffers. Another problem is lack of focus— many so-called M&A advisers really spend most of their time in other activities such as real estate brokerage or business valuation.

One way to avoid problems with inexperience and lack of focus is to request a list of recent deals closed by the intermediary, along with references to call. Just as in exploring any business relationship, past customers can tell you a great deal. By asking for a listing of recent deals you will also find out whether the intermediary knows your industry. At a minimum, someone on the team should know the industry issues.

Getting deals closed takes time. The person who will work with you day-to-day shouldn't be juggling more than one or two other major projects, or yours won't get enough attention.

Even if your M&A advisers have the experience and availability to serve you well, there is another necessary ingredient for success: a contact network. All the expertise in the world won't help much unless the right acquirer or target can be identified. Without a network intermediaries will turn to other intermediaries for matchmaking ideas. A daisy chain of intermediaries endangers confidentiality, adds fees, and can slow down the whole process.

Selling or purchasing a business is a personal process. The final test of your prospective M&A adviser should be how you get along. Someone who does not understand your needs will not be able to put the right deal together. Therefore, it's essential that you meet and get to know your adviser before committing. Again, it's important that the person you meet will be the person with whom you'll actually work.

What Should You Watch Out For?

There are traps for the unwary. Some traps—inexperienced advisers, lack of a network, poor sense of the M&A marketplace—

have been mentioned already. But there are others. For example, sellers shouldn't accept an intermediary's suggestions as to potential purchasers unless it is clear what the fee obligation will be, if any. Even a casual suggestion with respect to potential acquirers has, in the past, occasionally led to litigation.

Another problem is motivation. Intermediaries whose entire fee depends on closing a deal may be tempted to push too hard for a suboptimal deal in order to move on to the next one. Objectivity should be balanced carefully with the incentive and energy to close a deal.

A third problem is that word may get out. Confidentiality can never be guaranteed, but poorly thought-out contacts with potential purchasers or sellers can lead to rumors or worse.

A fourth problem is conflict of interest. Many intermediaries also act as principals in selected transactions. Purchasers and sellers should ensure that such intermediaries will put their obligation to their clients clearly above their personal interest in making an attractive investment.

How can you best avoid these and other traps? Once again, the people factor is crucial. If the adviser has the right personal qualities, these traps should not snare you.

Conclusion

Talented intermediaries add value to both sides of an M&A transaction. Dealing with intermediaries is risky, but the risks of not working with them—a poorly priced or structured deal or a failure to find the right purchaser or seller—are often greater. The best solution is asking the right questions before going forward, along with good old-fashioned people sense.

Letters of Intent

The M&A process has always been delicate and personal. Managing the M&A process is an essential element of business strategy. Changes in the tax environment, bidding contests, fear of litigation and the like have created new hurdles to getting deals done. Once two parties have begun discussions, they and their advisers should consider anything that may help. This section outlines whether, when, and how a letter of intent can help get the deal done.

Definition

Except as discussed below, a letter of intent is defined as a written but nonbinding outline of preliminary understandings between the principals. Letters of intent may also be called proposals, bid letters, or agreements in principle. Many M&A deals, particularly smaller deals and transactions between two closely held companies, take place without letters of intent. In such cases, the principals proceed directly from conceptualizing and negotiating

55

key points to the drafting of a definitive agreement or contract.

Benefits

A letter of intent can help or hinder the M&A process depending on the circumstances and the people doing the deal. Putting an understanding into writing can determine whether a deal even makes sense. A letter of intent can force issues or misunderstandings into the open that will otherwise fester silently while time passes and professional fees mount. A classic example: A buyer intends to purchase only the essential assets of the seller's business, which may pose tax and business risks to the seller. Without a letter of intent, the seller would probably assume (somewhat optimistically) that the buyer plans to purchase the seller's stock.

In addition, the letter of intent can enhance deal stability and commitment early on when both sides may feel least sure of their mutual interests, and it can establish the time frame for the proposed deal.

Letters of intent can especially benefit the prospective purchaser in at least two ways. First, the purchaser may find that raising money to do the deal is easier if lenders know that both sides have committed a deal outline to paper. Second, the prospective purchaser may find that the letter of intent can commit the seller not to negotiate with other potential suitors for a specified time period, thus facilitating due diligence and cooperation.

The prospective seller can benefit from a letter of intent, too. Most sellers want to preserve confidentiality. Indiscretions can damage employee morale, force untimely public disclosures, or put proprietary data in the wrong hands. Letters of intent often contain either a two-way (buyer/seller) commitment to protect such data or reference to a separate confidentiality agreement, which is most often executed by both parties before the letter of intent is signed.

Drawbacks

Deals may be saved or helped along because there was a letter of intent, but there are many cases where such letters are counterproductive. For example, a letter of intent could be construed as a binding agreement between the parties. To avoid this possibility, wording and appropriate disclaimers in the letter must be carefully chosen. Another problem may be the psychological impact of the letter on the negotiations themselves; one or both parties may believe they have little more to negotiate, thereby removing the momentum toward a definitive agreement.

A third drawback is the tendency of letters of intent to remove flexibility from discussions and to reduce the pressure to get the deal done. This again is more psychological than factual. At any rate, one or both parties may feel frozen into positions expressed in the letter of intent. For example, one letter of intent contained a generous earn-out arrangement, carefully designed by the purchaser. The earn-out later had to be greatly altered when the prospective purchaser's accountants pointed out that the original version would have necessitated booking a liability on the prospective purchaser's balance sheet. The alteration doomed the deal. Rightly or wrongly, what the seller had seen on paper made the subsequent alteration seem unexpected and devious.

Seller's Trauma

Before drafting a letter of intent, a prospective purchaser should carefully consider the seller's frame of mind; most sellers have never sold a business before. Obviously this is less likely if a conglomerate is selling the target, but the issue is important. The privately owned seller may be forced into two time-consuming sets of discussions: one to draft a letter of intent and the next one to reach a definitive agreement. The time, cost, and emotional strain can destroy earlier feelings of mutuality between the parties.

Content

Once the parties to a proposed deal have weighed the pros and cons and have decided to draft a letter of intent, content is crucial. The letter will do no good—and can actually misdirect further discussions—if it fails to cover the key elements of the M&A process and the proposed transaction. Does this mean that attorneys should be involved from the outset?

To some degree, yes. Letters of intent work best when principals take the first stab at a draft followed closely by the review and comments of both attorneys. Absent any unusual complications, if the letter of intent is more than two or three pages long, perhaps both parties should instead proceed directly to a definitive agreement.

Each letter of intent is unique, reflecting how and why the deal has evolved. Letters of intent will normally cover most of the following areas:

1. An express statement that the letter doesn't constitute a binding agreement. (Often, the letter will nevertheless specify as binding the obligation of both parties to maintain confidentiality and the obligation of the seller not to negotiate with other suitors for a stipulated period of time.)

2. The legal structure of the proposed deal (for example, purchase of stock or assets—which assets, what percentage of the stock).

3. The price or price range along with an outline of the manner of payment (for example, cash, restricted shares of the purchaser's stock, nature of restrictions, and earn-out terms).

4. The proposed time frame for reaching a definitive agreement, completing due diligence, and closing the deal.

5. An outline of employment or consulting agreements or covenants not to compete, which may apply to the seller or the seller's principals or key employees.

6. Obligations of the prospective purchaser with respect to employees of the seller (for example, union contract, benefit levels, or profit sharing).

7. Reference to the inclusion of normal representations and warranties in the definitive agreement along with an outline of possible escrows, hold-backs, "cushions," or similar proposed arrangements.

8. Conditions and contingencies upon which the deal depends (for example, IRS rulings, regulatory approvals, or audits).

9. Requirements for, and source and identity of, any outside financing for the deal.

10. An outline of expected due diligence procedures.

11. Any unusual items (for example, allocation of transaction costs and other fees).

Conclusion

Letters of intent have the potential to define and drive forward a deal or to destroy it. The letter can uncover new issues, but may do so at the risk of rigidifying each side's position. The circumstances and the content of the letter are crucial. Ironically, letters of intent are often discarded in draft form, having accomplished their purpose of either preventing further pointless discussions or of starting the definitive agreement itself. Thus, understanding the likely impact of a letter of intent can raise the odds of a successful M&A strategy.

How to Cash Out and Stay In: Leveraged Recapitalizations

With all the press about leveraged buyouts (LBOs) these days—large and small, friendly and hostile—many private business owners think that an LBO offers them the only way to cash in without selling to a bigger company.

An LBO loads the business with debt while handing majority control to the LBO investor. Is there a different way? Years of deals-doing innovation along with the growing pool of money flowing to the M&A marketplace have spawned a financially less-risky offshoot of an LBO: the leveraged recapitalization or leveraged recap.

Compared with an LBO, a leveraged recap adds less debt, keeps greater ongoing control for the owner and management, and often liquefies the owner with less operating disruption. Owners and their executives should understand how leveraged recaps work, when and why these recaps make sense, what the drawbacks are, which businesses best qualify, and from what source the money will come.

Recaps Can Vary

The size and role of lenders and equity investors can differ. There are three types of recaps:

1. In a "limited" recap the company borrows a modest amount from a traditional lending

institution and uses the loan proceeds to pay a dividend or to buy back shares. Ownership often doesn't change. In a more leveraged version of a limited recap, an outside financial group makes an equity investment in the company while also providing funds in the form of senior and subordinated debt.

2. A "high-leveraged" recap (with debt/equity ratios of 8:1 and beyond) leaves the owner with less-than-complete control. Certain lenders or investors in a high-leveraged recap will receive warrants entitling them to a sizable minority interest. Although high-leveraged recaps can be attractive because they generate cash for the owner while preserving control, the high-leveraged recap leaves the company with a much riskier debt structure. Also, the outside investors or lenders will closely watch how the company's money is spent. There may be pressure to redirect spending toward interest and principal payments.

3. The third form of recap, on which this section focuses, is called a "low-leveraged" recap. This type of recap balances the need for liquidity and continuing control against the risks of added debt.

How Do Low-Leveraged Recaps Work?

At first glance, they resemble LBOs. A financial partner—possibly a financial institution rather than an LBO investor—invests equity in the form of preferred and common stock while arranging for a senior lender to provide the rest of the financing. Management invests whatever it can afford and gains a minority stake. Where does the money go? To the owner.

The resemblance between recaps and LBOs stops here. LBO debt can outweigh equity by 10:1 or more, compared with more conservative 2:1 norms for low-leveraged recaps. Also, LBOs usually sever the owner's equity role, whereas in a low-leveraged recap shareholders reinvest 10 percent to 20 percent of their proceeds in return for a continuing equity stake of up to 51 percent. This reinvestment is tax free if it's properly structured and meets certain other change-in-control requirements set by tax laws.

When and Why Do Recaps Make Sense?

A leveraged recap simultaneously achieves several objectives. First, the shareholders get cash. Each shareholder can cash in some shares, or certain shareholders can cash out entirely while others stay in.

Second, the company stays independent. Recaps may shuffle equity stakes and add a new shareholder, but the company escapes falling into the hands of a corporate purchaser. In fact, the company hasn't even ceded majority control since shareholders and management together will own more than 50 percent.

Third, a leveraged recap allows the company to save some of its borrowing power for future growth and acquisitions, while an LBO nearly exhausts that borrowing power. Management often must pay off debt first—this may take years—and grow later. A strong financial partner in a recap will facilitate acquisitions by acting as adviser and then providing more money. Owners can maintain their preacquisition ownership stakes by arranging for the financial partner to invest some of the new money in the form of nonvoting preferred stock.

Fourth, a leveraged recap gives each of the parties—shareholder, management, and the financial partner—the returns they want at a risk level they will accept. Shareholders want some cash to compensate for the ongoing risks of investing in their own company, which they would otherwise sell. Management wants to buy in, perhaps for the first time, and will reap the greatest rewards in the long term if the company succeeds in growing, paying off debt, and buying out the financial partner. Most executives will accept great personal financial sacrifice for such rewards.

The risk/return profile of the financial partner falls between shareholders and management. The financial partner looks for compounded annual returns of between 20 percent and 30 percent over four to six years, generated by repayment of invested capital, plus dividends or interest, plus the increased value of the company.

There are other benefits to recaps. For example, the credibility of the financial partner bolsters the company's chances of later going public. Also, since some shareholders will seek to cash out in times of low tax rates on capital gains, a leveraged recap may give these shareholders an exit without forcing them to sell the company.

Low-leveraged recaps don't take full advantage of the tax deductibility of interest since much of the money is invested in, rather than lent to, the company. These recaps still benefit the company, thanks to flexible dividend requirements on invested funds that the company would otherwise have borrowed at high rates.

What Are the Drawbacks?

Leveraged recaps won't always work. Owners and management often don't want the outside scrutiny of a financial partner. Also, favorable treatment of capital gains would persuade many owners to cash out entirely rather than risk a reversion to higher rates later on. Third, a leveraged recap threatens the tax advantages of companies that elect S corporation status. These companies, which normally pay no federal corporate taxes, aren't allowed to add certain kinds of equity partners. Fourth, borrowings incurred during a leveraged recap—while modest compared to LBO borrowing—do require repayment. Shareholder cash needs, which lead to leveraged recaps, are satisfied by creating formal creditor claims on future cash flow. Fifth, leveraged recaps remove the chance for today's owners to capture the full benefits of future corporate growth. By exchanging some of their shares for personal liquidity, owners let an outsider share the upside.

Who Qualifies for a Low-Leveraged Recap?

Not all businesses are right for recaps. According to BancBoston Capital-Equity Partners, companies meeting the following criteria have the best chance:

Competent and committed management

Consistent earning

Competitive advantage (for example, proprietary product)

Recession-resistant

Low technology risk

Valuation: $10 million to $75 million

Where Does the Money Come From?

Companies meeting these criteria can contact various financial groups and institutions specializing in equity investments. Players include certain LBO groups, affiliates of certain banks, equity funds, and merchant and investment banks (although many investment banks focus on larger recaps of public companies). These participants in recaps all see opportunities to share in private business growth while committing less up-front cash than an LBO requires—thanks to reinvestment by the shareholders.

Low-Leveraged Recaps: An Example

Low-leveraged recaps can meet four seemingly conflicting owner objectives, namely:

Personal liquidity

Ongoing control

Only modest borrowings to permit growth

A strong financial partner

The cast of characters includes:

Seller/CEO, a highly successful 60-year-old entrepreneur who owns 100 percent of the stock of a $50 million (sales) manufacturer with stable pretax margins and bank debt of $9 million

The management team, with which the seller wants to share ownership, but which doesn't have the financial means to do so

A financial partner, often a financial institution, which is legally forbidden from taking more than 49 percent of the voting stock

Their respective agendas:

Seller's wish list:
  Cash, to diversify and liquefy personal wealth
  Retain control with management
  Involve management

Grow through acquisitions and/or capital expenditures

Protect financial base, that is, limit debt

Cash out minority shareholders

Remain active as chairman while pursing outside interests

Management's wish list:

Run the company with operating autonomy/flexibility

Pursue growth with additional financial resources

Financial partner's wish list:

A sound investment controlled by a superior management team

A growing company

A four- to six-year exit strategy.

Conclusion

Leveraged recaps differ from the traditional alternatives facing private business owners such as an LBO, a sale to a corporate purchaser, going public, or keeping the status quo. Owners who qualify should consider recaps as a means of "cashing out while staying in."

Noncompete Agreements

Noncompete agreements help shape most of today's acquisitions, especially in people-intensive industries. These agreements, often called noncompetes, deter key executives of the acquired company from leaving and competing during a specified time period in a defined geographical region. Executives who sign noncompetes—in the case of privately held businesses this often includes certain selling shareholders—receive money in return, payable at or subsequent to the closing, which is taxed as ordinary income.

Noncompetes have taken on a special importance in today's M&A marketplace, thanks largely to the convergence of marginal tax rates for ordinary income and capital gains. The waves of tax reform begun in 1986 have eroded the tax planning opportunities created by acquisitions. Purchasers can amortize properly designed noncompetes for tax purposes, and selling shareholders are currently taxed at the same marginal rates on noncompete payments as on the payments that they receive for selling their shares. Therefore, purchasers often seek to assign the highest possible value to noncompetes (instead of to the shares or business assets) as a way of maximizing the value of the total package offered to both sides. This section addresses the following issues raised by noncompetes:

What determines whether a noncompete will withstand scrutiny by tax authorities?

How are noncompetes valued and amortized?

What drawbacks do noncompetes contain for purchasers or sellers?

Validity

The courts, in order to limit the potential abuse of noncompetes, have raised questions on two separate issues: When does a noncompete have substance and what is the noncompete's amortizable value? In considering the first question, the courts have formulated the following four tests:

The noncompete must not be so closely related to the goodwill of the company that it has no independent value. The noncompete cannot be simply part of the goodwill associated with the acquisition of the business.

Both the buyer and the seller should take into account all factors affecting the final amount allocated to the agreement, including taxes. Neither party can later contest the tax consequences of a noncompete because those consequences should have been considered when fixing the noncompete value.

Both parties must intend to allocate a value to the noncompete independent of the value of the company. If tax authorities challenge the noncompete, the burden of proof is on the buyer and seller to show that both wanted to assign some value to the noncompete and that the value was considered separately from the purchase price of the company.

The agreement must have a basis in reality. The seller must actually pose a competitive threat to the buyer.

The four tests are not considered to be equally important and may be weighted differently from one case to another.

A common mistake during early-stage discussions is to put in writing the intent of the purchaser to offer the seller a package comprising payment for the seller's stock or assets *along with noncompetes.* This invites tax authorities to challenge the noncompete on the basis of the first, third, and fourth points above. Noncompete negotiations should be kept as separate as possible from negotiations on price.

How Are Noncompetes Amortized and Valued?

The courts have not established specific valuation guidelines for noncompetes. They have, however, applied two tests to determine if an intangible asset is amortizable: (1) the asset must not be goodwill and (2) the asset must have a finite useful life.

Noncompetes are generally valued using the income method. The income method assigns a present value to the stream of future income or cash flow that the target would lose if key executives were to compete. The duration of the noncompete is crucial to assigning it a value. For example, a five-year life rather than a three-year life could greatly change the noncompete's value.

In any case, the valuation of noncompetes is highly judgmental and is not dependent on guidelines or standards.

Potential Drawbacks

In a sale of stock, if tax authorities successfully prove that the noncompete is overvalued, both the buyer and the seller can be affected, depending upon how many people held stock in the acquired company. If the acquired company had only one shareholder, the buyer will have to reclassify a portion of the noncompete payment—probably as nondeductible goodwill—and reduce any amortization accumulated on the agreement. The seller will reclassify a portion of the noncompete payment as part of the selling price, for example, a capital gain rather than as ordinary income. This won't matter unless capital gains are favorably taxed. If the acquired company had more than one selling shareholder, the buyer's and sellers' reclassifications will still be necessary. The selling shareholders, however, are now also affected in a second way. Unless each shareholder's noncompete allocation is proportional to the shareholder's former ownership percentage (which would probably invite challenge from tax authorities), one or more of the selling shareholders will be construed to have gifted a portion of the proceeds to other selling shareholders.

An example clarifies things: Assume Ms. Smith and Mr. Jones each sold 50 percent of the stock of the selling company. In addition to the selling price, Ms. Smith received a noncompete payment of $1 million while Mr. Jones received no payment. If the noncompete covenant is found to be invalid, the $1 million is then considered part of the selling price of the business. Since the two sellers should each have been paid 50 percent of the additional $1 million, or $500,000, the IRS considers Ms. Smith's $1 million to be her own $500,000 plus a $500,000 gift from Mr. Jones. Mr. Jones must now pay gift taxes on the $500,000 he "gifted" to Ms. Smith.

The noncompete can affect the purchaser in another way: The higher the value assigned to the noncompete, the lower the tax basis of the shares or assets that the purchaser bought. Should the purchaser later *sell* some or all of the purchased stock or assets, the gain, and consequently the taxes, would be higher. Thus, the purchaser's plans for disposing of the business or its assets affect the importance of allocating value to the noncompete.

The status of a purchaser as either publicly traded or privately held can make a difference, too. Publicly traded purchasers may prefer the rather modest earnings impact of amortizing goodwill, for example, over twenty to forty years, to the impact of amortizing a noncompete over three to five years. These public firms may hesitate to pay big noncompetes despite the tax benefits, depending on their attitude toward cash flow versus reported earnings.

There is another, ethical, drawback of noncompetes, which affects the selling shareholders. Noncompete payments to one selling shareholder may be viewed dimly by the other selling shareholders, who may view such payments as simply a disguised premium. Unfair

ers who decide to sell will keep a low profile to avoid distracting employees, customers, or vendors, or alerting competitors. Owners either firmly believe that they don't want to sell or haven't ever had to think about selling. Most attractive businesses aren't on the block for precisely the same reason that they're attractive: things are going well, so no one wants out.

Frustrated purchasers with narrow criteria can respond in two ways:

Continue with a passive acquisition strategy (the "shotgun" approach) while accepting longer time horizons

Shift to a dual active/passive strategy (the "rifle" approach)

An active acquisition strategy calls for the purchaser to identify methodically and thoroughly all companies meeting a set of broad and preliminary acquisition criteria, *whether or not these companies are known to be for sale.* Fortunately, in the United States and Canada there are many ways to translate acquisition criteria into a screen of corporate information. Such information even covers tens of thousands of privately held companies, although information on them is usually much less complete and reliable.

Successful hunting requires pinpointing the following preliminary criteria, which make initial screening easier:

Primary line(s) of business

Size (revenues and employees)

Location

Ownership status (public, private, or segment)

Breadth of activities

The federal government maintains a convenient system for defining the first criterion: standard industrial classification (SIC) codes, which neatly classify all U.S. economic activity in four-digit numerical form. Every company can be defined as functioning in one or more SIC code. An engineering firm is classified as being in SIC code 8711, a manufacturer of woodworking machinery in SIC code 3553, a life insurance company in SIC code 6311, and so on. A diversified company may be classified under several codes.

Purchasers can quickly screen corporate databases to rule out companies that don't fit the preliminary criteria. Purchasers can also apply these criteria to other sources such as trade associations, special filings with the Securities and Exchange Commission, and regulatory filings. To shorten what may be a lengthy list of companies, much discipline and judgment is needed in eliminating targets whose industry, size, location, ownership, and business mix *combine* to lower their attractiveness.

Information gaps, particularly on obscure companies, can be lessened, though not eliminated, by obtaining Dun & Bradstreet credit reports and SEC filings. These documents often reveal which owners face a selling decision. At some point, though, it will be necessary to contact these companies and to measure the owners' willingness to talk. Remember, most owners *haven't* decided to sell their businesses and may, in fact, have a powerful emotional commitment to their businesses.

While the search unfolds, the purchaser should simultaneously continue soliciting information on businesses known to be for sale. The "passive" discovery of such a candidate may render further active searching unnecessary.

Contact Tactics

The odds are that the right target won't present itself. Purchasers have to break the ice in order to cull the list of targets. A program of contact generally involves the following:

Deciding in which order to make contact (Should the best target be left for last? Or might this unintentionally result in early agreement on the acquisition of a second-tier candidate?)

Selecting an apparent contact point within each company (usually the controlling shareholder, although sometimes helpful information can be gained from discussion with others)

Choosing the method of initial contact (Telephone call? Letter followed by a telephone call? Social event?)

Identifying the best person to *make* the contact (Purchaser's CEO? Officer? Banker? Lawyer? Accountant? Investment banker?)

Tailoring each contact to the characteristics of the target (Should the purchaser's name be disclosed? Should the purchaser's specific investment preferences be outlined at first? How much should be mentioned about the purchaser and the rationale for a merger before an interest is clearly expressed by the target?)

Agreeing on the best next step (Expression of no further interest, based on the new information? An exchange of financial data? A lunchtime chat? A visit to the target's headquarters, or to the investor company?)

Popping the Question

The moment of initial direct personal contact between executives of the investor company and a desirable target can determine whether the deal has any chance of happening. The owner who has never seriously considered selling must develop chemistry with the purchaser. Otherwise, the purchaser won't have the credibility to persuade the target to join forces and won't convince the unprepared seller that the business is ready to be sold.

Beyond this point, if the interest of more than one attractive candidate has been aroused, the purchaser faces the pleasant problem of comparing several promising opportunities.

Conclusion

Many purchasers never get this far. Many active acquisition strategies fail to uncover the ideal candidate or even to find serious interest. The timing, the desired candidate characteristics, or the contact strategy were probably wrong. If they were, then a continued passive acquisition strategy would have failed, too.

This is exactly the point: Seeking targets by scouring a tightly defined universe of companies in a given size range, location, and line of business *without regard to initial interest in selling* assures the purchaser that nothing has been neglected. At the moderate expense of a concerted research effort, the purchaser drastically lessens the chance that the best acquisition opportunity slips by because no one knew. The best acquisitions can be the least predictable.

Successful Recasting

Preparing the Business for Sale

Today's business owner who decides to sell faces a tough time finding the right purchaser and structuring the best deal. Things become easier if the owner prepares the business—financially and operationally—for sale. The key is to realize that the new owner will run things differently and will measure financial results differently. Even the legal structure may change.

Owners and executives run the business with a blend of personal and financial goals in mind. The purchaser will think differently, probably focusing on returns on investment and on financial, operating, and/or tax synergies.

How can the seller prepare? By reviewing the financial and operating history of the business. The seller wants to highlight items that the purchaser might otherwise miss—or, at least, not fully understand. The seller also wants to clarify anything that might confuse or discourage the purchaser from going forward. This process is often referred to as recasting.

Properly done, recasting improves communications between seller and purchaser and helps both sides agree on price and terms. If the purchaser plans to value the seller's business based, in part, on multiples of earnings or cash flow, appropriate recasting may alter the eventual price by several dollars for each dollar recast.

This section outlines recasting steps that sellers should consider along with brief comments on each. The section doesn't necessarily cover every important item, but provides a starting point for successful recasting by dividing the process into:

Balance sheet

Income statement

Accounting policies

Operations

Balance Sheet

Step 1. Cash. Estimate the minimum, maximum, and average cash balances that the business needs during an operating cycle (for example, one year). Estimate the impact on the income statement (such as loss of interest income) if cash balances were to be cut.

Comment: Privately owned businesses often hold more cash than necessary. (This may not be true for S corporations, which can usually distribute extra cash without negative tax consequences.) The purchaser will want to know how far cash balances can be cut without hampering day-to-day operations. The purchaser and seller can easily treat part or all of the cash balances separately in negotiating a price and deal structure.

Step 2. Nonoperating assets. Identify assets (for example, excess land, idle equipment, company plane, investments in unrelated fields) not needed for operations. Estimate the salable values of these assets.

Comment. The seller may have had reasons for holding these other assets. The purchaser wants to know what investment of hard assets is really needed to run the business. Separating unneeded assets allows both sides to focus on the "true" operating entity.

Step 3. Borrowings. Review borrowings to identify unusually unfavorable or favorable terms (for example, municipally subsidized interest rates). These terms may imply that the

present value of debt obligations differs from their face value on the balance sheet. Consider displaying both the balance sheet and the income statement on a debt-free basis.

Comment. The purchaser will value the business differently depending on the cost and terms of debt that the purchaser will assume. Also, the purchaser will usually capitalize the business differently than the seller will. A debt-free presentation will help the purchaser focus on the operating entity, shorn of debt.

Step 4. Intangibles. Identify easy-to-recognize intangible assets. Consider whether such assets have definite useful lives and whether these assets generate measurable benefit to the business (for example, government-subsidized favorable ten-year leases).

Comment. The purchaser often seeks to identify and amortize intangibles for tax purposes in order to bolster post-transaction cash flow. Better cash flow can increase borrowing capacity. Furthermore, these intangibles help support the seller's price.

Step 5. Asset values. Estimate fair market values for hard assets (for example, land and equipment) used in the business.

Comment. Although the purchaser will need these assets to run the business, making their values at first seem unimportant, these assets values may help the purchaser find financing and pay a higher price.

Step 6. Unrecorded/contingent liabilities. Identify unrecorded/contingent liabilities (for example, pending litigation, warranty contracts, and so on) that may represent future claims on company resources. Estimate the potential cost of these liabilities to the business and their likelihood. (Cost and probability estimates in this area are never easy.)

Comment. The purchaser will value the business based in part on the claims that the purchaser agrees to assume following the sale. Certain potential claims won't be booked if there's a good chance the business won't have to pay them. If the claims are sizable and/or likely, the purchaser will want to consider them in analyzing the business.

Step 7. Noncompete/consulting/earnout agreements. Identify financial commitments arising from prior acquisitions. Estimate the amounts and timing of these commitments and their approximate present value if not recorded on the financial statements.

Comment. These commitments can affect both the balance sheet and the income statement. Often they are expensed as paid, distorting results of operations, while not having been recorded as liabilities.

Income Statement

Step 1. Owner compensation and perquisites. Compare actual amounts recently paid to or accrued for owners for services as executives to estimated amounts to be paid to or accrued for executives performing the same services under new ownership.

Comment. The purchaser may have a different compensation philosophy, may employ different executives, and may not feel the same personal motivations as the seller.

Step 2. Unusual or nonrecurring events. Identify such events as asset write-downs, strikes, plant closings, and one-time expansion costs. Estimate the impact of these events on past income statements.

Comment. Highlighting these events allows both the seller and the purchaser to focus on the ongoing operating earnings capacity of the business.

Step 3. Affiliate transactions. Identify transactions among commonly-owned businesses or segments. Decide whether these transactions affect the income statement (or balance sheet) differently than arm's-length transactions would.

Comment. The purchaser should analyze market-driven terms since these are the terms that will normally exist following a sale.

Step 4. Tax attributes. Identify tax attributes that affect the company's earnings (for example, S corporation status, loss carryforwards, tax credits, and so on). Estimate the impact on the income statement.

Comment. Tax attributes may change dramatically after a sale, especially if assets are sold.

Accounting Policies

Step 1. Inventory. Estimate how the method of inventory valuation (for example, LIFO versus FIFO) has affected earnings (and financial condition).

Comment. The choice of one method of inventory valuation over another can dramatically affect recorded inventory values, earnings, and financial condition. The purchaser may plan to use different methods.

Step 2. Capitalizing versus expensing. Identify past expenditures that were expensed thanks to aggressive expense-versus-capitalization policies. Estimate how less-aggressive policies would have affected the income statement and balance sheet. The decision whether to expense or capitalize can be subjective.

Comment. The purchaser's view of operating earnings power may depend on more conservative expense-versus-capitalization policies, especially if the purchaser trades publicly.

Step 3. Depreciation. Estimate the impact, if any, of accelerated methods of depreciation on the income statement compared with straight-line methods.

Comment. An accelerated method, for example, may overstate economic depreciation in the interest of minimizing taxes. Also, publicly traded purchasers may choose more conservative accounting methods in order to maximize earnings.

Step 4. Revenue/expense recognition. Identify revenues/expenses that may have been booked in fiscal periods that differ from the periods in which they were earned/incurred (for example, contract revenues).

Comment. These timing distortions can mask the ongoing operating earning power of the seller's business.

Operations

Step 1. Discontinued operations. Estimate the impact of discontinued operations on historical financial statements. Show how the income statement would have appeared had these operations *never* been part of the business.

Comment. The purchaser will focus on the operating entity as it is currently configured. Previously discontinued operations may distort the apparent earnings potential of today's operations.

Step. 2. Seasonality. Identify times of year when the business experiences operational "highs" and "lows." Develop year-to-year comparisons.

Comment. Seasonal fluctuations can confuse potential purchasers, and can even complicate the drafting of terms covering post-closing adjustments.

Step 3. Overhead allocations. Compare allocations to operating affiliates for services performed (for example, insurance, capital infusions, treasury) with the estimated "real" cost of replacing these services under new ownership.

Comment. The purchaser may allocate quite differently, or may plan to hire or invest in stand-alone services.

Step 4. Business environment. Identify significant changes that may be triggered by new ownership (for example, gaining a new customer or losing an old one). Estimate how such changes will affect sales, cost of sales, and so forth.

Comment. For personal, legal, and/or competitive reasons, customers, suppliers, and others may choose to do business differently with a company under new ownership. A careful purchaser will want to understand what may happen.

Conclusion

A thorough recasting helps position the operating business for sale. The intent is to educate rather than mislead the purchaser, who will usually want to understand the earnings history and financial condition of the ongoing operating entity.

Some recasting steps require little effort on the seller's part and can be done informally. Others may require outside accounting or financial expertise. The investment in time and cost is often well worth the effort and can lead to a successful sale at a fair price.

Going Public Versus Selling Out

Today's business headlines make the M&A arena seem like the best place for business owners to cash out. There's also talk of private placements, which will become much easier if, as expected, the SEC changes certain of its rules. Whatever became of going public?

The strategically astute business owner shouldn't assume that an initial public offering (IPO) is no longer a viable alternative. While IPOs are tougher now than they were in the early 1980s—and, as always, the IPO market is fickle—IPOs still solve many problems facing businesses and their owners. To decide what to do, owners must know who can go public, the pluses and minuses, what will happen, and when to take other paths such as selling the business.

IPO Advantages

Businesses most often go public to raise equity capital without greatly diluting corporate control. Public stockholders rarely intrude in day-to-day operations, whereas other sources of capital look more closely. Also, IPO proceeds can be applied to R&D or marketing activities for which banks may lend only reluctantly.

Third, most IPOs bolster stockholders' equity and therefore debt capacity. Such IPOs are triply effective since the company obtains

IPO funds, access to extra bank money—and cheaper rates. A fourth advantage of an IPO—if successful—is the momentum it creates. If the stock rises, the company can raise still more money with secondary offerings, each of which will dilute control less than the IPO. A strong share price can also underpin executive and employee compensation plans.

A sixth advantage of going public is that the company's stock can become an acquisition "currency" for purchasing other businesses. Target-company shareholders will sometimes consider payment in the form of the purchaser's shares rather than in cash, since such shares are liquid (they trade publicly) and since target company shareholders receiving the purchaser's shares may be able to defer capital gains taxes. Finally, the IPO confers on the purchaser visibility and credibility with its suppliers, markets, and customers.

IPO Drawbacks

Does this mean that an IPO usually makes sense? Not at all. Most privately held businesses that could go public choose not to. Why?

First, IPOs destroy privacy, which most owners value almost as much as their independence. Once-confidential company information will be known to customers, competitors, suppliers, and anyone else who chooses to read required company filings. The time and cost to report and file quarterly results, major changes in the company's operations or business, sig-

nificant transactions, and the like constitute an additional drawback to IPOs.

Earnings performance pressures will increase, too. All eyes focus on the trading price of the company's stock. Quarter-to-quarter earnings trends compete with long-term plans for the attention of management. Without immediate growth prospects, the stock price may suffer.

Fiduciary issues also confront post-IPO management and employees, including insider trading rules and greater risks of personal liability arising from perceived breaches of responsibility to shareholders than before the IPO.

Yet another problem with IPOs is their near irreversibility. Once public, businesses can go private again only after extensive disclosures—and the risk of a hostile suitor.

Finally, IPOs don't usually put much cash in the pockets of pre-IPO shareholders, as the chart on page 78 shows. Investors want their money to go to the company, rather than its owners. Founders can't count on cashing in more than 10 percent to 15 percent of their shares in an IPO.

Who Can Go Public?

Businesses across a wide economic spectrum have gone public, but investors greet each new offering differently. Industries go in and out of favor. Investors usually look for compelling earnings progress for at least the previous two years. Most IPO candidates are relatively small companies with the potential to become major players in their industry. Annual sales of $10 million to $25 million with good margins and historical and projected earnings growth of 20 percent a year will often attract investor interest.

In a bullish IPO market, financial history may not matter as much. In such markets, companies with little or no operating history—but in "hot" industries and with well-credentialed managers—can go public. During IPO bull markets, investors care most about what management has done, how well they know the competition, whether they can successfully market the company's products or services, and how tightly they control cash flow.

During 1989, before the October correction, the market for IPOs was selective but viable. The outlook for more IPOs depends largely on the strength of over-the-counter (OTC) markets where most newly public companies trade. OTC trends lead IPO activity, which recovers only slowly from market shocks such as the October 1987 crash and the October 1989 correction. Constant and sometimes sudden shifts in the IPO market require management and owners to tread with care.

How to Go Public

Securities are usually sold to the public with help from an investment banking firm that underwrites the sale of the securities. While securities can be sold to the public without an underwriter, doing so is uncommon. A good underwriter provides a network for selling the company's securities and guides every step in the IPO process.

Underwriters usually handle an IPO in one of two ways. In a "firm commitment" transaction, the underwriter agrees that it will purchase the issue from the company for resale to the public. In a "best efforts" transaction, the underwriter merely agrees that it will do what it can to sell the issue directly to the public. Firm-commitment underwritings therefore entail less financial risk for the company and its owners.

Choosing the right underwriter is essential. Underwriters differ markedly in size, ability, and willingness to work with smaller companies. Except in a bullish IPO market, larger underwriters usually turn down offerings under $10 million and require prior-year after-tax earnings of at least $2 million.

Some firms will underwrite smaller companies with exciting potential. These underwriters' names appear in IPO announcements or reference sources such as the *Investment Dealers Digest* or the *National OTC Stock Journal.*

A good underwriter provides support after the IPO. Aftermarket support includes open-market share purchases and research on the company's performance. Aftermarket support ensures an orderly market in which selling isn't likely to push down share prices abruptly. The underwriter's research prowess helps since research reports can stimulate investor interest and reduce uncertainty. Finally, the underwriter's financial strength matters more

A Sample IPO

Pre-IPO sales[1]	$40 million (two-year compound growth: 15 percent)
Pre-IPO net earnings[1]	$3 million (two-year compound growth: 20 percent)
Pre-IPO stockholders' equity[1]	$10 million
Pre-IPO number of shares[1]	4 million (five founders, 800,000 shares each)
Post-IPO number of shares[2]	5 million (founders have 700,000 each, public has 1,500,000)
Number of shares floated to public	1.5 million (500,000 founder shares, 1,000,000 new shares)
IPO price per share	$10 (based on underwriter/founder negotiations)
IPO size	$15 million (before $1,500,000 in fees)
Proceeds to founders	$4.5 million
Proceeds to company	$9 million
Use of company proceeds	New facilities, debt repayment
Post-IPO stockholders' equity	$19 million
Post-IPO net earnings after tax	? (higher, thanks to new facilities and lower interest costs)
Percentage of each founder's stake liquefied	12.5 percent

[1]For the 12 months preceding the IPO.
[2]After a 1,000:1 stock split.

than ever, thanks to today's added market volatility. When underwriters go out of business, the smaller company stocks they supported often suffer.

Underwriters usually base their fees on the size of the IPO. Underwriter fees are regulated by the National Association of Securities Dealers (NASD). The underwriter sometimes asks for stock purchase warrants (rarely more than 5 percent to 10 percent of fully diluted shares) as incentive to provide aftermarket support. The IPO candidate pays printing costs, accounting and legal fees, and other associated offering costs, which may range from $170,000 to $250,000 on the smallest IPOs.

An IPO requires filing of a registration statement with the Securities and Exchange Commission (SEC) and the NASD. The registration statement details the company for investors and other interested parties. Preparing this document is one of the toughest parts of the IPO process. The registration statement requires management, the underwriter, lawyers, and accountants to work together closely and smoothly. Does this mean staying with long-standing advisers? Not always. The IPO may require some changes so that the team has the right IPO track record.

During the drafting of the registration statement, the underwriter and corporate attorney complete their due diligence on the company. The SEC and the NASD require such due diligence to ensure that the filing is thorough. Due diligence questions cover management, customer and supplier references, industry and competitor evaluation, financial analysis including management's projections, and hidden or contingent company liabilities.

The company then files its completed registration statement with the SEC and the NASD.

The underwriter's sales force distributes part of the registration statement, called the preliminary prospectus, to potential investors. Advance sales of stock can't be made during this phase of the offering, but the underwriter can get indications of investor interest. While the preliminary prospectus circulates, the SEC reviews the entire registration statement. The SEC often requires modifications to the original draft.

Once satisfied, the SEC declares the registration statement effective. The underwriter then determines how many shares to underwrite, along with the per-share price. The size and pricing of the offering are usually set by reference to the valuations of similar companies in the public securities markets, but the underwriter also subjectively measures the appetites of potential investors. Offer size and price occasionally become the subject of company/underwriter disputes.

To reduce the chance of a poor investor reception, shares are priced 10 percent to 15 percent *below* the underwriter's assessment of a stable trading price. Within several weeks after the registration statement's effective date, a closing takes place, at which time the underwriter conveys the proceeds of the offering to the issuing company.

Alternatives to Going Public

Going public often isn't the right solution. Most companies finance the earlier stages of their growth in other ways. Borrowings and internally generated funds finance growth. Rapid growth, ironically, imposes limits on both of these sources of growth capital. Corporate equity—scarce at young companies—often caps debt levels while growth can actually devour working capital rather than generate internal funds.

Other sources of financing include venture capital, corporate partners, or private equity placements. Each of these alternatives injects outsider expectations of profits and growth; each also dilutes corporate independence, ownership, and—sometimes—control. All of these other financing sources can bring in business skills, experience, and contacts, which are desperately needed by growing businesses.

Additional alternatives range from various state and federal loan programs to intrastate forms of exempt equity offerings. The Small Business Administration loan program is tailored to meet the needs of cash-starved companies. Many states have similar programs that provide incentives for local businesses to remain in-state. Several states also encourage businesses to raise equity capital through intrastate securities offerings. Such offerings must be limited in size and distribution to sidestep federal securities regulation.

Only if none of these ideas works should business owners consider selling their companies. Why should a sale be a last resort? Because anecdotal evidence implies that most acquisitions disappoint both purchasers and sellers. The process is personal and disruptive, and usually irreversible.

Conclusion

Few choices matter more for small businesses than whether to go public. The reasons for going public usually differ so vastly from the reasons for selling that the two paths shouldn't be considered as solutions to the same problems. Every business owner should carefully weigh financing alternatives and should understand when IPOs make sense.

Changes in the Private Placement Market— Rule 144A

The Securities and Exchange Commission adopted new rules in 1990 that make it easier to trade unregulated, privately placed securities. If, as expected, a brisk new market evolves, owners of many private businesses will have a new place to seek capital. This new capital source may change the way M&A deals are done, and provide an alternative to selling out entirely.

Rule 144A and related changes mark a departure from the SEC's traditional role as a zealous investor watchdog. For nearly six decades, the SEC's philosophy has required maximum public disclosure by sellers of stocks and bonds. The SEC's action was spurred in part by the growth of global trading and the heightened need for streamlined securities

regulation. The net effect of the SEC's changes should be reduced capital costs for both U.S. and foreign companies.

The Private Placement Market

Junk bonds, often publicly held, attracted most of the publicity surrounding the explosive growth of debt markets in the 1980s, but it was privately placed debt that grew to be half the size of all publicly traded corporate debt in 1989. While $25 billion in junk bonds were issued in 1989, the figure for private placement debt is over five times higher, with more than $137 billion in new issues. This doesn't include approximately $12 billion of debt placed without the aid of intermediaries. According to IDD Information Services, private placement issues totaled $170 billion last year, including convertible securities and common and preferred stock. Privately placed debt is a hybrid instrument, somewhere between a loan and a bond. It has certain characteristics of a bond, although often with stricter covenants and call protection than public bonds, but can be tailored to the borrower like a loan. The perception that junk bonds cut substantially into the private placement market is clearly wrong: Private placements grew tenfold during the 1980s.

It is estimated that there is another $170 billion in private placement money waiting to be tapped. The new SEC rules, which encourage a trading market, may draw this capital into the marketplace. Accordingly, commercial and investment banks have been building their private placement departments in anticipation of a boom in new private issues.

Rule 144 and 145 Amendments

On April 19, 1990, the Securities and Exchange Commission adopted Rule 144A and related amendments to Rule 144 and Rule 145. Rule 144 and Rule 145 permit the public resale of restricted securities when certain conditions, including a minimum holding period, are met. Under the amended rules, the required holding period of restricted securities is redefined to begin when the securities are sold by the issuer or its affiliate, rather than when the holder acquired the securities. Rule 144A provides a "safe harbor" from the registration requirements of the Securities Act of 1933 for resales of restricted securities to "qualified institutional buyers" as defined below.

Qualified Institutional Buyers

For the purposes of Rule 144A, qualified institutional buyers is defined to include the following:

Institutions, excluding banks and savings and loans, that in the aggregate own and invest, on a discretionary basis, $100 million or more in securities of issuers that are not affiliated with the institution

Banks and savings and loan institutions with an audited net worth of $25 million or more in addition to owning and investing on a discretionary basis $100 million or more in securities of unaffiliated issuers

Registered broker-dealers that own and invest, on a discretionary basis, $10 billion or more in securities of unaffiliated issuers, or broker-dealers acting as riskless principals for qualified institutional buyers

Regulation S

The SEC also approved Regulation S, which clarifies that the registration provisions of the Securities Act of 1933 do not apply to the offer and sale of securities outside of the United States, provided certain specified conditions are met. To qualify under Regulation S, both the sale and the offer relating to that sale must be made outside the U.S. In addition, there can be no direct selling efforts conducted in the U.S. in connection with an offer or sale of securities made under the safe harbor provisions of Regulation S.

PORTAL Computer System

Along with the amendments, the SEC approved PORTAL, a screen-based computer and communications system proposed by the National Association of Securities Dealers. The system will ease primary placements and the secondary trading of securities that qualify under Rule 144A. PORTAL will provide a centralized market for Rule 144A securities and support the negotiation, clearance, and settlement of private placements.

Eligible Securities

To prevent the new private placements from directly paralleling the public market, a series of restrictions applies to Rule 144A securities. Eligible securities must not be of the same class, when issued, as securities listed on a U.S. securities exchange or quoted on NASDAQ. Common equity securities will be considered to be of the same class if holders enjoy substantially similar rights and privileges. Preferred equity and debt securities will be deemed to be of the same class as registered preferred equity securities and debt securities, respectively, if their terms are substantially identical. A convertible security would be considered to be of the same class as the underlying security unless, at issuance, it is subject to an effective conversion premium of at least 10 percent. Warrants will also be treated as securities of the same class as the underlying security unless the warrant has a life of at least three years and an effective exercise premium of at least 10 percent. The test would be applicable to warrants, either trading as part of a unit with another security or separately.

Rule 144A would be available to securities issued by foreign companies that are listed on foreign securities exchanges, but are not listed on a U.S. securities exchange or NASDAQ.

Issuer Information

The safe harbor exemption from the registration requirements under the Securities Act of 1933 requires at least certain amounts of financial and other information from the issuer. For domestic and foreign private issuers that already comply with the periodic reporting requirements under the Securities and Exchange Act of 1934, no additional disclosure is required. Foreign private issuers currently applying the Rule 12g3-2(b) exemption also will not be required to provide additional information. Other foreign private issuers that have securities traded on a non-U.S. securities exchange should be able to meet the informational requirement under Rule 144A by furnishing information otherwise required to be made public by the home country or by the non-U.S. securities exchange.

For all other issuers, including a foreign government not eligible to register securities under the Securities Act, the Rule will require that certain information about the issuer be available to the holder and the prospective purchasers and that the prospective purchaser receive such information if so requested. The Rule requires a brief statement of the nature of the issuer's business, its products and/or services offered, and its most recent financial information, including statements of financial condition, profit and loss, and retained earnings. Financial information is also required for the two preceding fiscal years, or from the issuer's inception if less than two years. The financial information should be audited to the extent reasonably available. The information must be "reasonably current," which will be satisfied if:

The balance sheet is dated no earlier than sixteen months before the date of resale and profit and loss and retained earnings statements for the two years then ended are provided. If the balance sheet is dated more than six months prior to the date of resale, profit and loss and retained earnings statements covering a period from the balance sheet date to a date no more than six months prior to the resale date would also be required.

The statement of the nature of the issuer's business, its products, and its services offered is as of a date within twelve months prior to the date of resale; or, for foreign issuers, the required information meets the timing requirement of the issuer's home country or principal trading markets.

Conclusion

Business owners considering an acquisition or sale will find new financing strategies and deal structures as a result of these new rules. The SEC's changes should benefit issuers of securities by lowering their cost of capital. A new market will develop in the United States for foreign issuers that have previously avoided the U.S. public capital markets because of onerous registration and disclosure requirements. U.S.- and foreign-based companies alike, whose stocks and bonds are traded solely in the private placement market, will not be required to meet the rigorous initial and continuing disclosure requirements of the SEC applicable to companies operating in the public capital markets in the U.S. Rule 144A and the related amendments will increase the liquidity and efficiency of the U.S. private placement market, creating downward pressure on borrowing rates. This, coupled with lower registration and disclosure costs, will allow corporations to raise funds more quickly and less expensively.

5

Going Public

The term "going public" generally refers to a closely held company's first interstate sale of securities to the general public. In order to go public a company is required to file with the Securities and Exchange Commission (SEC) a registration statement that is in compliance with the Securities Act of 1933 (the '33 Act).

The '33 Act mandates certain disclosures for registration statements. Its objective is to ensure that a company selling securities on an interstate basis discloses relevant information about its business, financial condition, results of operations, officers, and principal shareholders. The purpose of the disclosures is to allow investors to make informed decisions about whether to invest in the company's securities.

The SEC administers the '33 Act and reviews all initial public offerings. The SEC does not judge the merits of an offering but acts to ensure that all of the required disclosures have been made in the registration statement.

What Are the Typical Characteristics of Companies That Go Public?

Sound management is the most important characteristic if a company is to be successful in obtaining public financing. Underwriters and the investing public look first to the quality, integrity, and experience of management as a key indicator that an investment will be protected and enhanced. Companies with relatively inexperienced management have gone public successfully but usually only under exceptional circumstances such as when a company's products or services are considered to have extraordinary potential.

Other important characteristics are the company's size, earnings performance, and potential for growth. In evaluating whether the public will be interested in purchasing your securities, you should review your company's sales and earnings performance over the past five years, or since inception if your company is less than five years old. If your company's performance shows sustained growth of greater than 20 percent a year with the potential to maintain or exceed that growth rate over the next several years, the investing public will generally be very interested in purchasing your securities.

Compare your sales and earnings performance to successful public companies of similar size in your industry. The greater your company's growth potential, the less importance is placed on historical sales and earnings performance by the investing public. Generally, the investing public is most receptive to companies that have annual revenues in the range of $20 million, net earnings of $1 million or more for the company's most recent year, and the potential of achieving revenues of $100 million or more in five to ten years. However, many companies that did not meet this size test have gone public. These companies overcame their lack of a proven operating history

with some significant compensating factors that attracted the investing public. Examples of such factors include a unique product with a substantial growth potential and a management team with a proven track record of developing successful companies.

Should My Company Go Public?

Businesses go public for a variety of reasons, but most growing companies consider a public offering to obtain additional capital for corporate growth. Before deciding to go public, consider the advantages and disadvantages.

The Advantages

Unrestricted use of funds. Use of the proceeds from a company's sales of securities is generally unrestricted. The funds may be used for research and development, acquisition of property, plant and equipment, reducing existing debt, or increasing working capital.

Compensation vehicle. Stock-based compensation plans for a publicly traded company provide an excellent compensation strategy for attracting and retaining managers and key employees.

Improved financial condition. The sales of equity securities will increase the company's net worth and generally improve its borrowing capability. If the company's stock does well in the public market, additional equity can be raised on favorable terms. Management thus increases its financing alternatives.

Acquisitions. A company with publicly traded stock is in a position to make acquisitions by offering its own stock, thereby not incurring additional debt.

Prestige. By taking a company public management is undertaking a long-term commitment. Some suppliers and customers may prefer to do business with companies whose financial statements are publicly available.

Marketable holdings. Once a company goes public and a market is established for its shares, the shareholders can readily determine the market value of their holdings. The market for the share establishes a high level of liquidity for the shareholders' investment.

The Disadvantages

Stock price management. To fully realize the benefits of going public management needs to maintain and then increase the market value of the company's stock. This is normally accomplished by achieving consistently increasing quarterly profits. The pressure to maintain this earnings trend sometimes results in delays and cancellations of necessary research and development or other long-term expenditures. This potential problem can result in the sacrifice of long-term projects for short-term earnings results.

Life in a fishbowl. When a company is publicly owned, the public has a right to know some of its most closely guarded information. Management is required to disclose executive salaries, related-party transactions, competitive positions, related affiliates, and significant customers and suppliers, among other things. This information is required in the initial registration statement and is updated at least annually. Management will need to take into account the practical and legal considerations of being a public company before making any significant business decisions. As an example, a major decision could result in a filing of a descriptive report with the SEC, a press release, and a vote by the board of directors and shareholders.

Expenses. The expenses incurred with the initial public offering include the underwriter's commissions, filing fees, and out-of-pocket expenses. The underwriter's commissions generally range from 7 percent to 10 percent of the total offering amount, depending on the size of the offering. Out-of-pocket expenses can range between $170,000 and $500,000. In addition, the ongoing expense of being a public company, depending on the company's circumstances, can be significant.

Loss of control. Depending on the size of the initial and subsequent offerings, the owners may be threatened with the loss of control of the company.

Before deciding to go public you must weigh

the advantages and disadvantages in light of the plans and goals you have for yourself and your company. We also encourage you to discuss the matter with investment bankers, your attorney, accountants, other professional advisers, and executives of other companies that have gone public in the past few years.

Overview of the Going Public Process

Before deciding to go public you should have a good understanding of the going public process, which usually takes several months to complete.

Sequence of events. The first task in the going public process is the selection of an underwriter. The underwriter purchases the securities from the company and sells them to the public through a syndicate. Management must demonstrate to the underwriter that the company is qualified to go public. The sales price per share and the number of shares offered are negotiated with the underwriter.

Once the underwriter is on board the next step is preparing the registration statement. As previously noted, the registration statement is the disclosure document filed with the SEC. It consists of two parts, the prospectus and the supplemental information section. The prospectus is the document that is distributed to potential purchasers of the securities. The supplemental information is filed with the SEC for public inspection. Preparation of the regis-

tration statement is the most time-consuming event in the process of going public.

Once the registration statement is completed in draft form it is printed and filed with the SEC. The underwriter then distributes copies of the preliminary prospectus. Although the underwriter cannot take orders or deliver securities until the registration statement becomes effective, most of the underwriter's selling effort takes place during this period. The managing underwriter first forms a sales and distribution syndicate. This syndicate of underwriters uses its salespeople to distribute the preliminary prospectus to clients and to orally obtain indications of interest. Although these indications are not binding, they do represent investor interest.

After receipt of the registration statement the SEC reviews the document and responds (usually in four to six weeks) with comments about disclosures that the SEC staff reviewers believe need clarification. After the SEC is satisfied with responses to their comments and the related modifications are made to the registration statement, the SEC will declare the registration statement effective.

Once the SEC is satisfied with the registration statement but before it is declared effective, ordinarily you will complete negotiations with the underwriter regarding the share price and number of shares to be offered, and a final amendment on the registration statement (called the "pricing amendment") is filed. Sometimes these negotiations are not concluded until after the effective date of the registration statement and the price is reflected in the final prospectus. Once the pricing has been completed the final prospectus is printed and sent to the underwriters' customers along with the confirmation of sale.

The final step in the process is the closing. The closing is held about one week after the effective date, giving the underwriter time to receive most customers' payments. The underwriter gives the company a check for the proceeds from the offering, and the company gives the underwriter the stock certificates.

What professional assistance do I need to go public? Because of the complex nature of the securities laws and the requirement for audited financial statements, the company will need the assistance of legal counsel with extensive securities law experience. It will also need an accounting firm, preferably one that has been involved in a number of initial public offerings and is familiar with your industry.

Role of the attorneys. It is of the utmost importance that the company's legal counsel be well versed and up-to-date in SEC matters and public offerings. There are serious penalties for issuing registration statements containing material misstatements or omissions. If your present attorneys are not qualified in the securities area, it could create a sensitive relationship problem. It is not uncommon, however, to retain special SEC counsel to work with existing counsel. SEC counsel's primary role is to advise management of its responsibil-

ity and liability under the securities laws and to coordinate the preparation of the registration statement. In addition, SEC counsel has further responsibilities:

Serving as the primary contact with the SEC and the financial printer of the registration statement

Acting as the liaison with all parties in the registration process (that is, management, underwriter, underwriter's counsel, and accountants)

Conducting corporate housekeeping—reviewing and completing all minutes of the board and shareholder meetings

Ensuring proper authorization, amount, and class of stock (that is, recapitalizing the company if appropriate)

Reviewing and revising articles of incorporation and bylaws

Reviewing all contracts and leases

Reviewing the ownership status of all major assets

Monitoring the activities of the company very closely during the period between the filing and effective dates for any developments that would affect the offering

Role of the accountants. The accountants can assist you in the going public process by:

Auditing the company's financial statements. The SEC requires three years (from inception if the company is less than three years old) of audited financial statements for initial public offerings in excess of $7.5 million. Some underwriters, as a practical matter, like to see five years of audited historical financial statements to assist them in their investigation of the company.

Assisting the company in determining the appropriate accounting principles within its industry and those principles that the SEC will accept. This is necessary because at the time of an initial public registration the company is given a one-time option under the accounting profession's rules to retroactively change accounting principles.

Assisting the company in the preparation and review of the financial information included in the registration statement prepared by the client

Assisting the company in responding to any questions raised by the SEC

If you are considering going public in a few years, you should have audits done on an annual basis even though they are not presently required. This preparation will allow you to choose the most advantageous time (the window) for going public without the time-consuming delays of a cumulative three-year audit.

The CEO's role. The CEO will be actively involved in planning the public offering, from making the decision to go public to selecting the underwriter and the other professionals. Once preparation of the registration statement begins many long and tedious meetings will be held to discuss, review, or revise the registration statement.

Although the registration statement tasks assigned to the company generally become the responsibility of the chief financial officer, the chief executive officer must be involved. For example, the CEO's overall perspective on the company's activities and objectives is very important to the preparation of the sections of the prospectus describing the business and use of proceeds. Furthermore, all parties involved are subject to civil and criminal liabilities under the '33 Act for misstatements or omissions in the registration statement and prospectus. Therefore, everyone must read the entire registration statement and consider the implications of all revisions. In this regard many CEOs who have been through the process say that they underestimated the time required to prepare a registration statement.

The cost of going public. The largest cost of the offering is the underwriter's discount or commission. The discount generally ranges from 7 percent to 10 percent of the gross proceeds from the offering. The discount is reviewed for fairness by the National Association of Securities Dealers, Inc. (NASD). The underwriter determines the discount by taking into account several factors such as the size of the offering, the type of commitment, and the type of securities being offered. Underwriters generally do not consider the discount percentage to be negotiable outside of a narrow range.

In addition to the underwriter's discount you will incur legal fees, accounting fees, printing costs, and other costs. These costs can vary significantly depending on the circumstances of the offering.

Legal fees normally range from $50,000 to $150,000 depending on the orderliness of the legal records and the amount of time the company's counsel spends in drafting the registration statement and participating in the going public process.

Accounting fees (excluding audits of the financial statements) range from $40,000 to $80,000 depending on the time the accountants spend in drafting the registration statement and participating in the going public process. If audits are required, expect to add $50,000 to $200,000 depending on the size of the company, the condition of the records, and the number of years required to be audited.

Printing costs range from $50,000 to $180,000 depending on the number of proofs required between the initial proof and the final document. Other costs, including the filing fee, "blue sky" fees, transfer agent fees, and miscellaneous fees can range from $30,000 to $100,000.

The following table summarizes the estimated lower and upper range for the above-discussed costs:

The Cost of Going Public		
	Lower	Upper
Underwriter's discount (assuming $10 million offering)	$700,000	$1,000,000
Legal fees	50,000	150,000
Accounting fees (exclusive of audits)	40,000	80,000
Printing costs	50,000	180,000
Other costs (filing fee, blue sky fees, transfer agent fees, miscellaneous)	30,000	100,000
	$870,000	$1,510,000

These expenses for the most part are paid out of the proceeds from the public offering. Underwriter counsel's fees are typically paid by the underwriter with the exception of the review of the blue sky laws (that is, state securities laws) as they affect the offering.

The tax consequences of going public. For most private companies there are no significant advantages or disadvantages in being a publicly held company from a corporate tax perspective. Before going public it is strongly recommended that management evaluate the company's tax accounting exposure areas and make appropriate changes.

As a public company your tax practices are much more visible because of disclosures in your financial statements. In addition, disputes with federal and state taxing authorities that involve material amounts would need to be disclosed in your financial statements. Keep in mind that claims by taxing authorities tend to cast a negative light on the company.

Experience has shown that in many situations the market value of the shares of a private company that goes public will increase substantially. It is critically important that the major shareholders of a private company involved in an initial public offering develop a comprehensive personal tax strategy. Matters that should be considered in this strategy include the following:

The gifting of shares to children and/or other members of the family unit prior to the public offering to reduce gift, estate, or income taxes

The timing of the offering and the amount of gain to be realized from the sale of shares if a secondary offering is contemplated by the major shareholders

The change in cash compensation and employee benefits (for example, insurance or stock options) to be received from the company as a result of the offering

Assessing a Management Team and Board of Directors

The most important characteristic that must be present if a company is to be successful in obtaining public financing is the quality of its management. One of the required disclosures in the prospectus is the identification of the senior members of management and the board of directors. The disclosures encompass each management member's work experience for the past five years. The management team and board of directors must be salable to the investing public. Therefore, the most difficult decision to be made by the CEO of a private company contemplating going public is whether the company has the right management team—one that is capable of developing a small, private company into a larger, successful public company that consistently generates earnings.

The CEO needs to realistically assess his management team as well as his own capabilities. Below are several factors to be considered in making this assessment:

The company needs to be professionally managed. Growth will necessitate more delegation of duties and authority.

As a public company, management will be taking on new legal, accounting, administrative, and public relations problems. This new undertaking will mean a whole new perspective in doing business.

From the analyst's and investor's point of view, the company's focus should be on consistent increases in quarterly earnings, which translates into favorable stock prices.

Planning a Compensation Strategy

Because of the importance of attracting and retaining outstanding officers and directors for your company, you must devise a compensation strategy. There is strong competition among business entities to attract, motivate, and retain high-caliber executive talent. This competition is reflected in the multitude of arrangements various entities have developed to compensate their executives.

Most executive compensation programs involve four general categories of compensation. Although some executive compensation packages place different emphasis on specific aspects of the compensation program, most of them include all or a combination of the following.

Deferred salary and supplemental retirement income arrangements. These are arrangements that allow participants to defer the receipt and taxability of a portion of their current compensation and arrangements where a company agrees to provide supplemental income to an individual in certain future periods if specified conditions are met.

Awards granted pursuant to capital accumulation plans. These awards provide participants with the right to receive cash, the right to receive or acquire capital stock, or the right to receive and/or acquire a combination of cash and capital stock as consideration for performance of personal services. The types and characteristics of capital accumulation plans have become increasingly complex over the past several years because of a desire by companies to design and implement plans that are responsive to the objectives of both the enterprise and its participating employees. The design of such plans requires a thorough understanding of such objectives as well as an understanding of relevant accounting principles and current tax laws.

Qualified deferred-compensation arrangements. These are funded pension and profit-sharing plans in which substantially all full-time employees participate.

Although individual circumstances may dictate specific executive compensation packages, the overall objective of a sound compensation program is to ensure that compensation is externally competitive, internally equitable, and defined by a compensation strategy that in turn is linked to the company's business plan.

A review of recent prospectuses and annual proxies of similar-sized public companies within your industry will give you a good indication of what compensation programs are considered effective.

Consideration should be given to when your company's compensation program should be put in place. It is much easier to have your compensation program approved by your shareholders while you are a private company than when you are a public company.

Selecting the Professionals

You should become knowledgeable about the going public process before making contact with the professionals. Selecting the right professionals and being knowledgeable enough to make sure they do a top-quality job should be major objectives. First, it is important for you to select the right underwriter. In addition to the underwriter you must select accountants, attorneys, and a printer.

Accountants. Accountants are critical players in the going public process. It is essential that you present a clear financial picture to both the underwriter and investors. You should establish a relationship with accountants and, if possible, have financial statements audited several years before a possible public offering. In selecting accountants it is, of course, very important to choose a firm that is experienced in SEC reporting matters, understands your industry, and is acceptable to the underwriter.

A common approach in selecting accountants is to interview several firms and request proposals. The proposal should disclose the accounting firm's public offering experience within your industry, describe individuals to be assigned to your engagement, and estimate the range of fees and expenses for all audit work and assistance in the offering.

Printer. Selection of a qualified, experienced financial printer is very important to a successful public offering. All printers are not experienced in the requirements for printing a registration statement to be filed with the SEC. The SEC has specific presentation and format guidelines that it expects in all offering documents. Only a select group of financial printers in the country understands the registration process and can handle this type of work.

Because of their experience, attorneys and underwriters are in a good position to recommend or select the printer. Therefore, you should consult with these professionals before making your selection. Selection of a printer can be postponed until after you have chosen your SEC counsel and the underwriter.

Financial Statement Considerations

Is my accounting system in order? Public companies must maintain adequate accounting and financial records and a system of internal accounting control for several important reasons. The financial analysts and the investing public will insist that the company report timely results of operations for each quarter and year end. The analysts will also push for quarterly and yearly projections of operating results. To establish credibility with the public marketplace, the company's results-of-operations releases must be reliable, meaningful, and timely.

Most companies that file a '33 Act registration statement are also required to be registered under the '34 Act. The '34 Act registrants are required to file periodic reports with the SEC. For example, the '34 Act requires that within forty-five days of the close of each of the company's first three quarters a Form 10-Q be filed with the SEC, and within ninety days of the fiscal year end a Form 10-K must be filed.

In addition, the Foreign Corrupt Practices

Act of 1977 (FCPA) requires all companies that are registered or filed reports under the '34 Act to devise and maintain a system of internal accounting control sufficient to provide reasonable assurance that:

Transactions are executed in accordance with management's authorization

Transactions are recorded as necessary to permit preparation of financial statements in conformity with generally accepted accounting principles (GAAP), and to maintain accountability for assets

Access to assets is permitted only in accordance with management's authorization

The recorded accountability for assets is compared with the existing assets at reasonable intervals and appropriate action is taken with respect to any differences.

In consideration of the statutory requirements and the demands for timely financial information, it is important that the company's accounting system be in place and working before going public.

Financial statement audits. Because of the SEC's extensive audit requirements you should have annual audits performed even though they may not be presently demanded by shareholders or lenders. If your financial statements have not been audited, however, we suggest that you immediately arrange for your accountants to perform the required audits. (See discussion of the registration pro-cess, page 102.) You should be prepared for several potential problems.

First, it may not be possible to audit your financial statements for the period required in a registration statement. For example, if you have significant inventories, your auditors generally must observe and test your annual physical inventory counts for each of the years under audit. Since this cannot be performed after the fact, your auditors may be unable to issue an unqualified opinion on your company's financial statements. The investing public expects an unqualified opinion and the SEC will not accept an audit that is limited in scope.

Second, the results of an audit may affect your company's financial statements significantly. Your financial statements are used as a basis for the preliminary discussions with the investment banking firms. If after the auditors have completed their procedures the necessary adjustments adversely affect your earnings or trend of earnings, the changes could cause the underwriter to cancel or delay the public offering. It is extremely important for the company to have reliable financial statements when discussions are held with the investment banking firms.

Related-party transactions. Related-party transactions (transactions between the company and insiders) will be fully disclosed in the registration statement and to a lesser extent in the financial statements. Disclosure of these transactions may cause embarrassment and can make your company less attractive to underwriters and investors. It makes sense that you, with the help of your attorney, depersonalize your company. That can be done by making the necessary revisions in the terms of all contracts (leases, employment contracts, stock option plans, and so forth) with related parties. The SEC defines related parties as principal owners, management and members of their immediate families, equity investees, trusts for the benefit of employees that are managed by management, and the registrants' affiliates or other parties who control or significantly influence management or operating policies of the company.

Full disclosure. The transition from a private company to a public company can be painful. Proprietary information considered the company's "secret of success" may now be disclosed publicly. Unless the company is willing to make full disclosure in compliance with both the letter and the spirit of the law, going public is not advisable.

In addition to management's remuneration and related-party transactions, there are a number of other required disclosures the company may deem to be sensitive. Examples of these types of disclosures to be made in the registration statement are as follows:

General development of the business over the past five years

Financial results of the company broken down by segments

Principal products, markets, and methods of distribution

Source of raw materials

Importance of trademarks, franchises, licenses, and so forth

Amount and nature of research and development expenses

Identification of major customers

Dollar amount of backlog orders

Competitive conditions in the business, registrant's position in the business, number of competitors

Financial results broken down by foreign and domestic operations

Amount of export sales

In addition to required disclosures the company would also be required to provide copies of material contracts as exhibits. However, the SEC has adopted a rule providing for confidential treatment of contracts or portions of contracts if it can be demonstrated that disclosure of the documents will impair the contracts' value and that confidential treatment is necessary for protection of the investors.

Encouraging Public Interest

Prior to considering a public offering you probably have not spent a great deal of time pondering whether or not your company has a public image. In all likelihood, however, you have worked hard to create a favorable image for your product(s) with customers and others in your industry.

A public company needs to develop a public image. The desired public image motivates investors to purchase your shares and investment analysts to recommend your securities. A study of companies that have gone public supports this notion. The study indicated that over three out of four of the CEOs surveyed had established or were currently establishing a communication program with security analysts and newspaper and periodical business editors.

Given your circumstances, your underwriter can help you determine what type of communication program you require and whether or not you need a public relations firm.

The Underwriter

Role of the underwriter. For all practical purposes an underwriter's participation in an initial public offering is essential. An underwriter can make the most important contribution toward the goal of a successful public offering. The underwriter is the conduit through which the company's securities will be sold to the public.

Underwriting services for initial public offerings are normally performed by investment banking firms. An underwriting generally consists of an investment banker purchasing securities from a company and/or the company's major shareholders and selling those securities to the public.

The investment banker who takes the lead in purchasing these securities is referred to as the managing underwriter. The managing underwriter forms a syndicate of other investment banking firms that participate in the purchase of securities from the company and any of its major shareholders and in the sale and distribution of those securities to individual and institutional investors.

A company does not have to sell securities through an underwriter; however, the chances of a successful initial public offering would be significantly diminished without one. The benefit of an underwriter lies in the firm's knowledge of market conditions and ability to successfully price the securities and to arrange for their sale and desired distribution. Underwriters also provide invaluable market support for your securities after they have been sold.

Selection of a managing underwriter. The selection of a managing underwriter is a critical step in the going public process. Many large reputable investment banking firms generally are not interested in initial public offerings. However, there are numerous investment banking firms that handle initial public offerings. These firms vary broadly in reputation, in experience, and in their ability to provide services. The criteria for selection of a managing underwriter are as follows:

Reputation and distribution capability. Your managing underwriter's name should be well known and respected in the financial marketplace. The managing underwriter should have a reputation for successful initial public offerings in your company's industry. The better the reputation, the easier it is to sell your shares. Individual and institutional investors consider the association of the managing underwriter with your offering as one of the most important factors in deciding to purchase your shares.

An underwriter with a good reputation can assemble a strong underwriting syndicate. The strength of the syndicate is important to the company as it relates to the sale and distribution of the securities. Depending on the size of the offering, the underwriting syndicate can consist of ten to twenty investment banking firms.

For most companies an optimal distribution of securities would result in a security-holder base made up of a large number of investors holding relatively small quantities of stock. A broad distribution of securities results in a larger trading market for the company's securities. If distribution were limited to a few investors, they could strangle the market for those securities, seriously depress the value of the securities by selling in large quantities, and position themselves to take control of your company.

Other desirable distribution capabilities, depending on the requirements of your company, include broad or selected geographic markets, and quality individual and institutional investors. It is not necessary that your managing underwriter possess all of these distribution capabilities. Capabilities not possessed by the managing underwriter may be available through selected members of the underwriting syndicate.

Experience. Your managing underwriter should have experience in initial public offerings and expertise in your company's industry. Most investment banking firms specialize in certain industries and technologies. It is important to have a managing underwriter who understands the nature of your company's products and where the company is positioned within its industry.

Selection of an underwriter who is conversant with your industry will obviate the need for a time-consuming effort to learn the nuances of the industry. As a result, the going public process will be smoother because the underwriter will be better able to price your securities, sell the offering to the syndicate, and convince analysts and institutional investors of your company's merits.

Aftermarket performance. An important service the managing underwriter should provide to your company is aftermarket support for your shares. Aftermarket support consists of the managing underwriter's "making a market" in your shares after the offering and helping to maintain the financial community's interest in the company. The term "making a market" refers to the managing underwriter's buying and selling of your shares for its own account, after the offering, in order to maintain a tradable market.

As long as a market for your shares exists, your company's new shareholders will enjoy liquidity, investor interest, and market conditions permitting a stable or rising stock price. If the managing underwriter's firm is experienced in your industry, in all likelihood the firm's research analysts will be recognized as knowledgeable in your industry. The managing underwriter's research analysts' role should be to maintain the flow of current information on the company and its industry to the investing public with timely, periodic reports.

Ongoing financial advice. To avoid the need to reeducate a new underwriter or financial adviser about your company, consideration needs to be given to the selection of an investment banking firm that meets your long-term as well as your current needs. Ideally, your relationship with the investment banking firm that serves as managing underwriter in your initial public offering will be long term. The investment banker can advise you and your company on the types, amount, and timing of future public or private offerings and assess potential merger and acquisition candidates, among other services.

Cost of underwriting. The largest cost of the public offering is the underwriter's discount or commission. In selecting among several reputable investment banking firms, the discount will not differ significantly nor will these firms consider the discount percentage to be negotiable except within a narrow range. During your interviews with investment banking firms you should discuss with each firm the discount percentage they intend to charge.

Do your homework before contacting any investment bankers. Identify investment banking firms that have underwritten initial public offerings for companies similar to yours. Sources of information include recent prospectuses, business periodicals focused on initial public offerings, and recommendations from your bankers, lawyers, accountants, or the venture capitalist involved with your company.

Once you have obtained the names of potential candidates, contact the management of the companies for which they were underwriters and solicit comments as to the selection criteria stated above. Review the market performance of the initial offering shares they underwrote.

Based on the results of your homework, reduce your list to four investment banking firms. Obtain an introduction to these four prospective investment banking firms through a respected, credible third party such as a reputable accounting firm, law firms with securities law expertise, large commercial bankers, or venture capitalists. This is important because investment bankers receive hundreds of unsolicited calls or letters; accordingly, your chances of gaining their attention are improved with a proper introduction.

When four firms have expressed an interest in meeting with you to discuss going public, inform each of these firms that you are also considering other firms. This competition will bring out the best each of the investment banking firms has to offer your company.

Some underwriters warn against "shopping around," which is loosely defined as a company talking to many investment banking firms and letting it be known that the business goes to the firm making the highest bid for the securities.

The investment banker must invest a significant amount of time and expense in preliminary discussions and investigation before determining whether a company is ready to go public and at what price range a company's securities should be offered to the public. Shopping around will discourage an investment banker from performing a thorough preliminary investigation. This lack of thoroughness could result in last-minute surprises (for example, a delay or cancellation of the offering or a stock price outside the range indicated during preliminary discussions).

The Investment Banking Firms

The investment banking firms that have expressed an interest in your company and its prospects will perform preliminary investigations of your company. At this stage the investment banking firms want to make a reasonable and responsible investigation to determine if they want to take the company public.

The preliminary investigation can take several weeks to perform and will include discussions with management, suppliers, customers, competitors, the company's counsel, and ac-

countants. The company's management should be prepared to sell the merits of the company to the investment bankers, who look for typical characteristics of companies that go public. The matters the investment bankers will investigate include the following:

The quality, integrity, and experience of management

The company's financial position and results of operations for the past five years

The company's position within its industry, the quality of its products, and its growth potential

Sources of supply and nature of customers

Related-party transactions

The intended use of proceeds from the initial public offering

The amount of secondary offering contemplated by major shareholders

If the investment banking firms are satisfied with the results of their investigation, they will be in a position to have definitive discussions with the company about the proposed offering. At this time the company should have all of its questions answered regarding the capabilities of these investment bankers.

If one investment banking firm does not fulfill all of the company's requirements, a co-managed underwriting should be considered. This situation may arise, for example, where the company wants an investment banking firm that specializes in its technology and another firm that has a strong institutional customer base. The co-managed underwriting arrangement is not the most desirable to investment bankers. Co-managing results in the splitting of certain underwriting compensation.

Discussions with the investment bankers after their successful preliminary investigation should cover the following topics.

Types of underwritings. The two basic types of underwriting agreements are "firm commitment" and "best efforts." In a firm commitment the managing underwriter agrees to purchase all of the securities being offered by the company and by any selling shareholders at an agreed-upon price. If the managing underwriter cannot sell all of the securities to the public, it will keep the unsold securities in its own account and sell them at a later date. Firm-commitment underwritings are the most advantageous from the company's perspective. They assure that the desired funds will be raised by a specific date. This type of underwriting is handled by the larger, more widely known firms.

As part of this firm-commitment agreement with the company, the underwriter usually is entitled to an overallotment option. This option, commonly referred to as a "green shoe," enables the managing underwriter to purchase from the company and/or selling shareholders securities in addition to those covered in the firm commitment. The amount of optional securities is an agreed-upon percentage of the quantity covered by the firm commitment. The purpose of the green shoe option is to enable the managing underwriter to cover any excess orders following the offering. This option can be as high as 15 percent of the total shares offered.

Under the best-efforts agreement the underwriter agrees to make best efforts to sell the company's securities but does not agree to purchase the unsold securities for its own account. There are several variations of best-efforts agreements. "All or none" agreements are ones where the offering is canceled if the entire offering amount of securities cannot be sold. Other variations set a minimum number of securities that must be sold for the offering to be completed. From the company's perspective, best-efforts agreements are not nearly as desirable because of the uncertainty as to the amount of securities that will be sold. Smaller investment banking firms typically handle best-efforts underwritings.

Offering price. At the conclusion of the preliminary investigation of the company, the investment banker will have formulated a proposed range of prices at which the company's securities can be sold to the public. The range of prices will be based on present market conditions and the results of the preliminary review. This range of prices is subject to change as a result of further investigation by the investment banker as part of the registration statement process and market conditions up to the day the company's securities can be sold to the public. The exact offering price ordinarily will be set on the day before the registration statement is declared effective by the SEC or very shortly thereafter. The effective date is when the company can commence its offering. The price is set by agreement between the company and the managing underwriter.

The type of security offered in most initial public offerings is common stock. However, initial offerings have been made of preferred stock and debentures or common stock with warrants. Until a public market exists for the company's common stock, a convertible security is not a practical alternative. Basic economics is the driving force behind the preference for common stock in initial offerings. In addition to the advantage of offering common stock, there are no mandatory interest or dividend payment requirements.

There are numbers of variables considered by the investment banker in determining the price of the stock to be offered. No one formula is used. The investment banker will first value the company in its entirety. The company's value is determined in large part by comparison with similar public companies within an industry or closely related to it. The investment bankers will first project what impact an infusion of capital from the proposed offering will have on the company's financial position and operating results. The company's projected financial statements are then compared with those of public companies with a similar-sized asset, revenue, and earnings base within the industry. Comparison would be based primarily on key financial

ratios used within the industry. Examples are as follows:

Leverage ratios—debt to equity; number of times interest earned

Earnings ratios—net earnings as a percentage of sales; net earnings to net worth; net earnings as a percentage of assets

Efficiency ratios—sales per employee

In most situations a company that is exactly comparable will not be found and the differences are taken into account. The following types of differences are considered:

Experience and quality of management

Historical and projected growth rate of sales and earnings

Product innovations and/or track record of research and development successes

Operations base—regional or national

The length of time the company has been in operation (that is, an operating history)

Once similar public companies are found and the differences considered, the investment bankers will review these companies' price-earnings ratios and determine the approximate market value of your company. The investment banking firms like to see a minimum market value of $30 million to $40 million. They usually recommend selling 25 percent to 33 percent of the company in the initial public offering.

Your managing underwriter probably will recommend that you price your shares between $10 and $20. They will advise you that the stock with a price below $10 is generally viewed by the public market as speculative. A stock price in excess of $20 will dissuade some individual investors from buying because of the higher purchase price of a round lot (100 shares).

The exact offering price is often set at a 10 percent to 15 percent range less than the anticipated aftermarket price. Although the company and its selling shareholders may want the highest possible offering price, it is not necessarily to your company's advantage. If the initial offering price of your stock is perceived as too high by the investing public, a weak aftermarket could result and the price of the company's shares could fall below the offering price.

Once the market value of your company has been estimated and the share price selected, you will probably have to adjust the number of shares the company has authorized prior to the offering. This can be accomplished through either a stock split or a reverse stock split. Your managing underwriter will advise you to offer enough shares to obtain a broad distribution, to provide liquidity in the aftermarket, and to interest institutional investors. Institutional investors often make their purchases in 10,000-, 20,000-, and 50,000-share blocks. A minimum offering of 750,000 shares is acceptable to most underwriters.

Secondary offering. Agreement should be reached with your managing underwriter as to how many shares, if any, will be offered by selling shareholders. Generally, a large secondary offering will be viewed by the investing public as a "bailout."

A secondary offering can assist the company in creating more shares to attain a broad distribution. In addition, it can lesson the impact of the total offering on the company's earnings-per-share computation.

The Registration Process

Once the managing underwriter has been selected, the company should arrange for a planning meeting. The purpose of this meeting is to devise an overall detailed plan to sell your securities. This meeting should be attended by your underwriter and its counsel, your SEC counsel, your independent accountants, and the corporate personnel who will assist in the registration process.

At this planning meeting (generally known as an "all-hands" meeting) a timetable is developed. The managing underwriter will take the lead in setting this timetable, which will cover the entire registration process from the first all-hands meeting to the closing date of the offering. Each of the parties attending this meeting will be assigned responsibilities. The entire registration process can take from two to four months depending on your company's circumstances.

The most time-consuming activity in the

registration process, as evidenced by the time-table presented below, is the preparation of the registration statement. Your SEC counsel should coordinate the drafting of the registration statement. The company's CEO and other personnel also will be devoting a substantial amount of time to drafting this document. The underwriter, its counsel, and the company's accountants will critically review the statement during its preparation.

A timetable example. On pages 104–105 is a typical proposed time and responsibility schedule for a hypothetical company, Advanced Communications Corporation. In our example, the first all-hands meeting was held on May 16, with a target filing date of July 15, and a target offering date of August 14. The example also assumes that all of the corporate housekeeping is completed and the necessary audits performed.

The activities in the timetable are described in the glossary on pages 117–20.

Due diligence. Misstating or omitting required disclosures in a registration statement filed in compliance with the '33 Act can result in both civil and criminal prosecution. The upper limit of the civil liability could be as high as three times the sales price of the shares issued. This liability could apply to all the directors and officers who signed the registration statement, the company, the underwriter, and all experts associated with the registration statement (for example, auditors and other professionals).

The company has absolute liability for not correctly stating or for omitting the required disclosures in the registration statement. All other parties associated with the registration statement can avail themselves of a "due diligence" defense against this liability. Due diligence consists of an investigation of all statements made in the registration statement that will provide a reasonable basis for the persons conducting the investigation to conclude that the statements made in the registration statement are true and do not omit any information that would be misleading.

It is important that all parties involved in the preparation of the registration statement read the entire document. Your SEC counsel and underwriter's counsel will conduct an intensive investigation of the company and will scrutinize the registration statement text in carrying out their due diligence procedures. The underwriter will request a comfort letter from your independent accountants. This comfort letter details the procedures the underwriter would like carried out by the accountants. The letter covers unaudited financial data in the registration statement as well as the findings by the accountants as a result of comparing tables, statistics, and other information to the accounting records of your company.

The registration statement. The SEC rules will dictate what form of registration is to be used for an initial public offering depending on the company's circumstances and the size and nature of the offering. Most initial public

Advanced Communications Corporation Initial Public Offering Proposed Time and Responsibility Schedule

Parties involved:		
	Advanced Communications Corporation	ACC
	Selling shareholders	SS
	Company's counsel	CC
	Underwriter	U
	Underwriter's counsel	UC
	Accountants	A

Tentative Date	*Activity*	*Responsibility*
May 16	Organizational meeting to discuss parameters of offering, schedule, prospectus format, and responsibilities; due diligence.	All
June 23	A first draft of prospectus distributed.	ACC/CC
June 24–25	Drafting session; due diligence meetings; customer and supplier lists available.	All
Week of June 23	Preparation of draft underwriting agreement, agreement among underwriters, power of attorney, underwriter's questionnaire, officers', directors', and selling shareholders' questionnaires, and preliminary blue sky memorandum.	UC
	Select and notify registrar, transfer agent, and financial printer.	ACC
	Arrange for preparation of stock certificates by banknote company.	ACC
	Distribute officers', directors', and selling shareholders' questionnaires. Establish custodian arrangements and powers of attorney for selling shareholders.	CC
June 30	Distribute second draft of S-1 and draft underwriting documents to working group.	CC/UC
July 1–2	Drafting session. Continue due diligence.	All
July 3	Distribute first printed proof of S-1 to working group.	CC
July 7–8	Drafting session.	All
	Review market conditions, timing, filing date.	U
	Send revised S-1 and underwriting documents to printer.	CC/UC
	Continue due diligence activities; discuss comfort letter with accountants.	U
Week of July 7	ACC officers, directors, and selling shareholders return completed questionnaires.	ACC/SS
	ACC board meeting to approve issue, establish pricing procedure, approve forms of S-1 and underwriting agreement.	ACC
	Officers, directors, and selling shareholders sign S-1 execution pages.	ACC/SS
	Review proposed syndicate list.	U
July 11	Distribute second printed proof of S-1 to working group.	CC
July 14	Final working session at printer's to review new proof; make final changes in S-1 and other documents.	All
	Accountants sign report and consent included in S-1.	A
July 15	File S-1 with SEC and NASD.	CC/UC
	Press release issued.	ACC/U
Week of July 21	Syndicate invitations sent.	U
	Begin blue sky qualification.	UC
	Arrange NASDAQ listing.	ACC/CC
Week of July 28	Domestic road show.	ACC/U
	Underwriter's information meeting in New York.	ACC/U
	Prepare underwriter's advertising.	U
	Review market conditions.	ACC/SS/U
	Complete blue sky qualification.	UC

Tentative Date	Activity	Responsibility
	Prepare selling shareholders' letters setting out reasons for sale.	CC
	Accountants deliver draft comfort letter.	A
Week of August 4	European road show.	ACC/U
Week of August 11	Receive comment letter from SEC, review SEC comments, and prepare responses.	All
	Acceleration requests.	ACC/SS/U
	Distribution report from underwriters.	U
August 13	Pricing meeting.	ACC/U
	File final amendment.	UC/CC
August 14	Execute underwriting agreement and agreement among underwriters.	ACC/SS/U
	SEC declares issue effective; commence public offering.	U
	Issue final press release announcing offering.	ACC/U
	Supplemental blue sky memorandum distributed.	UC
	Complete blue sky and NASD filings.	UC
	Accountants deliver comfort letter.	A
August 15	File ten prospectuses with SEC.	ACC
	Begin stabilization reporting to SEC.	U
August 18	Underwriter provides breakdown for stock certificates.	U
	Registrar and transfer agent authorized to deliver stock certificates to New York City for inspection.	ACC
August 20	Preclosing.	CC/UC
	Certificates available for inspection in New York City.	ACC
August 21	Closing. Payment and delivery; accountant's second comfort letter; execution of other closing documents.	All

offerings for amounts in excess of $7.5 million are filed on Form S-1. The SEC rules also govern the content of the registration statement. The SEC expects the company not only to comply with the required disclosures but also to provide potential investors with any disclosures that the company believes are germane to an investment decision.

The registration statement consists of two parts: the prospectus and the supplemental information section. The prospectus is the document that is distributed to the potential purchasers of the securities. The supplemental information is filed only with the SEC for public inspection.

The prospectus has a dual—and what appears at times to be conflicting—purpose. The prospectus is used by the underwriter to sell the company's securities. A company might be inclined to highlight only its positive aspects, but the prospectus is also a disclosure document that must contain all the material facts a reasonable investor would consider in making an investment decision. The omission or misstatement of such facts could lead to liability. In order to reduce the risk of potential liability, your SEC counsel and the underwriter's counsel will insist that the registration statement be written in a manner and style that assure full compliance with the applicable laws.

Following is a brief summary of some of the items required in Part I of the registration statement, the prospectus.

Outside front cover. This page highlights key features of the offering, including the name of the company, title, amount, and a brief description of the securities; a table showing the price to the public, underwriting discounts and commissions, and proceeds to the issuer; and date of the prospectus.

Inside front and outside back cover. A table of contents and information concerning price stabilization and distribution of prospectuses are provided on these pages.

The company. This section provides a brief background statement about the organization and location of the company and a description of its business.

Risk factors. A discussion of risk factors such as the absence of an operating history, the nature of the company's business, the company's financial position, and other pertinent items should be provided, as appropriate, for a high-risk or speculative offering.

Use of proceeds. The company must state the principal uses of the net proceeds of the offering and the approximate amount intended to be devoted to each purpose. If there is no specific plan for use of the proceeds, this fact and the reasons for the offering must be disclosed.

Determination of offering price. The company should describe the various factors considered in determining such offering price.

Dilution. When there is a significant disparity between the price paid by the existing shareholders and the price to be paid by prospective purchasers for the securities, the dilution that will occur in the prospective purchasers' equity interest must be shown.

Plan of distribution. The distribution plan will typically disclose the names of the principal underwriters, the amount of each underwriter's purchase, the underwriting method (for example, whether on a firm-commitment or a best-efforts basis), and any material relationships, compensation, or indemnification arrangements that exist between the underwriters and the company.

Description of securities to be registered. The description should address such matters as dividend rights, conversion or redemption provisions, voting rights, liquidation and preemption rights, and any restrictions that apply to the securities.

Capitalization. The company's debt and equity capital structure, both before and after the offering, is typically disclosed in tabular form.

The business. A detailed description of the company's business is required. The principal disclosures will include information concerning:

General development of the business over the past five years

Operating plan for the following year if the company has not had operating revenue for all of the last three fiscal years

Financial information relating to industry segments

Principal products produced and services rendered by each industry segment

The principal markets and distribution method for each industry segment's principal products and services

The status of new products or industry segments about which public announcements have been made

Sources and availability of raw materials

The importance, duration, and effect of all patents, trademarks, licenses, franchises, and concessions held

The extent to which the business is or may be seasonal

Practices relating to working-capital items (for example, required inventory levels to meet customer needs, customer return-of-merchandise rights, extended payment terms)

Substantial dependence on a customer or a supplier or a limited number of customers or suppliers

Dollar amount of firm order backlog

Government contracts subject to renegotiation or termination

Competitive business conditions

Research and development expenditures during each of the past three fiscal years if such amounts are material

Any material effects or costs associated with compliance with environmental protection laws

Number of employees

Financial information about foreign and domestic operations and export sales for each of the past three fiscal years

Description of properties

Status of any material pending legal proceedings

Selected financial data. Summarized financial data are required for each of the past five years. In addition, it has become custom and practice to provide such data for any interim period since the last year end and the corresponding period of the preceding year. The purpose of this information is to highlight certain significant trends in the company's financial condition and results of operations. Financial data for periods other than those required should be presented if it is necessary to keep the information from being misleading.

Management's discussion and analysis of financial condition and results of operations. This discussion and analysis should promote investor understanding of the company by providing information on trends in the company's operations, liquidity and capital resources, commitments, expected sources of capital, and future plans. The discussion should relate to the last three fiscal years and any interim periods. Additional periods may be included if meaningful.

Management and certain security holders. This section requires the company to provide background information on its directors and principal officers with respect to such matters as:

Their business experience

The amount of their compensation (including information about stock options, profit-sharing plans, and other benefits)

The extent of both their security holdings and the holdings of principal shareholders (holders of more than 5 percent of any class of shares)

Family relationships and the nature of certain related-party transactions between them and the company

Loans to related parties or to their immediate families

If the company has existed for fewer than five years, certain transactions with its promoters must also be disclosed

Other. Other information will include the identification of attorneys who have furnished legal opinions, the identification of experts relied

upon in the preparation of the registration statement, and reference to the availability of other information filed with the SEC in Part II of the document.

Financial statements. The financial statements required to be included in the prospectus are as follows:

Audited balance sheets as of the end of each of the two most recent fiscal years

Audited statements of income, changes in stockholders' equity and cash flows for each of the three fiscal years preceding the date of the most recent audited balance sheets

Unaudited interim financial statements, on a comparative basis with the preceding fiscal year, that end within 135 days of the effective date of the registration statement

The registration statement may require financial information relating both to unconsolidated subsidiaries and to businesses that the company has acquired or probably will acquire. Pro forma financial information may also be required to give effect to certain types of actual or contemplated transactions on an "as if" basis in the financial statements.

Part II of the registration statement will contain information that is available for public inspection but is not required to be included in the prospectus. That information will include the following:

Other expenses of issuance and distribution

Indemnification of directors and officers

Sales of unregistered securities within the past three years

Various exhibits (for example, underwriting agreements, corporate charter and bylaws, material leases) and financial statement schedules

Form S-18

As previously noted, most initial public offerings are filed on Form S-1. Form S-1 requires an extensive amount of disclosure as described above. If your company is contemplating an offering for an amount not to exceed $7.5 million, Form S-18 may be available to the company.

Form S-18 is a simplified form of registration statement that requires less extensive disclosure: an audited balance sheet as of the end of the most recent fiscal year, statements of income, changes in shareholders' equity, and cash flows for the two most recent fiscal years. These financial statements need to be prepared in accordance with generally accepted accounting principles and are generally not subject to the additional disclosure requirements of Regulation S-X. The five-year summary of selected financial data and management's discussion and analysis of financial condition and results of operations need not be presented. In addition, other sections of the registration require less detailed disclosure.

Filing with the SEC

When the registration statement is completed (that is, all parties associated with the drafting and review are satisfied), it is filed with the SEC. The registration statement must be signed by specific company officers and a majority of the board of directors. The filed registration statement's prospectus is printed and then distributed to the underwriting syndicate. This preliminary prospectus will not have a final offering price but will include an offering price range. The preliminary prospectus is referred to as a "red herring" because it must have the following statement, printed in red ink, on the front cover:

Information contained herein is subject to completion or amendment. A registration statement relating to these securities has been filed with the Securities and Exchange Commission. These securities may not be sold nor may offers to buy be accepted prior to the time the registration statement becomes effective. This prospectus shall not constitute an offer to sell or the solicitation of an offer to buy nor shall there be any sale of these securities in any state in which such offer, solicitation, or sale would be unlawful prior to registration or qualification under the securities laws of any such state.

The review of your registration statement is performed by the staff of the SEC's Division of Corporation Finance. This staff comprises accountants, attorneys, analysts, and engineers. Your registration statement is assigned to those staff members who are responsible for filings in your industry. An initial filing with the SEC is given an in-depth review, which is a thorough analysis for compliance with all required disclosures. In addition, in its review of your registration statement, the staff will consider current developments, business practices, and accounting policies within your industry and the company's economic condition to determine if the appropriate disclosures have been made or if additional emphasis is required. The staff does not comment in any manner on the merits of the offering nor does the fact that the SEC declares an offering effective imply Commission approval.

After the staff has reviewed your registration statement, the SEC will respond in writing to the company or to your SEC counsel regarding any deficiencies that have been noted. Most initial public offerings receive comments.

Depending on the nature and extent of the matters in the "comment letter" from the SEC, your SEC counsel, the underwriter's counsel, and your accountants will advise you on how the company should respond. If the company is required to make significant changes, an amended registration statement must be filed with the SEC. In some cases this may require the reprinting and redistribution of the preliminary prospectus to the underwriting syndicate as well as to potential investors who have received copies of the preliminary prospectus. This process is referred to as a full recirculation.

If the changes resulting from the SEC's comments are not significant, the company would not have to recirculate the preliminary prospectus. The company may be able to respond to insignificant changes by sending the SEC a copy of the printer's proof of the registration statement with all the recommended changes or by a letter advising the SEC on how the company intends to respond to the insignificant changes, indicating that these changes will be included in the pricing amendment.

Examples of recurring disclosure deficiencies are as follows:

Management's background and experience is misstated or not fully disclosed. Prior legal problems of management and prior business failures in other companies need to be disclosed.

The current status of the company's business and its products. All known problems of a new or existing product are required to be disclosed. Problems could occur with development, production, delivery, and customer dissatisfaction.

Related-party transactions are not properly disclosed.

Management's discussion and analysis is lacking substance in its description of the company's operations.

Detailed financial statement disclosures are missing or need to be expanded.

The pricing amendment is the final amendment with all corrections made and the final offering price information included in the registration statement. Once the SEC is satisfied that all the necessary disclosures have been made and the company, your SEC counsel, and accountants have determined that the registration statement does not have to be updated for developments subsequent to the filing date, the pricing amendment is filed and your registration statement becomes effective.

Practically speaking, the company needs to be in agreement with the SEC comment letter if the registration is to be declared effective. The '33 Act provides that final registration statements automatically become effective twenty days after they are filed with the SEC; however, the SEC does have the right to accelerate the effective date. The price for your securities will be fixed based on market conditions at the close of business on the day the pricing amendment is finalized. Since market conditions are subject to change, your underwriters will not want to wait the twenty days after determining the offering price before they can begin to sell your securities. Therefore, most companies comply with the SEC's comments and have the effective date accelerated to the date the pricing amendment is filed. As soon as you are satisfied that the SEC has granted your request for acceleration, the printer will begin printing the final prospectus.

Blue sky filings and NASD clearance. In addition to filing a registration statement with the SEC, your company would need to qualify the securities to be offered under the blue sky laws. These blue sky laws are the individual state securities laws. (The term "blue sky" refers to pervasive fraud schemes of the early 1900s that were characterized as "selling building lots of blue sky." The result of these fraudulent schemes was the enactment of state securities laws.)

The primary difference between the state laws and the '33 Act is that many of the state laws pass on the merits of an offering. The state laws allow for a prohibition of the sale of a security in a given state even if all the required disclosures have been made. Some state authorities will take exception to related-party transactions (particularly those involving the issuance of stock and stock options), "excessive" dilution for public investors, "excessive" management compensation, and too many outstanding options, among other things.

The underwriter will be able to determine in what states the securities will be sold. Underwriter's counsel will take care of the filings in each of those states.

In addition, the National Association of Securities Dealers, Inc. (NASD), will determine if the underwriting arrangements are fair and reasonable. The NASD reviews the underwriting discount and all other forms of compensation to be received by the underwriter in connection with the offering. Underwriter's counsel will take care of this filing.

Offering Completion

The selling effort. Prior to the initial filing of the registration statement no public offering is permitted either orally or in writing. For this purpose, publicity about the company or its products may be considered an illegal offering in the sense that it is designed to stimulate an interest in the securities even if the securities themselves are not mentioned.

In the interval between filing with the SEC and the effective date (the so-called waiting period), the company and the underwriter may distribute preliminary prospectuses.

During the waiting period only oral selling efforts are permitted. No written sales literature is permitted other than the preliminary prospectus. Tombstone advertisements (so-called because the permissible limited notice of the offering is often presented in a form resembling a tombstone) are not considered selling literature and may be published during the waiting period. It is much more common, however, for them to be published after the effective date. Through the use of a preliminary prospectus and by making oral solicitations by telephone or otherwise, the underwriter may offer the security and may accept "indications of interest" from purchasers prior to the effective date. As indicated, however, no sales can be made during the waiting period.

The SEC is sensitive to all public statements made by the company during the waiting period. The company should discuss with its counsel and managing underwriter all press releases before they are issued.

As part of the selling effort, the managing underwriter will arrange for a series of meetings to be held in various cities to promote the company's offering. This tour is referred to as a road show and can cover as many as ten cities in the United States as well as selected cities in foreign countries. The purpose of this essential tour is to sell your company's potential and display your management team's abilities. These meetings are a unique opportunity for you to tell your company's story.

The road show will include the following:

Meetings with the managing underwriter's account executives (This will be done in person. In some cases, a videotape will be prepared for distribution to retail offices that are not visited.)

Meetings with account executives of the syndicate

Group meetings with institutional investors

One-to-one meetings with institutional investors

Meetings with analysts

The meetings give the audience the opportunity to raise questions about the company and to clarify any information in the preliminary prospectus. The managing underwriter will accompany you to all of the meetings and will help you to prepare for the types of questions expected and how to respond to them. The road show can take a week to prepare for and one to two weeks to complete.

Going effective and closing the deal. The binding underwriting agreement is not normally signed until within twenty-four hours of the expected effective date of the registration statement—often on the morning of the date of effectiveness. Thus, throughout the process of preparing the registration statement and during the waiting period, your company will have incurred very substantial expenses without assurance that the offering will take place.

Experience indicates that reputable underwriters rarely refuse to complete an offering once preparation of the registration statement has begun. It is possible, however, that the underwriters could refuse to complete the offering if the market drops sharply during the waiting period, especially if the offering is small or highly speculative or there are significant adverse developments in the company's affairs. It is more common, however, for the offering to be completed at a lower offering price and/or with fewer shares being offered. On the other hand, a sharply improved market could result in a higher offering price and perhaps more shares being offered.

The day before the effective date the managing underwriter and the company will agree on the final offering price to the public. On the morning of the date the registration statement is declared effective, the underwriting agreement will be signed by the company, the managing underwriter, and the selling shareholders, if any. The underwriting agreement will include the offering price of the stock, commissions, discounts, and expense allowances, if any.

The closing is a meeting attended by all parties involved in the offering and it usually takes place seven to ten days after the registration statement becomes effective. This period allows the underwriter time to collect the funds from its customers. The purpose of the meeting is to exchange documents, certificates, checks, and receipts. During these exchanges, the underwriter gives the company a check for the proceeds from the offering, net of the underwriting compensation. In addition, the registrar and transfer agent give the underwriter the stock certificates.

A Public Company

Your commitment as a public company. Once your company becomes public you have the obligation of keeping your shareholders apprised of all significant current developments affecting the company. Your decision-making process for company matters will now be more complicated. Management will need to consider if a significant business decision needs approval by the board of directors or the shareholders, if a timely press release is appropriate, or if a current report needs to be filed with the SEC. The accounting impact of this decision also needs to be considered. If an adverse accounting impact results, the stock price could suffer. Decisions can no longer be made in a vacuum.

Your new shareholders' primary concern is the value of their stock. Management will be pressured to maintain and then increase the market value of the company's stock. This increase is normally accomplished by consistently improving quarterly profits. The pressure to maintain this earnings trend sometimes results in delays and cancellations of necessary research and development or other long-term expenditures. The result can be the sacrifice of long-term projects for short-term earnings results. Management's lifetime challenge will be to balance the pressures of short-term earnings impacts with the long-term development of the company.

As noted earlier, it is important for you to sell the merits and potential of your company to the investment bankers and then later during the road show to the potential buyers of your securities. The promotion of your company does not stop after the offering. It is very important to continue to take advantage of all opportunities to tell your company's story. The more widely the company is known, the better the opportunity for a broader market for the company's shares. You should make every effort to seek out groups of research analysts and investment advisers to promote your company. A positive image with the investment community is crucial to the development of a public company.

Use of proceeds. You are required to use the proceeds substantially as described in the prospectus. If not, the SEC may proceed against you for having filed a registration statement that included an untrue account of a material fact. If the registration statement was your company's first filing under the '33 Act, you generally will need to file with the SEC a Form SR, which is a report on the use of proceeds. A Form SR must be initially filed approximately three months after your registration statement goes into effect and once every six

months thereafter, with a final form filed within ten days after the proceeds have been fully applied.

Compliance with the '34 Act. Once your registration statement becomes effective, the company is required to file certain periodic reports under section 15(d) of the '34 Act. The requirement to file such periodic reports continues for the remainder of the company's fiscal year in which the registration statement became effective and for any subsequent fiscal year in which the security registered is held by three hundred or more shareholders of record at the beginning of such fiscal year.

Other sections of the '34 Act provide that if your shares are listed and traded on a national securities exchange or on NASDAQ, you need to be registered, and if your shares are traded over the counter and the company has more than five hundred shareholders and $5 million in assets, the shares need to be registered under the '34 Act.

Periodic reporting. As stated above, you are required to file periodic reports for your first fiscal year. After the first year, however, your obligation to file periodic reports can be suspended under certain circumstances. If the number of shareholders falls below three hundred or if after the first two fiscal years subsequent to going effective there are less than five hundred shareholders and the company reported less than $5 million in assets on the last day of each of the previous three years, then the company's obligation to file periodic reports will be suspended. Those companies with securities listed on national securities exchanges or NASDAQ are subject to the periodic reporting rules regardless of the number of shareholders and the amount of assets.

The routine periodic reports required to be filed with the SEC in compliance with the '34 Act are as follows:

Form 10-K, which must be filed annually within ninety days of the company's fiscal year end. Form 10-K is designed to update, on a continuing basis, the disclosures in your registration statement. Accordingly, Form 10-K includes the latest audited financial statements and a somewhat condensed version of the information disclosed in Form S-1.

Form 10-Q, which must be filed quarterly within forty-five days after conclusion of each of the first three quarters. This report contains unaudited quarterly financial statements, management's discussion and analysis, and disclosure of certain specific reportable events.

Form 8-K, which must be filed within five business days of a change in independent accountants or certain resignations of directors and within fifteen days of (1) a change in control, (2) the acquisition or disposition of a significant amount of assets not in the ordinary course of business, (3) bankruptcy or receivership, or (4) a determination to change the company's fiscal year end. Other events that the company considers important to shareholders must be filed promptly on Form 8-K after the occurrence of the event.

It is very important that the company make every effort to meet all of the due dates for these periodic reports. Failure to do so could result in adverse consequences for the company.

Proxy solicitations. There are selected events during the life of a public company that require a vote by the shareholders. Examples of such events may be the election of directors and approval of major acquisitions or divestitures.

When company matters require a vote by the shareholders, it is not practical to assemble all of the shareholders; the process is usually accomplished through the proxy system. The company will solicit from the shareholders the authority to vote their shares at a meeting. The SEC's proxy rules specify the content of the proxy statements that are used in the solicitation process.

The proposed proxy statement must be filed with the SEC ten days prior to the date that the proxy materials will be mailed to shareholders.

In addition to a proxy statement, the company is required by SEC rules to send a copy of an annual report to each shareholder in connection with an annual or special meeting. The SEC specifies the content of the annual report.

Tender offers and reports by 5 percent shareholders. The SEC regulates both the manner in which tender offers for any class of securities can be made and the tactics management may employ to resist a tender offer. If any person acquires a 5 percent or more equity security interest in the company, that person is required to file prescribed forms.

Insider reporting and "short swing profits." The SEC rules require each officer, director, and holder of more than 10 percent of any class of equity security to file a report, Form 3, with the SEC before the initial public offering becomes effective. This report discloses all beneficial holdings of all equity securities of the company. Once the Form 3 is filed, any change in the reporting person's beneficial holdings occurring during any calendar month must be reported on Form 4 within ten days after the end of such month.

Persons required to file Forms 3 and 4 are subject to the "short swing profits" provisions of the '34 Act. The provisions require that any profits realized by reporting persons on the purchase and sale or sale and purchase of the company's equity securities within a six-month period must be turned over to the company, without offset for losses. This provision applies regardless of whether the reporting person's trading was based on material inside information or whether such person's trading losses exceeded his trading profits. If the company does not sue to recover those profits, any shareholder may do so on behalf of the company.

The '34 Act prohibits reporting persons from making "short sales" (i.e., selling shares they do not own) or "sales against the box" (i.e., selling shares they do not own but don't deliver within twenty days after the sale).

The antifraud provisions of the '34 Act impose an affirmative obligation on company insiders to disclose material nonpublic information before participating in securities transactions. A company officer, director, or controlling stockholder is considered an insider. An insider who is in possession of material nonpublic information concerning the company must either disclose this information to the investing public or abstain from trading in or recommending the securities of the company while this inside information remains undisclosed.

Insiders cannot pass on undisclosed company information to an outsider to exploit this information for their personal gain. "Tipping" is viewed as a means of indirectly violating the "disclose or abstain from trading" rule which applies to all company insiders. The person who receives the information from the insider is known as the tippee. The tippee has an obligation not to trade on this information if the tippee is aware that the insider has breached a fiduciary duty to the shareholders.

The Insider Trading Sanction Act of 1984 gave the SEC the authority to seek a civil penalty of up to three times the amount of profits gained or losses avoided by a person who knowingly trades on material nonpublic information.

Rule 144—resale of restricted securities. Securities acquired directly or indirectly from an issuer in a transaction that did not involve a public offering, securities acquired subject to the resale limitations of Regulation D, or securities acquired in a transaction meeting the requirements of Rule 144A are known as restricted securities. Restricted securities may not be resold in the public marketplace unless they are registered under the '33 Act or sold in compliance with Rule 144.

To avoid triggering a Rule 144 violation, the company's securities must be subject to the '34 Act for at least ninety days and all of the requisite periodic reports filed. The rule permits a person who owns fully paid restricted stock for at least two years to sell during any three-month period the greater of:

One percent of the securities of that class outstanding

The average weekly reported volume of trading for the securities on all national exchanges or reported on NASDAQ

If sales of restricted stock within a three-month period exceed 500 shares or have an aggregate sales price of more than $10,000, Form 144 must be filed with the SEC.

Persons who are not controlling stockholders and have owned fully paid restricted stock for a period of three years or more are not subject to most resale restrictions.

The provisions of Rule 144 are complex and subject to constant interpretation. SEC counsel should be consulted before any Rule 144 sales are made.

Listing Securities on a Stock Exchange

CEOs offering their companies' securities for sale in the public marketplace may seek a listing on the New York and American stock exchanges. These exchanges have specific listing requirements, however, and few emerging companies can meet these requirements immediately after an initial public offering.

Instead, emerging companies completing their initial public offerings often list their securities in an over-the-counter market. The NASDAQ system, sponsored by the National Association of Securities Dealers, is such a system. It provides the benefits of electronic price quotations and trading volume information for a significant number of over-the-counter securities. The NASDAQ over-the-counter markets have grown rapidly in recent years. Most major newspapers publish the NASDAQ national listing of securities and total NASDAQ trading volume has been very significant. Many NASDAQ-traded companies, in fact, may prefer to remain on the NASDAQ over-the-counter market.

Glossary

Aftermarket: State of the financial community's interest in the company after the public offering.

Agreement among underwriters: Agreement signed by the underwriting syndicate authorizing the managing underwriter to sign a purchase agreement with the company seeking an offering.

"All-hands" meeting: Planning meeting to prepare for drafting the registration statement, involving the CEO, the management team, the underwriter, the accountants, and the attorneys.

Bail out: Offering in which management and/or shareholders sell their shares of the company's stock.

Best efforts: Underwriting agreement in which the underwriter agrees to make best efforts to sell the company's securities but does not agree to purchase the unsold securities for its own accounts.

Blue sky fee: Registration fees paid in compliance with state laws governing the interstate sale of securities.

Blue sky laws: Individual state securities laws to protect investors against securities fraud.

Capitalization: Total amount of the stocks issued by a company. Includes all short- and long-term debt.

Closing: Meeting to exchange documents, certificates, checks, and receipts seven to ten days after the registration statement becomes effective.

Comfort letter: Accountant's letter to underwriter describing the results of procedures performed on the financial information included in the registration statement.

Deficiency letter: SEC letter describing deficiencies observed in its review of the registration statement.

Dilution: Reduction of one's relative interest; for example, the sale of additional shares dilutes the percentage of one's ownership.

Directors' questionnaires: Tool used by the company's attorneys and the underwriter's attorneys to gather information about the directors prior to registration. The questionnaires verify information to be disclosed in the registration statement.

Due diligence: Investigation performed by the underwriter, attorneys, and accountants to ascertain that information in the registration statement is accurate and complete.

Effective date: The day the registration statement is declared effective by the SEC. The underwriting agreement is then signed by the company, the managing underwriter, and the selling shareholders.

Financial printer: Printer specializing in the printing of prospectuses and registration statements.

Firm commitment: Agreement by managing underwriter to purchase all of the stock being offered by the company and by the shareholders at an agreed-upon price. If the underwriter cannot sell all of the stock to the public, he or she will sell it at a later date.

Form 8-K: Form filed with the SEC noting change in the condition of the company.

Form S-1: Comprehensive, complex form generally used in application to the SEC for registration of securities in an initial public offering.

Form S-18: Simplified form generally used in application to the SEC for registration of securities.

Form 10-K: Form used to file annual report with the SEC, in compliance with the '34 Act.

Form 10-Q: Form used to file quarterly report with the SEC. Usually contains unaudited quarterly financial information.

Green shoe: An option in a firm-commitment underwriting agreement allowing the underwriter to purchase additional shares of stock from the issuer or the selling shareholders to cover overallotments.

Intrastate offering: Offering and sale of securities exempt from registration, sold only to residents of the state where issuer is doing significant business.

Investment banker: Individual who purchases securities from a company and/or the company's major shareholders and who sells those securities to the public. Also known as the underwriter.

IPO: Initial public offering.

Letter of intent: Preliminary, nonbinding agreement stating underwriter's intent to proceed with an offering.

Making a market: Efforts by a dealer to maintain trading activity in a particular stock by offering firm bid and asked prices in that stock on the public market.

Managing underwriter: Underwriter who leads the offering effort and who forms a syndicate of underwriters.

NASD: National Association of Securities Dealers, an association of brokers and dealers in the over-the-counter market. Reviews underwriters' compensations for fairness and reasonableness.

NASDAQ: National Association of Securities Dealers Automated Quotations. Computerized system containing information on all NASD-listed securities.

Over-the-counter market: Market made up of dealers who buy and sell securities not listed on an exchange, typically between buyers and sellers over telephone lines.

Pricing amendment: Amendment to the registration statement stating the price of the offering.

Private placement: Offering of securities exempt from registration with the SEC.

Prospectus: Publication describing the company, management, and the nature of the business of a company making a public offering. Serves as the company's "selling" document.

Proxy solicitation: Form used to authorize an individual voting on another's behalf.

Red herring: Preliminary prospectus with a cover printed in red ink signaling that the registration statement has not become effective.

Registrar: Agency issuing certificates to new shareholders, checking transfers of stocks, and reconciling new stocks issued with number of stocks canceled.

Registration: Filing with the SEC to offer a company's securities for sale to the public.

Registration statement: Document submitted to the SEC containing the prospectus and financial information.

Regulation D: Provisions of the '33 Act containing rules that govern private placements.

Regulation S-K: Instructions for preparing nonfinancial information for inclusion in the registration statement.

Regulation S-X: Instructions for preparing financial information for inclusion in the registration statement.

Road show: Presentations by CEO, management, and the underwriter on a tour of the United States and/or foreign financial communities.

Rule 144: Exemption established in the '34 Act that allows, under certain conditions, the sale of restricted and control stock in the public market without registration of that stock.

SEC: Securities and Exchange Commission, a federal body administering federal securities laws.

Secondary offering: Offering in which securities of previously unregistered stock are offered for sale by shareholders.

Securities Act of 1933: Federal act regulating the offering and selling of securities in interstate trade and through the mails.

Securities Exchange Act of 1934: Federal act regulating securities markets and practices.

Short-swing profits: Profits realized in a six-month period by reporting persons on the purchase and sale or sale and purchase of the company's securities.

Syndicate: Group of investment bankers/underwriters who work together to distribute an offering.

Tender offer: Offer to purchase shares of stock from shareholders.

Tombstone ad: Advertisement of an offering of securities that indicates how the prospectus may be obtained.

Transfer agent: Agency that maintains official records of the transfer of stocks from one individual to another.

Underwriter: Individual or group of individuals who serve as intermediary(ies) between the company issuing securities and the public investing in securities: an investment banker.

Underwriter's counsel: Attorneys retained by the underwriter to perform due diligence, review the registration statement, advise on state and federal laws, and review the agreement between the underwriter and the company.

Underwriter's questionnaire: Survey circulated among members of the underwriting syndicate to determine names and addresses of underwriters and relationships with the issuers.

Underwriting agreement: Agreement between the underwriter and the company stating the terms of the offering, the method of underwriting, the offering price, and the commission.

Waiting period: Period during the registration process between filing with the SEC and becoming effective.

6

Compensating Your Employees

Employee Plans and Benefits

What is Compensation?

Compensation can mean different things to employees and employers. To your employees, compensation is more than a regular paycheck; it's an entire "value" system of rewards for performance. In this context, value has a double meaning since compensation has both tangible (monetary) and intangible (satisfaction) value to employees. Compensation fills basic human needs for fair pay, good working conditions, personal recognition, incentives to strive and grow, and security.

To the CEO of a middle market company, compensation is a method of attracting, motivating, and retaining qualified people to successfully operate and build the business. It is part of any good management system. Compensation has been viewed solely as a cost but, in fact, it should be viewed as a means of motivating people and boosting the performance of the company. The chart below indicates how particular employee groups are typically compensated:

121

Compensation Strategy

Senior Management	PREREQUISITES
All Employees	BENEFITS
Senior Management or Executives who have impact on long-term results of company	LONG-TERM INCENTIVES STOCK / PERFORMANCE PLANS
Senior/Middle Management and also possible rank-and-file employees whose performance can be measured against specific business goals and their contribution to these goals	SHORT-TERM INCENTIVES BONUS / ANNUAL MANAGEMENT / SALES
All Employees	BASE SALARY

Variable cost (LONG-TERM INCENTIVES, SHORT-TERM INCENTIVES)
Fixed cost (BASE SALARY)

Designing a Compensation Plan

A successful compensation plan rewards employees for both short-term and long-term contributions to the business. Many companies are myopic about this. Some owners assume that their employees are interested exclusively in short-term rewards, meaning salary and bonus. Others make the mistake of thinking that top managers, like the principals, are interested primarily in long-term rewards, so they think they are willing to trade current salaries for stock and other long-term incentives. True, many employees—especially managers—are attracted to a company by the possibility of significant future wealth-building opportunities, but they also need short-term rewards that fulfill basic human needs such as security, personal recognition, and good working conditions.

The emphasis that companies put on each component of compensation is dependent on the stage of the company's growth. Consider the following guidelines.

Relationship of Employee Compensation
Mix to Business Stage

| Business Stage | Base Salary | Compensation Programs | |
		Short-term Incentive	Long-term Incentive
Start-up	Low	Moderate–High	Moderate–High
Growth	Low–Competitive	High	Moderate–High
Mature	High	Moderate	Moderate
Reorganization	Competitive	Moderate–High	Moderate

Compensation Programs

In an attempt to create a "win/win" solution for both the company and its employees, many CEOs use a mix of the following types of compensation:

Salary, generally in the low end of the range in the company's geographic area

Cash bonuses, companywide or by work group as well as additional bonuses for employees exhibiting exceptional performance

Stock options or other long-term incentives in amounts determined by job responsibilities, base salary, and performance

These elements are discussed below in detail.

Salary

Salaries are a favorite topic of conversation among company employees, and your employees will likely talk salary with their counterparts in other companies, too. Even if you cannot pay top or even median salaries, you can show employees that you're making a serious attempt to be competitive.

Obtain information on what other employers in your industry are paying in your area. The local chamber of commerce, other CEOs, trade associations, and business and trade publications are all sources for salary data. How does what you're paying now compare with what other employers offer?

Compensation		
Fixed Compensation	*Variable Compensation*	
Base Salary	*Annual Incentives*	*Long-Term Incentives*
Rewards individuals for distinct position responsibilities	Rewards individuals for their *direct contribution* to assisting a business meet its *annual business objectives*	Rewards *senior executives* for their direct efforts to assisting the business meet its *long-term and strategic business objectives*
Typically reflects competitive market salary levels as well as a position's importance within a business's hierarchy	Size of awards typically reflect competitive market levels as well as a business's ability to share in its bottom-line results	Size of awards typically reflect competitive market levels and level of importance within the organization
Increases in base salaries are pegged to market salaries (which typically is a function of supply and demand and/or cost of living increases) as well as an individual's actual performance within the job	Type of awards are commonly in the form of cash	Type of awards are either in the form of cash and/or company stock
Represents an expense item that generally will not vary significantly from year to year	May vary widely from year to year and will be based on an individual's actual level of contribution as well as a business's actual financial results	Depending on the type of award, it may represent an expense item supported by long-term business results. If award is given in certain types of stock it would have a dilutive effect on company stock ownership
	Represents an expense item with significant cost variances to be supported by business results	

If you're paying less than average rates for similar positions and are having problems attracting and retaining employees, you should do everything in your power to make salaries competitive. (One caveat: Be sure you're meeting other employee needs, such as good working conditions and personal recognition before you identify low salaries as the sole source of low morale and turnover.)

If you are currently paying competitive salaries, you should be able to use incentives such as bonuses to reward superior performance. This gives the highest compensation to the best-performing employees without raising fixed costs (the underlying salary base).

Another important pay issue is an internal one among old and new employees. In a competitive labor market, employers often must offer more to new hires than what they are already paying existing employees in similar positions. Many employers have learned the hard way after serious falls in existing employee morale or increased turnover that the best strategy in these cases is to "bite the bullet" and make adjustments for current employees.

Salaries should be reviewed on a regular schedule (usually three to six months for first review, then annually) based on objective criteria (performance compared with previously agreed-upon goals or job description). *Consistency is important.* Morale is seriously impaired when some employees get regular reviews and others do not, or when some employees have job descriptions or work goals and others do not.

Also, difficult as it may be, employees who are not performing adequately should be given a reasonable amount of time to improve before being terminated. If you set performance standards, be ready to review and enforce them. It's a drain on the morale of those who are achieving to see marginal employees carried on the payroll (or even given raises) because management won't act to review and terminate them.

Overtime pay is another issue you'll probably encounter. In general, "nonexempt" (hourly) employees *must* be paid for overtime work. Your local Department of Labor office can help you with questions on legal requirements for overtime pay.

Annual Incentives

Annual incentives are becoming popular because they are easy to administer and generally provide immediate gratification to recipients. They are popular with companies because they are "pay for performance programs." From the employee's perspective, he or she is being rewarded for hard work and takes pride in receiving a reward. There are a number of different types of incentive plans:

Senior management incentives generally reward executives for the company's bottom-line performance.

Middle management incentives typically reward managers for their departmental or divisional performance.

Employee incentives reward individuals or groups of individuals for performance that is within their control.

Guidelines to consider for the use of annual incentives:

The performance measures should reflect the most important activities that are *controllable* by the participants.

The performance indicators must be measurable by the company and communicated to the participants. Whatever measures are reflected should be affected by the participants within one year or less. The idea is to link performance to reward.

To be an effective incentive, the plan should be communicated at the beginning of the year.

The plan should be easy to understand and administer.

Clear, objective measurement criteria should be established for granting cash bonuses that are tied to meeting product development, sales, or other productivity goals.

Individual bonuses or special awards are a way to further reward employees who have made significant personal contributions to the company. For example, the telemarketer who makes the largest number of sales in a quarter, the technician who brings in a bug-free product ahead of schedule, or the mailroom employee who discovers a way to cut mailing costs may each receive a cash bonus for his or her effort.

In addition, both employer and employee may benefit from deferring annual cash bonuses. The employee enjoys the tax advantages of deferred compensation while the employer can put off the out-flow of scarce cash. Any employer who offers this option should be sure to explain to employees that deferred compensation is unsecured debt and therefore is not guaranteed in the event that financial problems develop within the company.

Long-term Incentives

When you are thinking about granting long-term incentives, three key questions have to be answered:

Is the company contemplating going public?

If it is not going public, is the company willing to grant real equity (stock) to employees?

Is the company unwilling to grant equity?

If the company is going to go public, it will typically want to grant stock options to its senior employees.

There are two types of stock options available, incentive stock options (ISOs) and non-qualified stock options (NQSOs).

Incentive stock options (ISOs). With an ISO, employees are taxed only when they sell their stock—not when they exercise the option (buy the stock).

Tax is paid only on the difference between the original exercise price and the proceeds from the sale of stock at current market value.

125

For example, if the exercise price is $2 per share and the market value when the employee *exercises* the option is $3 per share, the employee will pay no income tax on the $1 difference at the time of exercise. However, if the employee *sells* the stock two years later at $10 per share, he or she will report taxable capital gain on the $8 difference between the option price and market value of each share.

Caveat: ISOs have certain restrictions. To receive capital gain tax treatment, the employee cannot dispose of the option (or stock if option is exercised) within two years after the option is granted and must hold the stock for at least one year from exercise.

Nonqualified stock options (NQSOs). Generally, when an NQSO is exercised, the difference between the market value of the shares purchased and the exercise price is fully taxable to the employee. If the market value of shares at the time of exercise is higher than the exercise price when the employee sells them, this difference is taxable at the time of sale. Thus, if the employee exercises the option at $2 per share when the market value is $3 per share, he or she will report the $1 as ordinary taxable income when the options are exercised. Then if the employee sells the stock two years later at $10 per share, he or she will report an additional $7 capital gain per share.

NQSOs give the company a tax advantage. When the employee exercises the option, the company receives a tax benefit equal to the employee's taxable gain from the transaction.

There are three major differences between ISOs and NQSOs:

There is no tax due at the exercise (purchase) of an incentive stock option because the employee is allowed to defer reporting income (capital gain) until the shares are sold. When the employee exercises nonqualified stock options, he or she must report ordinary income at exercise equal to the difference between the exercise price and fair market value on the date of exercise.

The gain that results from the exercise and sale of incentive stock options is treated as capital gains by the employee, and the company receives no tax benefit. The gain that results from the exercise of nonqualified stock options is treated as ordinary income by the employee, and the company receives a tax benefit equal to the ordinary income reported.

To qualify for preferential tax treatment (capital gains), incentive stock options must be granted at 100 percent of fair market value, while nonqualified stock options may be granted at any price deemed suitable by the company's directors. (If nonqualified stock options are granted at a discount from the fair market value, the discount is charged as compensation expense over the required service period.)

The value of stock in a nonqualified stock option plan in a private company should be based either on an independent valuation or on some formula that approximates the value of the shares on the market (such as a multiple of earnings). Plans based solely on book value will incur a charge to earnings.

If the company is not willing to go public but is willing to grant equity, stock incentives remain one of the most important executive motivators for a middle market company. Although much of the stock is usually given in the form of options and outright purchases are usually at a very low price, some cash can flow through to the company from employee payment for the stock.

However, be aware that giving or selling stock to employees is far from free to the company. There are often substantial costs in several areas:

Loss of control. As more and more stock is issued, the ownership percentage of the original founders and initial management team becomes diluted. Venture capital may also be harder to obtain since venture firms like to see strong, limited, centralized management ownership of the company and the resulting commitment from the management team that this ownership brings.

Future Worth. Although the stock of a start-up may be worth very little in the beginning, as the company grows, makes a profit, and perhaps eventually goes public, the stock value can skyrocket. The same initial amount of debt rather than equity financing would return far less to the employee but would ultimately be less costly for the company since

debt does not dilute the ownership of the original shareholders.

Many companies have schedules for vesting stock over time, which allow them to reward employees and minimize losses should the employee leave. For example, if an employee receives stock options for 900 shares with a six-year vesting schedule, he or she would actually own only 150 share options the first year, 300 the second year, and so forth, until all 900 share options are fully vested in year six. If the employee left the company before all share options were vested, he or she would forfeit the unvested options.

Although most employees are pleased with stock options, they do assume certain responsibilities and risks with such plans including the following:

Cash outlay. It is generally necessary to exercise options or purchase stock with cash.

Price volatility. Over time, changes in the market for a company's stock may cause the exercise price of "underwater options" to be above the actual value of the stock. Similarly, stock that was purchased may later have limited marketability or may decline in value.

Tax liabilities. Programs have varying degrees of employee tax liability either at the time of exercise or upon any sale of the stock itself.

Vesting. Most companies require employees to achieve a certain length of service or certain performance goals before they can qualify for stock option or ownership plans. Even after vesting, if an employee leaves the firm there may be a buy-sell agreement or strict time limits imposed on exercising any options.

If the company is unwilling to grant equity, it has two basic choices: phantom stock plans and performance unit plans.

Phantom stock plans. Phantom stock, which is the right to the appreciation in a share/unit defined by book value or some other indicator of company growth, is the most common form of long-term incentive compensation in privately held companies. Under this arrangement, the executive receives a cash payout of the appreciation in the share/unit at the end of a specified period. A charge to earnings to the company is directly tied to the annual appreciation of the share/unit.

Many private companies with phantom stock plans use book value of the common stock to determine company growth. While this may seem a reasonable approach, there are potential problems with using book value as an indicator of company growth in a phantom stock arrangement:

Book value takes into account historical cost treatment as presented on the balance sheet of the company; for example, real estate is valued on the balance sheet at the original purchase price. Thus, book value can significantly underestimate the real value of the company.

Book value is calculated by dividing the owners' equity by the number of shares of common stock outstanding. In private companies, this capitalization can easily be skewed by additional stock grants as well as by repurchases of stock by the company.

Book value also takes into account certain charges to the company's income statement that are not directly tied to operating results. For instance, if the company had goodwill from a prior acquisition, the amortization of this goodwill would negatively affect book value.

In any case, book value is very seldom the same as fair market value. Therefore, a transaction at book value would favor one side or the other in comparison to transactions based on fair market value.

To circumvent these inherent problems with the use of book value, companies often seek an independent valuation of the market value of their shares/units. This unit value becomes the basis for the initial price of the company stock, and its increase determines the amount of compensation an executive will receive under a phantom stock plan.

There are a number of advantages to seeking an independent valuation when setting up an executive compensation plan:

Since the share/unit valuation price reflects the market value of the company, employees who participate in the plan will have an incentive to work toward the same long-term growth objectives as the owners.

An independent valuation takes into account such things as potential growth of markets and potential for product/service profitability, which a strict analysis of current financial statements does not include.

When an independent valuation is conducted on a periodic basis, employees can see the results of their efforts to increase the value of the business. In addition, an independent periodic valuation makes "cashing out" of the plan easier to calculate and administer.

Performance units plans. Performance units are most appropriately used when a company has a defined strategic plan and is able to set reasonable long-term (three- to five-year) quantifiable goals on which it can base an award system. In these types of plans, employees are granted units whose value will vary based on the degree to which the company's long-term goals and objectives are met. If performance exceeds target levels, the units are worth a greater amount than if the targets are not met or are only partially met. Neither ownership nor "phantom" ownership is implied by these plans. No independent valuation of the company is required for performance unit plans because the value of each unit is fixed at grant based on a total predetermined target payment.

While long-term incentive plans are more frequently used by public companies, they can

also be a powerful vehicle for attracting, retaining, and rewarding key employees of closely held companies. Naturally, the tax and accounting issues vary from plan to plan and need to be addressed when determining which type of plan is most appropriate for use in any given situation.

While some plans may be tied to book value instead of fair market value of the securities involved, a fair market value relationship can have decided advantages in employee compensation programs. A plan that uses fair market value will be perceived by employees as reflecting the market's view of the organization's results over time.

Other Fringe Benefits

Fringe "benefits" are a bit of a misnomer. Today, many employees take them for granted as much as they do salary.

Fringe benefits are not free, but they can be money savers for both employees and employers. Certain types of fringe benefits are tax free to employees (perhaps allowing an individual to stay in a lower tax bracket than if he or she received the benefit's value as salary). The cost of fringe benefits to employers is less than the gross salary that would be needed if an employee were to purchase an equivalent benefit. For example, a health insurance premium of $50 per month paid directly by the company to the insurer would be the equivalent of $71 per month in gross salary for an employee in the 30 percent tax bracket. Actually, the value of a benefit as perceived by employees is often higher than a similar amount of salary—thus an employee is often more pleased with the $50 benefit of employer-paid health insurance than with another $71 gross per month that would buy the equivalent insurance.

Common employer-paid taxable and nontaxable fringe benefits can include the following:

Medical insurance

Dental insurance

Vision care

Disability insurance

Life insurance

Legal and financial counseling

Use of company automobile

Paid holidays

Vacations

Compensated time off

Sick days

Not all companies offer all benefits. Even though many employees perceive them as "free," they obviously are not. Increasingly, companies are requiring employees to contribute to the cost of their benefit plans. In addition to a company's cash contribution are the time and expense necessary to establish and administer the benefits program.

To be competitive and motivating, a growing company should offer at least medical, disability, and some life insurance (more for senior managers than for support staff) and paid vacation and holiday time. As soon as they are able, most employers add dental care and additional life insurance. Local practices normally will dictate the order or necessity of other benefits. For example, if every manufacturer in your area gives child care benefits, you may need to provide them also.

Finally, whatever package you offer, be sure that all benefits are clearly described in an employee handbook. Be specific so there are no ambiguities as to how vacation days are earned, what constitutes "comp" time, and how other benefits are provided.

Company Retirement Plans

At first glance, qualified retirement plans and other deferred compensation arrangements may seem less attractive to both business owners and employees now that the maximum individual tax rate is down to 28 percent. Such a view, however, underestimates the long-term value of these plans, according to Peter I. Elinsky, a tax partner in Peat Marwick's Washington National Tax Practice.

"We're hearing individual taxpayers say that they'd rather take the cash now as income and pay a comparatively low tax on it rather than have it invested in a qualified retirement plan," he says. "They're assuming, of course, that tax rates are going to go back up—and they're overlooking the long-term value of retirement plans. These plans are still a very important part of individual tax planning."

Similarly, Elinsky finds that a business owner may consider eliminating the employee retirement plan to avoid the cost of funding it. He encourages almost anyone considering such a move to hang on to the tax deduction the company gets for funding the plan. "Qualified retirement plans are a tax-efficient way to provide compensation," says Elinsky. "Eliminate the plan and you'll not only lose a valuable deduction, you'll also lose one means of competing for employees—who really value these plans. They'll turn around and demand some other form of compensation or they'll leave."

In the descriptions of four qualified retirement plans below, Elinsky explains the pros and cons. The Internal Revenue Service calls these plans "qualified" because in each case the company gets a tax deduction for its contributions and the employee pays no income tax until he or she receives the funds.

Defined benefit pension plan. With this arrangement, the company calculates a pension using a formula that takes into account the employee's years of service and average compensation over a certain period. The plans are attractive to employees because the future benefit is a function of a set formula and is not affected by fluctuations in the marketplace. "The drawbacks are that the company must contribute to the plan every year—whether or not it is profitable—or be penalized by the IRS; and because the retirement benefit is 'defined,' the company must bring in an actuary to deter-

mine how much it must contribute," notes Elinsky. "Company turnover, life expectancies, interest rates, and other factors are all a part of the equation. With employees who are relatively young, for example, a company's contribution will be comparatively low since it has more time to build the pension fund before they retire than would a company with an older work force."

In contrast, the other three plans are defined contribution plans, which differ from defined benefit plans in that they do not fix the future retirement benefit.

Profit sharing plan. Under this plan, the company makes discretionary contributions to a fund based on its profits—or other variables of its choosing. (The Tax Reform Act of 1986 enabled companies to fund such plans even if they had no profits.) The company determines each year how much (or whether) it will contribute, and the employee's pension is based on the fund's growth. "This arrangement offers the employer more flexibility than the defined benefit plan," says Elinsky.

Stock bonus plan. This plan is like a profit-sharing plan except the payout is in the form of company stock. It may save the company the cash currently required to fund a plan while preserving its tax deduction for doing so. "Closely held companies often shy away from these plans, however, because they prefer not to dilute their ownership,"

Elinsky says. "One option is to arrange to buy the stock back from the employee when he or she retires, although the company must always offer the employee the stock first."

401(k) plan. With this arrangement, a company offers the employee the option of deferring a portion of his or her pretax salary each year, subject to current IRS regulations. (Adjusted each year for increases in the cost of living, this cap was $7,979 in 1990.) In general, the tax code stipulates that the average percentage of compensation that highly compensated employees contribute must meet either of two tests: (1) It does not exceed one and one-quarter times the average percentage that non–highly compensated employees contribute; or (2) it neither exceeds by more than two percentage points, nor is more than two times the average percentage contributed by non–highly compensated employees.

Other pension plans. Certain middle market companies do not use pension plans because they find them expensive to administer and not appropriate for a young work force. An exception is the simplified employee pension (SEP).

Simplified employee pension (SEP). The SEP is actually a variation of the individual retirement account (IRA). To implement the SEP, employees must establish an IRA, which can be the same as, or separate from, any regular IRA

accounts they may have. Employers then make discretionary SEP contributions directly to the employee's IRA account. Thus, there are no employer administrative expenses. Employers may contribute annually up to the lesser of 15 percent of employee cash compensation or $30,000 per employee, at their discretion. Employer SEP contributions are regarded as part of the employee's taxable income; however, the SEP amount may be deducted from gross income on personal tax returns. SEPs vest immediately, accumulate interest tax deferred, and are controlled by employees subject to federal IRA regulations.

A drawback to SEPs is that they require cash. Clearly, if the company has not generated profits, the SEP won't get funded and, hence, can have a demotivating rather than incentive effect. If you do set up a SEP, be sure you can contribute to it.

CODA-SEP. A SEP may offer a cash or deferred arrangement (CODA) to participants of plans sponsored by certain small employers. This operates similarly to a 401(k) plan and must meet nondiscrimination tests.

Money purchase pension plan. A money purchase pension plan is fairly easily understood by employees because a percentage of salary is contributed to the plan and each participant has his or her own account. At retirement this amount may be paid in a lump sum or used to purchase an annuity that provides the employee with known retirement income.

Administrative expense is lower for this type of plan than for a defined benefit plan.

Target benefit plan. A target benefit plan is one in which a separate account is maintained for each participant. Retirement benefits are based solely on the amount accumulated in a particular participant's account at retirement. Unlike a normal money purchase pension plan, however, contributions to a target benefit are not made on the basis of a given percentage of each participant's compensation. Instead, like the defined benefit plan, contributions are based on the retirement benefits a plan expects to provide. Since contributions under a target benefit plan are calculated in the same way as those of a defined benefit plan, the contributions are heavily weighted toward older and highly compensated participants. Administrative expenses will be lower than for a defined benefit plan but will be higher than those of a typical defined contribution plan. Annual contributions on behalf of a participant in a target benefit plan are limited under the defined contribution annual addition limits, which may be lower than contribution limits to defined benefit plans.

Employee stock ownership plans (ESOPs). ESOPs are very much in the financial news today because of the many advantages they offer employers and employees alike. ESOPs were introduced to encourage the acquisition by employees of an equity interest in their employer's business and to provide employees with a source of retirement income. In effect, ESOPs give employees a double benefit: a pool of retirement funds accumulating on a tax-deferred basis and an opportunity to share in their employer's growth. Employers may reap the rewards of increased worker incentive and improved morale as a result of employee equity involvement in addition to the tax and other potential benefits that ESOPs provide.

An ESOP is a tax-qualified defined contribution plan. It can take the form of a stock bonus plan or a stock bonus plan combined with a money purchase pension plan. In either case individual accounts are maintained on behalf of each plan participant. Employer contributions are allocated to individual accounts in accordance with a nondiscriminatory formula such as one based on annual compensation. As with all defined contribution plans, investment risk is borne by the participant. Within limits contributions to the plan are deductible by the employer and neither the contributions nor the earnings attributable thereto are included in an employee's income until distributed from the plan. Upon distribution certain favorable tax benefits may inure to the participant, provided tax law requirements are met.

ESOPs are distinguishable from more conventional defined contribution plans in two ways: (1) Most defined contribution plans invest in a diversified portfolio of equity, debentures, and fixed-income securities and cannot invest more than a nominal amount of plan assets in the stock of the plan sponsor (except for certain profit-sharing and stock bonus plans), whereas ESOPs may invest up to 100 percent of plan assets in company stock of the plan sponsor; and (2) while tax-qualified retirement plans generally are prohibited from borrowing funds on employer credit, an ESOP is permitted to finance the entire acquisition cost of company securities through a loan originated by or guaranteed by the company.

The marked increase in popularity of ESOPs in recent years can be attributed to several factors. The law provides significant tax incentives to the owners of closely held businesses who transfer share ownership to employees through an ESOP. As a result, shareholders who sell their stock in closely held businesses to an ESOP can now receive a distribution of corporate-earned surplus in a tax-deferred manner while increasing the diversity and liquidity of their personal holdings at the same time.

Other improvements over the past few years have also made ESOPs more desirable to employees. Vesting, voting rights, and put-option provisions have been improved. ESOP participants have been given diversification rights with respect to their accounts and receive further protection through independent appraisal requirements for the valuation on ESOP shares of closely held companies.

On the downside, other recent legislation has cut back on some of the tax incentives for ESOPs. Employees' perceptions of their companies' ESOPs are diverse. If management is highly regarded and the company is growing,

employee reaction to an ESOP is usually favorable. But the opposite is true if management is poorly regarded or if the company's financial performance is not good. Employee communications, both oral and written, are useful in explaining this rather complex and novel arrangement. In the absence of good communications, employee perception of the plan will almost certainly suffer.

Of course, a plan that invests primarily in employer securities renders an employee's retirement income acutely sensitive to the performance of his or her employer's company. For this reason, ESOPs are frequently intended to provide supplemental retirement income above and beyond the retirement income that an employee may expect from additional sources (such as retirement plans, Social Security, IRAs, and so forth).

Health Care Cost Containment

The rising cost of employer-sponsored health care plans is a major concern for middle market business owners. Redesigning a company's benefits package to encourage a more economical use of health care is often the best way to begin controlling these costs. A properly designed plan cost-effectively matches employee needs with an employer's ability to finance the cost.

Key objectives in a redesign effort are to restrict the use of expensive benefits with questionable value as well as to make the plan more resistant to inflation. Plan redesign includes the following steps:

Evaluate the existing plan. How much does the current plan cost? What has been the trend in cost increases? What are the high cost areas that would be most responsive to cost containment? How well does the company's benefit package compare with those of similar companies?

Identify problems. What is the company's employee benefits philosophy? How are plan costs affecting the profit margin? Does the benefit package meet the needs of a diverse work force? Is excessive coverage being provided in some cases?

Involve the employees. What types of benefits do the employees want? What types do they need? Do the employees appreciate the benefits being provided? Is a survey of employee attitudes worthwhile?

Get senior management support. Would plan redesign have the support of top management?

Make design recommendations. The redesigned plan should be tailored to meet the unique needs of the company. It should alter employee patterns of behavior in order to encourage less costly services. A short-term dollar investment may be needed to realize long-term savings.

Communicate and implement the program. Communicating the program will be the most important aspect of redesign. Brochures, newsletters, and seminars should gain the employees' attention and be presented in a simple and clear fashion. Face-to-face sessions allow the employee to ask questions and have points clarified. The objective is to explain what changes were made, why plan redesign is necessary, and how the plan will enhance quality of care and cost effectiveness. The employees must be educated to take greater responsibility for their own health care and to be more prudent consumers of health care services.

Evaluate the plan periodically. Cost containment is a long-term commitment for both the employees and the employer. Criteria for performance measurement should be set, and the plan should be evaluated on a periodic basis to determine how effective the plan is in meeting its objectives. Management reports will help track the effect of plan changes on cost and use patterns. The claim system must provide data essential to produce profiles of use, costs, and provider patterns that can be compared with normative data.

To be cost effective a health care benefit package should be as simple as possible. It should allow for risk-sharing through deductibles, coinsurance, and other methods. It should include incentives for less expensive but effective treatment and should strongly discourage unnecessary services and inappropriate treatment.

The value of deductibles and coinsurance was considered controversial until a 1982 study by the Rand Corporation, which concluded that use of medical services varies inversely with the degree to which employees participate financially in a benefit plan. Employees with high-cost sharing use their benefits far less than employees with full coverage.

A cardinal concept in the industry is that insurance is intended to protect the individual against large, unpredictable losses; individuals themselves can take care of smaller, more reasonable expenses. Employees should not be insulated from the impact of medical costs. Otherwise, providers become protected from competitive cost pressures.

Certain benefit designs have proven effective in reducing costs by changing employee behavior and giving employees incentive to choose more cost-effective forms of medical care. Some of the most commonly seen cost containment measures include the following:

Mandatory second surgical opinions

Preadmission testing

Ambulatory surgery

Hospice care, home health care, skilled nursing facilities, and birthing centers

Weekend admission limits

Hospital-use review, including prospective review and concurrent review

Large-claim management

Hospital-use review and large-claim management offer the greatest potential for cost saving. Large-claim management offers the greatest return on investment, but it cannot generally be implemented without prospective hospital-use review, which provides a reliable method of flagging catastrophic and chronic claims as early as possible.

While plan redesign is intended to produce short-term cost savings, it is also intended to encourage employees to be more prudent and cost-conscious consumers of health care and to avoid unnecessary and inappropriate treatment. Employees must realize that cost-containment efforts are in *their* best interest. Communication is a key ingredient in making the program succeed.

General Tax Issues Related to Compensating Employees and Business Owners

Deducting Compensation

Generally, compensation is deductible when paid or incurred for both accrual and cash-basis taxpayers. Prepaid compensation is not currently deductible but is usually taxable to the recipient. Year-end bonus accruals are exceptions for accrual-basis taxpayers but must be fixed and determinable by year end and paid within two and a half months of year end.

Special rules disallow deductions for the

employee/owner who is treated as related to employer. Generally anyone owning more than 50 percent of the company's stock *must* have his or her bonus paid by year end so that it may be deducted in that year. Watch attribution rules when calculating who owns more than 50 percent (that is, if the top 50 percent shareholders are joined in any type of partnership, then they would technically be considered owners of each other's stock and consequently own 100 percent).

The amount of compensation deduction allowed is limited to a reasonable amount. This is an important concern for profitable closely held companies. A reasonableness test is generally designed to prevent avoidance of double taxation of corporate earnings (that is, nondeductible dividend payment to a shareholder/employee) through payment of excessive compensation to individuals related to the shareholder/employee.

There is a subjective test by the IRS. Factors considered include the following:

Comparison to compensation paid for a similar position in similar businesses

Compensation paid to nonshareholders/employees

Consistency over years of salary and bonus plans

Dividends paid

Success of company

There is no deduction for *"excess* parachute payment" resulting from change in control. A nondeductible 20 percent excise tax is imposed on an executive receiving the payment.

General Requirements That Must Be Met to Provide Nontaxable Fringe Benefits to Employees and Business Owners

Fringe benefits that can generally be provided on a nontaxable basis to employees include the following:

Group term life insurance up to $50,000

Accident and health plans (insured and uninsured)

Dependent care assistance programs

Choices between the above benefits offered to employees (within certain dollar limits)—referred to as a "cafeteria" plan

Perquisites, including no-additional-cost services (such as airline tickets to airline employees), qualified employee discounts, working condition fringes (such as parking, business use of auto), de minimus fringes, and athletic facilities

Basic nondiscrimination rules generally must be met in order for most benefits to be provided on a nontaxable basis to employees. Insured health benefits can be offered on a discriminatory basis.

Sole proprietors, partners, and 2 percent S corporation stockholder/employees (self-employed) are not treated as employees for purposes of many of the excludable fringe benefits. Which fringe benefits can be provided for this group of "self-employed" taxpayers on a pretax or excludable basis?

Dependent care assistance program

Working condition fringes (such as parking, business use of auto, and so forth)

All other fringe benefits *cannot* be provided to self-employed taxpayers on a pretax or excludable basis.

Dealing with Reinstated Nondiscrimination Rules

The repeal of section 89 greatly relieved many business owners faced with completing a complicated series of tests to demonstrate that their benefit plans did not discriminate in favor of highly compensated employees.

"Employers need to remember, however, that the issue of nondiscrimination did not die with section 89," says Peat Marwick Washington National Tax Practice partner Deborah Walker, who played a key role in the repeal of section 89 as chair of the AICPA executive committee's section 89 task force. "The repeal reinstated various nondiscrimination tests in effect before 1989 for health and group term life insurance cafeteria plans (those plans that allow the employee to select from a number of options), and, to some extent, dependent care assistance programs. Employers whose plans do not meet these tests may subject certain employees to taxation."

The reinstated tests are summarized as follows:

Medical plans. Self-insured medical expense reimbursement plans are subject to nondiscrimination rules. A self-insured plan is one that an employer establishes to reimburse employees for medical expenses not covered by another accident or health insurance policy. Plans that reimburse employees for medical diagnostic procedures (for example, routine medical examinations) are not treated as self-insured plans and are therefore exempt from the nondiscrimination rules. No other medical plans are subject to nondiscrimination testing unless they are part of cafeteria plans, which, in general, must not discriminate in favor of highly compensated or key employees.

Group term life insurance plans. Before 1989, group term life insurance plans had to meet certain nondiscrimination rules with respect to key employees. These rules will continue to apply for subsequent years. In general, such a plan must not discriminate in favor of key employees with respect to eligibility and the type and amount of benefits provided.

Dependent care assistance programs. The nondiscrimination rules affecting dependent care assistance plans remain intact.

Reporting requirements. Prior to 1989, employers with health plans, group term life insurance plans, and dependent care assistance programs generally were not required to file Form 5500 with the IRS if the plans had fewer than one hundred participants. Until future guidance is issued, these welfare benefits plans will continue to be subject to the rules in effect before 1989.

Analysis of the circumstances of each taxpayer will help determine if it is cost effective to make the plans nondiscriminatory (that is, provide the fringe benefits to more of the *non*-highly compensated group). The alternative is to pay the executive in the highly compensated group more salary to pay the additional taxes on the fringe benefits that are now taxable.

OBRA 1990: Extensions of Expiring Benefit Provisions

Exclusions for employer-provided educational assistance and group legal services now expire for taxable years beginning after December 31, 1991. Excludable reimbursements can be made for graduate-level educational assistance. The maximum educational assistance exclusion remains at $5,250. Employers should adjust employment tax withholding that may have occurred after September 30. Educational assistance that exceeds the $5,250 maximum may still qualify for exclusion the education meets certain job-related requirements.

The 25 percent deduction for health insurance for self-employed individuals or eligible S corporation shareholders is extended and will now expire for taxable years beginning after December 31, 1991.

In addition to withholding from employees, beginning in 1991 employers are required to contribute 1.45 percent of wages up to $125,000. This will increase employment tax costs for employees earning in excess of the current taxable wage base of $51,300.

The 0.2 percent surtax that was to expire after 1990 for federal unemployment tax (FUTA) is extended through 1995 beginning with wages paid on or after January 1, 1991.

General Attributes of Various Types of Qualified Retirement Plans

The major tax benefits of qualified plans include a current deduction (within limits) by the employer for contributions and deferred income recognition and tax on plan earnings until benefits are distributed.

The requirements for qualification are complex. Generally, a trust that forms a part of a stock bonus, profit-sharing, or pension plan of an employer for the exclusive benefit of a broad-based group of employees shall constitute a qualified trust.

Attributes of different types of plans are as follows:

Pension plan. A pension plan is established and maintained by an employer primarily to systematically provide for the payment of definitely determinable benefits to his or her employees over a period of years, usually for life.

Benefits are generally determined by or based on such factors as compensation and years of service. Contributions are not contingent on profits and must be made annually. Pension plans are divided into two major types—the defined contribution plan and the defined benefit plan:

A *defined contribution plan,* which is also referred to as a money purchase or target benefit pension, provides for fixed contributions to each employee's account. The employee receives whatever size retirement benefit can be purchased with the funds accumulated in his or her account. The maximum annual contribution to a defined contribution plan for 1990 is the lesser of $30,000 or 25 percent of compensation.

A *defined benefit plan* provides fixed benefits the size of which are determined by a predetermined formula. The annual contribution necessary to fund these benefits is determined actuarially. The maximum benefit that may be funded is the lesser of $90,000 (inflation adjusted) or 100 percent of the participant's average compensation for his or her high three years.

Profit-sharing plan. A profit-sharing plan provides for the sharing and allocation of profits to employees on a predetermined basis. The plan must provide for allocating the contributions made to the plan among the participants and for distributing the funds accumulated under the plan.

Contributions are discretionary each year and are generally limited to 15 percent of compensation.

A profit-sharing plan is often the first plan a middle market company will implement because the discretionary contributions do not burden management with an annual monetary commitment.

Stock bonus plan. A stock bonus plan gives employees a proprietary interest in the employer and thus may act as an incentive to improve performance. The plan must provide a definite predetermined formula for allocating the contributions made to the plan among the participants. Employees must have the option to receive benefits in employer stock.

Section 401(k) plan. A section 401(k) plan is also known as a cash or deferred arrangement. It is a qualified plan under which an employer gives employees the choice of being paid a specific amount of cash as current compensation or having the amount contributed to a qualified profit-sharing or stock bonus plan. IRS regulations permit most employees to contribute a set amount to a 401(k) account annually. The amount one may contribute is based on contributions made by the non–highly compensated group of employees and could not exceed

$7,979 in 1990 (adjusted for cost of living increases in subsequent years).

Simplified employee pension plan (SEP). SEPs were created to provide a tax-favored plan easier to administer than a qualified plan. Contributions are paid into separate individual retirement accounts (SEP-IRAs) opened in the name of each participant. Contributions are generally limited to the lesser of 15 percent of compensation or $30,000. SEPs generally require that a broad base of employees be covered.

Employee stock ownership plan (ESOP). An ESOP is a qualified retirement plan designed to invest primarily in employer securities. An employer is allowed a deduction for contributions to an ESOP, within limits.

An ESOP can borrow on employer credit to finance an acquisition of employer securities without violating prohibited transaction provisions generally applicable to other qualified plans. Dividends received on stock held in an ESOP can be deducted if paid out immediately to plan participants. Recent legislation provides other incentives for the use of ESOPs.

ESOPs are being used in management-sponsored leveraged buyout situations. Also, considerable income tax benefits exist for the owner of a middle market company.

Basic Tax Ramifications of Nonqualified Deferred Compensation Plans

The types of nonqualified deferred compensation plans are as follows:

Employee salary deferral plan. This plan provides for the voluntary deferral of what would otherwise be cash compensation to employees. The employee is typically 100 percent vested in the deferred amount, plus interest is credited to the account. The election to defer should be made prior to the rendering of services and the promise to pay the deferred amount must be unsecured and nonassignable (employee's claim is that of a general creditor).

Excess benefit plan. This plan amounts to a promise to pay additional benefits up to and above the maximum benefits that can be provided through qualified pension plans. Typically, vesting occurs over a period of time (similar to defined benefit plan vesting but not subject to any minimum requirements). The amount of benefit is typically based on a percentage of final compensation and the promise to pay must be unsecured and nonassignable.

Golden parachute plans. A golden parachute plan is the payment to an executive upon a takeover of a company.

The basic tax and business issues for nonqualified deferred compensation plans include the following:

In order for the employee to defer current taxation of the value of the employer's promise to pay the deferred compensation, the promise must be unsecured (general creditor). If the promise is secured in any way, the employee will have an economic benefit and the compensation will be taxable immediately. (Rabbi trusts can be used to protect against hostile takeover but not against bankruptcy.)

The timing of the tax deduction to the employer will follow the timing of when the executive includes it as income (generally when paid).

The positive aspects of nonqualified deferred compensation plans are as follows:

The employee is not taxed currently.

Substantial discrimination and flexibility are allowed: There are no minimum benefits and lower paid employees cannot participate. The employer can be very selective in who participates.

The employer has no fiduciary responsibility for investment of funds.

Negative aspects of nonqualified deferred compensation plans are as follows:

The employer is allowed no current deduction.

The corporation must continue to exist so the promise to pay can be fulfilled.

Risk of bankruptcy or hostile takeover potentially threatens such plans.

Basic Tax Ramifications of Stock Option Plans

Incentive stock option (ISO). An ISO is an option to buy employer stock at a set price for a period of time. The exercise price should not be less than the fair market value at the time the option is granted. The ISO's benefits include the following:

Regular tax is deferred until the purchased stock is sold.

No regular taxable income is recognized by the employee at exercise; however, the difference between the fair market value of the stock at the date of exercise and the exercise price is included in alternative minimum taxable income.

If the taxpayer pays alternative minimum tax (AMT) as a result of the ISO exercise, the AMT incurred is creditable (it represents a prepayment of regular tax ultimately due upon sale of the stock).

Upon the sale of the stock acquired through the exercise of the ISO, sales proceeds in excess of the exercise price are treated as capital gain (which can be offset by capital losses). *Note:* The basis of the stock will be different for regular tax and AMT.

The employer does not receive a tax deduction upon exercise of the stock option or sale of the stock by the employee.

Special disqualifying disposition rules apply if the employee disposes of the stock before a prescribed holding period (that is, ordinary income to employee and deduction to the corporation).

With the recently enacted differential between tax rates on ordinary income and capital gains, the tax benefits of ISOs have been increased.

Nonqualified stock option (NQSO). An NQSO is a capital accumulation plan in which an employer grants the employees the right to purchase a specified number of shares of employer stock at a stated price for a period of time.

Under this plan, ordinary income will be recognized by the executive upon the exercise of the option. The amount of income will be the excess of the fair market value of the stock at date of exercise over the exercise price.

The employer generally is entitled to a tax deduction at the date of exercise in the amount of ordinary income recognized by the employee. The employee's tax basis in the stock will be equal to the fair market value of the stock at date of exercise. Special section 83 rules could defer the recognition of income and the employer's deduction if the employee is subject to SEC [section 16(b)] insider trading rules and the stock is otherwise subject to a risk of forfeiture.

Restricted stock. Restricted stock is defined as stock that is subject to a substantial risk of forfeiture (that is, if the employee does not stay with the company for five years, he or she will have to sell the stock back to the company for what he or she paid for it).

The special rules of section 83 will control when the employee recognizes the value of the stock received in income. Income is deferred until the substantial risk of forfeiture lapses (that is, the employee reaches his or her five-year anniversary) and the income is measured based on the fair market value (FMV) of the stock at that date. Alternatively, the employee could recognize income currently (making a section 83(b) election) and measure the income based on the FMV of the stock at date of transfer (ignoring the impact of the substantial risk of forfeiture on its FMV).

The employer's deduction will follow the timing and amount of income recognition by the employee.

Restricted stock is often granted in start-up situations and the employees often use the section 83(b) election because the value of the stock is usually minimal at the time of grant but could be substantial at the time the substantial forfeiture lapses. However, this often-used strategy must be reconsidered because ordinary income and capital gain tax rates are now so close (31% vs. 28%) that deferral of taxation may outweigh the cost of taxing the future value of the stock.

Stock appreciation right (SAR). An SAR is a capital accumulation plan that allows the employee to be awarded units entitling him or her to share in appreciation of the employer's stock. At maturity the employee receives the appreciation of the units from the grant date to the maturity date in cash or stock.

The employee is not taxed at the time of the grant, but at maturity the appreciation received is taxed as ordinary income. The company receives an income tax deduction at the same time the employee recognizes income.

SARs are often issued in tandem with ISOs or NQSOs. The employee will typically have the choice at certain points in time to take the SAR in cash (which will cancel an equivalent amount of stock options) or exercise the stock option (which will cancel an equivalent amount of SARs). This can solve problems with SEC section 16(b) insider trading rules when the employee wants to turn the appreciation in the stock option into cash but does not want to be at risk for fluctuations in the value of the stock over a six-month waiting period.

Phantom stock. A phantom stock plan allows employees to "own" the equivalent of stock in the company without actually buying the stock. Under this plan the employee's account could be credited whenever dividends are paid. After a specified period the employee receives cash equal to the value of the stock and accumulated dividends.

The employee typically must recognize taxable income when the cash is paid from the account. The employee should have no ability to control distribution from the account, or taxation will occur immediately. The employer is allowed a deduction at the time the employee recognizes the income. This can work well in an S corporation environment where limited ownership of stock is necessary.

7

Tackling Your Taxes

For middle market business owners, personal and corporate tax issues frequently coincide. This section addresses some of the pertinent questions these taxpayers must consider when developing personal and business tax plans and strategies.

Structuring Your Business for Tax Purposes

The table below presents tax attributes of different forms of business that may be helpful in selecting the optimum structure of your business.

S Corporations

In recent years S corporations have become increasingly popular, mostly because they avoid the dual taxation to which most corporations are subject: Generally, there is no federal income tax at the corporate level. Instead, for federal tax purposes, all income is taxed directly to the shareholders. State tax treatment varies among the states. But there are many things you should know about S corporations, both positive and negative.

	Sole Proprietor	Partnership	S Corporation	Regular Corporation
Restrictions on type or number of owners	Not applicable	None	Only individuals, estates, and certain trusts can be owners. Maximum number of shareholders limited to 35.	None
Incidence of tax	Individual owner recognizes income (loss) in personal return.	Entity not subject to tax; partners in their separate capacity subject to tax on their distributive share of income.	Entity generally not subject to tax. Depending on the date S-corp status was elected, certain "built-in gains" can be subject to tax for a ten-year period and certain capital gains for a three-year period. Other income is taxed to shareholders based on their stock ownership. Also subject to tax on any excess passive investment income.	Income subject to double taxation. Entity subject to tax and shareholder subject to tax on any corporate distribution received.
Maximum federal tax rate	31% (beginning in 1991)	31% (beginning in 1991)	31%; however; for any income also subject to corporate-level tax (see above) the combined rate is approximately 54%.	34%

	Sole Proprietor	Partnership	S Corporation	Regular Corporation
Choice of tax year	Any month-end coinciding with individual's tax year.	Selection restricted to coincide with tax year of principal partners or calendar year.	Selection restricted to calendar year unless IRS approved business reason for fiscal year. Optional election to use September, October, or November year-end, but a cash deposit may be required.	Unrestricted selection allowed at time of filing first tax return.
Timing of taxation	Not applicable; business and business owner share same tax year.	Partners must report their share of income in their tax year within which the partnership's tax year ends; partners in their separate capacity may be subject to declaration and payment of estimated taxes.	Shareholders must report their respective share of the corporation's taxable income in their tax year within which the corporation's tax year ends; shareholders are subject to payment of estimated taxes on corporate income.	Corporation subject to tax at close of its tax year; may be subject to declaration and payment of estimated taxes; distribution will be subject to tax at the shareholders' level in their tax year received.
Basis for allocating income to owners	Not applicable	Profit and loss sharing agreement; may provide for special allocations of deductions among partners, as long as such allocations have substantial economic effect.	Income is prorated among shareholders on a per-share, per-day basis (general rule).	Not applicable
Basis for allocating a net operating loss to owners	Not applicable	Profit and loss sharing agreement.	Prorated among shareholders on a daily basis (general rule).	Not applicable

Continued

	Sole Proprietor	Partnership	S Corporation	Regular Corporation
Limitation on losses deductible by owners	None	Partner's investment plus share of liabilities.	Shareholder's investment plus loans made by shareholder to corporation.	Not applicable
Tax consequences of earnings retained by entity	Taxed to individual when earned.	Taxed to partners when earned and increases their respective basis in partnership interest.	Taxed to shareholders when earned and becomes part of basis in stock.	Taxed to corporation as earned and may be subject to penalty tax if accumulated unreasonably.
Nonliquidating distributions to owners	Not applicable	Not taxable unless money received exceeds recipient partner's basis in partnership interest.	For an S corporation that was not a regular C corporation, not taxable except to the extent it exceeds recipient shareholders stock basis. For a former C corporation, same as above if out of undistributed S corporation earnings (known as AAA). Taxable as dividend income if out of accumulated C corporation earnings and profits.	Taxable in year of receipt.
Fringe benefits	Not deductible	Cost of partner's benefits are not deductible as a business expense unless treated as a guaranteed payment to the partner.	Cost of benefits for shareholders owning more than 2 percent of stock is treated as if shareholder is a partner.	Cost of share-holder/employee's benefits is generally deductible as a business expense.

Background

The Subchapter S Revision Act of 1982 significantly altered the manner in which shareholders of a corporation electing S status are taxed on income earned by the corporation. The 1982 Act designated such corporations as S corporations; previously, they were known as Subchapter S corporations. Subchapter S corporations were first allowed in 1958 to minimize the effect of federal income taxes as a factor in the choice between operating a small business as a corporation or as a partnership. However, Subchapter S as originally enacted actually created a third type of business organization—an organization that was different from both a corporation and a partnership in its tax consequences. For tax purposes, an S corporation is a hybrid of both the corporation and the partnership.

The major purpose of the 1982 Act was to redirect Subchapter S corporations toward the original goal of treating the shareholders of such corporations as partners and the corporation as a partnership for purposes of taxing income, deducting losses, and allocating other tax items. The Tax Reform Act of 1986 added some complexities relating to the decision surrounding the S election—the new corporate-level tax on "built-in gains," for example. On the other hand, the Act also imposed a corporate tax rate higher than the individual tax rates. S corporations have proven to be very popular, but for a corporation that has been operating as a regular C corporation, the decision to elect S-corporation status can be a difficult choice.

What Is an S Corporation?

An S corporation is a corporation that satisfies certain prescribed eligibility requirements and has a valid S election in effect. An S corporation can have no more than 35 shareholders. They may include only individuals, certain estates, and certain types of trusts. Nonresident aliens are not permitted to be shareholders. Only one class of stock may be outstanding.

Certain corporations are ineligible to elect S status. They include corporations qualified to file consolidated returns, banks, savings banks, or S&Ls, insurance companies, DISCs, and former DISCs.

The S election must be made by the corporation and all shareholders must consent to the election. The election may be made in the preceding tax year or on or before the fifteenth day of the third month of the taxable year for which it is to be effective.

The S corporation acts as a conduit for its shareholders. Each shareholder includes on his or her income tax return (on a pro rata basis) each item of income, loss, deduction, or credit of the S corporation that can affect the computation of the shareholders' tax liability. Pass-through items also include capital gains and losses, Section 1231 gains and losses, charitable contributions, dividends, tax-exempt interest, foreign taxes, intangible drilling and development costs, and investment interest items.

Each shareholder's portion of an S corporation's income, loss, or separately stated items is allocated on a pro rata daily basis among the shares outstanding for each day. A special election is available where a shareholder terminates his or her entire stock interest during the year. With the concurrence of all shareholders, the corporation may elect to apply the pro rata allocation rules as if the taxable year consisted of two taxable years, with the first one ending on the date of the shareholder's termination. Shareholders of an S corporation can deduct net operating losses only to the extent that losses do not exceed adjusted basis in stock and adjusted basis in corporate debt owed directly to a shareholder. Losses in excess of adjusted basis of stock and debt are carried forward and are treated as incurred in the following taxable year. Losses will be carried forward indefinitely as long as the S election is in effect.

Summary of Advantages and Disadvantages of S Election

Operating income or losses. S corporation income and losses are passed directly through to the shareholders in proportion to their ownership interest. Losses are only deductible up to a shareholder's basis in his or her stock and loans made by the shareholders to the corporation. Further, shareholders who do not materially participate in the corporation's business throughout the year may be subject to the passive loss limitation provisions.

Tax rates. Effective January 1, 1991, the maximum federal income tax rate for individuals is 31%. The maximum corporate rate is 34%. Therefore, corporate earnings may be taxed at a lower rate if an S corporation is used exclusive of elimination of potential double taxation.

Alternative minimum tax (AMT). The corporate alternative minimum tax does not apply to S corporations. Therefore, the tax preference on business untaxed profits does not apply to S corporations or their shareholders.

Penalty taxes. S corporations are not subject to the personal holding company and accumulated earnings taxes. However, regular corporations that elect S-corporation status may be required to pay tax on excessive passive investment income and certain capital gains.

Choice of accounting period. An S corporation is generally restricted to a December 31 tax year unless a business purpose can be shown for a different year. If a change is made to S-corporation status, most companies will, more likely than not, be required to change to a December 31 year end. However, under certain circumstances, an S corporation may elect to use a September 30, October 31, or November 30 tax year by making a deposit with the IRS in an amount approximately equal to any deferred tax liability.

Retirement income and fringe benefits. This is an area where a regular corporation has certain advantages. Owners of more than 2 percent or more of an S corporation are treated like a partner in a partnership. Therefore, an employee who owns more than 2% of the S corporation's stock is not allowed to exclude from income certain fringe benefits that would be excludible if the corporation were a regular C corporation.

State and local income taxes. The S election will generally require nonresident shareholders to file income tax returns in all states in which the company does business in addition to its state of residence. However, some states permit S corporations to file a composite tax return on behalf of all out-of-state shareholders. Where available, this eliminates the need for each nonresident shareholder to separately file a return. Not all states recognize S-corporation status.

Tax imposed on built-in gains and long-term capital gains. The 1986 Act imposed a corporate-level tax on certain gains and income items recognized within ten years after the S-corporation election takes effect if the corporation was previously in existence as a C corporation. The tax will be limited to an aggregate "net built-in gain" at the time of the conversion to S-corporation status. The effect of the Act is to prevent a regular corporation from switching to an S corporation and then selling or distributing assets to avoid the double tax that regular corporations will be required to pay as a result of other changes in the Act. The Act indicates that this provision *will not* apply to elections made prior to January 1, 1987. However, corporations that elected S status prior to January 1, 1987, may still be subject to corporate tax on long-term capital gains in excess of $25,000. This latter tax will not be imposed if the election has been in effect for three taxable years preceding recognition of the gain.

Distribution of income to shareholder. Many regular C corporations contemplating S-corporation status recognize that it will be nearly impossible to distribute all taxable income to shareholders. Generally, the intent is to distribute sufficient cash to provide the shareholders the means to pay the tax on income allocable to them. To the extent that earnings are not distributed, the shareholders will realize an increase in the basis of their stock, thereby realizing less gain on the ultimate disposition of their stock.

How Long Should You Keep Your Tax Records?

As you put the finishing touches on your federal income tax return each year, you may wonder what records you should keep—and for how long.

For the most part the answer is three years. That is the usual time frame for the statute of limitations, the period during which the IRS may question your return. In other words, you may discard most records regarding your 1990 return after April 15, 1994—three years from the filing deadline. (In the case of a late return, keep records for three years from the date filed.)

Special Circumstances

Don't throw everything away automatically after three years. Records you should hold onto for a longer period of time include the following:

Your principal residence. When you sell your home and report the capital gain or loss to the IRS, you need as verification, records documenting the original cost, the cost of improvements or repairs, and the selling price. Also, keep indefinitely the form on which you report the gain or loss.

Transfer of assets. You should retain records pertaining to any assets/investments for as long as you own them. When you sell assets, you will need proof of your original purchase price as well as any other documentation affecting an increase or decrease in value. For example, if you reinvested dividends of a stock, you need proof of the amount reinvested.

Assets as gifts. If you inherit property, keep the portion of the estate tax return that contains the valuation of the asset in question to serve as proof of the basis should you sell the property.

Carryforward losses. Keep all documentation regarding carryforward net operating losses (NOLs) and net capital losses for three years after you use them to offset income (or, in the case of NOLs, until the fifteen-year carryforward term expires).

Nondeductible IRA contributions. You should retain all records pertaining to nondeductible contributions to your individual retirement account(s) until you receive the last of your earnings. Otherwise, you may end up paying tax on your after-tax contributions when you begin to make withdrawals.

Take note . . .

The government may assume the basis of an unsubstantiated asset to be zero. In other words, when you sell the assets, all proceeds can be considered taxable gains unless you can verify the basis.

You may want to retain records longer than the statute of limitations suggests. For example, you may need them if new tax legislation provides an opportunity to claim a refund with an amended return.

The IRS has six years in which to collect back taxes or take legal action if it discovers you failed to report more than 25 percent of your income. However, there is no limitation period in the case of a fraudulent return.

Save copies of your actual tax returns indefinitely.

Will Your Tax Return Trigger an IRS Examination?

Millions of taxpayers file their tax returns with relief—and then watch their mailboxes with foreboding. Most of these concerned citizens are not awaiting refunds, they are expecting to be asked to defend their interpretations of the tax law before a professional more universally dreaded than the dentist—an Internal Revenue Service (IRS) examiner.

Of the approximately 140 million tax returns filed with the IRS each year, fewer than 2 million are audited. The public's perception is that the IRS examines many more returns than it actually does. Indeed, audit horror stories help produce a high rate of voluntary compliance in the United States, as well as the misconceptions about the factors that will trigger an audit.

In most cases the IRS counts on its discriminant function (DIF) computer system to select audit candidates. The computer screens a return to determine how well it matches a statistical profile of a comparable taxpayer. It assesses the return's "tax change potential," assigning numerical values to items such as exemptions, deductions, and income adjustments. A high scorer is flagged for manual screening, which in turn may trigger an audit.

Some taxpayers are more likely than others to be audited. For example, self-employed individuals (who the IRS believes tend to overstate expenses and understate income) or those with annual incomes over $50,000 stand a better chance than other taxpayers of hearing from their local examiners. Owners of middle market businesses are increasingly subject to examination as well.

Small business owners should consider the following items that may prompt an IRS examination:

Inadequately explained business losses

Large acquisitions of assets without corresponding deductions for interest expense

Casualty and theft losses

Dual-use deductions (for example, those deductions that could be of either a business or personal nature such as expenses for entertainment and meals, country club dues, maintenance of a boat, and so forth)

A claim for an excessive refund or a claim for a refund in a past tax year

Investments that make it difficult to distinguish whether the taxpayer is an investor or a dealer (such as stocks and securities or land)

Failing to report income such as interest and dividends that are reported to the IRS by banks and brokerage houses

Filing inadequate or incomplete schedules (*Note:* Taxpayers who use the wrong table, make math errors, or omit an item will be corrected and notified, but such an occurrence is not an audit.)

Inconsistencies between real estate mortgage interest and the taxpayer's area of residence and illegal deductions for mortgage loan points

How to Handle an IRS Examination

Even though the odds of being examined by the Internal Revenue Service (IRS) have been getting higher over the past decade, your chances of being audited may soon start to increase. New revenue agents are being hired and existing agents are finishing long-running exams of tax-shelter cases. Fortunately, the deck isn't necessarily stacked against you—especially if you know what to expect and are prepared for the examination.

The complexity of the tax return determines whether an IRS audit is conducted via correspondence, in an agency office, or at the taxpayer's place of business (known as a field examination). Taxpayers audited by mail are usually asked simply to submit documents such as receipts or bank statements, allowing the examiner to check, for example, deductions that exceed the average for a particular tax bracket.

The IRS initiates an office interview by writing a letter to the taxpayer giving the date and time of the examination, information on appointing a representative, and a list of the items that need to be substantiated. Documentary proof of your calculations includes invoices, canceled checks, bank statements, deposit slips, credit card receipts, and tax return worksheets. You have the option of rescheduling the exam; a valid reason to do so would be to allow more time to assemble the necessary information. Reschedule the exam early in the morning since afternoon appointments are more often delayed.

A word about your representative: Using one is advisable, but keep in mind the IRS tends to be insistent that the taxpayer also be present at all examinations as a way of enforcing its long-standing policy that the taxpayer is being audited—not just the return. Let the representative do most of the talking. An experienced professional speaks the same language as the IRS. You don't want to talk yourself out of a perfectly good deduction.

However, if you prefer to have your representative handle all aspects of the examination, you are totally within your rights to do so. In fact, the IRS cannot require a taxpayer to accompany his or her representative to an interview unless an administrative summons is issued.

Be aware that your return may not be assigned to an examiner until the day of the interview. This means the agent will have little time to review it, and unless something comes up during the examination, the scope of the audit will be limited to the items described in your letter from the IRS. In any case, prepare carefully for the examination. Summarize your documentation on a worksheet or attach an adding machine tape. The key is to make it easy for the examiner to follow the flow of the numbers and get through the return quickly and easily. Be helpful and cordial, but do not volunteer information.

Field examinations are conducted in most audits of business entities. Field examiners generally have more experience and training than their office counterparts—and more time to review the taxpayer's returns and other information they deem pertinent. Most agents will insist on meeting at the taxpayer's place of business rather than at the accountant's office so they can observe the business and its owners in action. Agents who wish to gauge how the physical operation of the business corresponds to its owners' books should be escorted through the premises to talk with designated employees.

At the conclusion of any audit the examiner will either accept the return as filed by the taxpayer, provide a refund, or assert that money is due. A taxpayer who disagrees with the examining agent may appeal to a higher level within the IRS. Take advantage of the appeals process. But be sure you have the guidance of an experienced professional. In summary, the best defense is a good offense.

Estimated Corporate Taxes

As April 15th approaches, calendar-year corporate taxpayers should be preparing themselves to make their first quarterly estimated tax payment. This prospect represents a drain on cash flow for many, but perhaps not as much for those who are aware of alternatives existing within current law.

There are ways of minimizing the cash flow problems associated with estimated tax payments while avoiding penalties. But beware of the restrictions that are now in place. Recent tax code changes make it more important than ever to have accounting systems that can make close approximations of taxable income at any point in time.

Calendar-year corporations are required to make federal estimated tax payments in four installments: April 15th, June 15th, September 15th, and December 15th. Estimates for fiscal-year corporations are due on corresponding dates adjusted for the actual fiscal year. Failure to make estimated payments can result in penalties.

There are two basic ways of figuring what the four payments should total. In the simplest alternative, a corporation can pay 100 percent of the tax shown on the return of the corporation for the preceding taxable year. This is the safest method, and for a corporation that is doing better in its current year than the year before, it will be a way of deferring taxes. If the corporation is not doing as well this year, however, the cash drought created by paying 25 percent of last year's taxes each quarter can only make matters worse.

Computing estimated taxes based on last year's tax is not permitted for corporations whose previous taxable period was less than twelve months or corporations that paid no taxes the previous year. Large corporations, as later defined, can base only their first quarterly estimate on last year's tax. Any deficiency in estimated taxes resulting from the required use of the second method described below must be repaid in the second required installment.

The second method of calculating the amount of estimated tax necessary to avoid penalties is open to all corporations. This entails paying in four equal installments that equal at least 90 percent of the actual tax that will ultimately be shown on the return for that year. Corporations wishing to avoid being smothered by their good fortune in the previous year will find this alternative useful.

A variation of the second alternative eliminates some of the guesswork. Referred to as the "annualization method," it allows all corporations to annualize income already received during the year and to use that amount as a basis for making their quarterly estimated tax payments. This is particularly attractive for corporations with seasonal income earned in the latter part of the year.

Using this method, the first installment is 22.5 percent of the tax that the corporation projects it will owe based on what it has earned so far; the second installment is equal to an amount that when combined with the first installment is 45 percent; the third is cumulatively 67.5 percent; and the fourth is cumulatively 90 percent.

Rules for large corporations. As previously mentioned, other than for the purposes of a first-quarter estimate, large corporations are no longer permitted to make estimated tax payments based on 100 percent of the prior year's taxes. A corporation is considered "large" by the IRS if it or any predecessor corporation had taxable income of $1 million or more during any of the three taxable years immediately preceding the taxable year involved.

Method of payment. Corporate estimated tax payments must be accompanied by federal tax deposit coupons (Form 8109) and deposited with an authorized financial institution or a Federal Reserve Bank according to the instructions in the coupon book. A timely payment is a deposit received before the deadline.

Alternative minimum tax

The Tax Reform Act of 1986 introduced the alternative minimum tax (AMT) for corporations as well as a new distinction between the adjustments and the preference items that affect its calculation.

Alternative minimum taxable income (AMTI) is regular taxable income increased by tax preference items and adjustments, although adjustments may also result in reductions, as discussed below. In calculating the potential AMT liability (which all corporate taxpayers other than S corporations must do), corporations are entitled to an exemption of $40,000, which is phased out at the rate of 25 percent of the amount by which AMTI exceeds $150,000. The minimum tax is 20 percent of AMTI, reduced to a limited extent by investment and foreign tax credits. Having computed both regular tax and AMT, the taxpayer pays the higher amount.

Tax preference items always increase AMTI. But adjustments may either increase or decrease your alternative minimum taxable income—which brings us to the new concept called *netting*.

Here's how netting can work to your bene-fit. When computing AMT, the taxpayer recalculates specified adjustment items (listed below), using a different method than is used to determine the regular tax deduction. The number that results is substituted for the number that was used to determine regular taxable income.

For example, in the case of depreciation, an asset costing $100 placed in service in June 1987 and depreciated over five years yields the following deductions under each system.

The table shows that the concept of netting permits a negative adjustment to AMTI in years 4 through 8. The reduction resulting from these negative adjustments may be used to offset positive additions to AMTI from other preferences and adjustments. For example, the negative adjustment to AMTI of $6.13 in year 8 from this asset could be used to offset a tax preference in that year resulting from, for example, intangible drilling costs (see list of preferences below). The old law would also have required an addition to AMTI in years 1

Year	Regular Tax (200 percent D.B.[1] 5-year)	AMT (150 percent D.B. 7-year) A.D.S.[2]	Net Adjustment to AMT
1	$20.00	$10.71	$ 9.29
2	32.00	19.13	12.87
3	19.20	15.03	4.17
4	11.52	12.25	(0.73)
5	11.52	12.25	(0.73)
6	5.76	12.25	(6.49)
7		12.25	(12.25)
8		6.13	(6.13)

[1]Declining balance
[2]Alternative depreciation system

through 3. In later years, however, when regular depreciation was less than AMT depreciation, the earlier preference was not reversed (that is, no subtractions were allowed).

Preferences include:

Depletion allowance

Intangible drilling costs

Certain tax-exempt interest

Contributions of appreciated property

Depreciation on certain property placed in service before 1987

Adjustments include:

Adjusted current earnings

Depreciation on property placed in service after 1986

Mining, exploration, and development costs

Alternative tax net operating loss deduction

Amortization of pollution control facilities

Installment sales of certain property

Passive activity losses for certain corporations

Merchant marine capital construction funds

Special deduction for Blue Cross/Blue Shield types of organizations

Writing Off Bad Debts

What is a bad debt? How can you prove it is uncollectible? What qualifies for the bad debt write-off?

In determining deductibility, the length of time a debt is outstanding is not as important as the effort expended to collect it. While the month-old debt of a now bankrupt company will likely be deductible, an account delinquent for six months or more may not qualify unless there was a prudent effort to recover funds.

To preserve bad-debt deductions, companies are advised to take a systematic approach toward credit and collections. Consider this six-point program:

Bill accounts well in advance of the due date, clearly spelling out your payment terms and conditions.

Send a follow-up invoice soon after the payment date, reminding the debtor of his or her obligation.

If payment has not been received within forty-five days, send a reminder notice. Follow up on or about day seventy-five with a warning that the account will be turned over for collection.

After ninety days, refer the account to a collection agency or an attorney specializing in debt collection.

A debt must be deducted in the year it becomes worthless. A delay in taking the write-off may result in a loss of the bad-debt deduction.

Carefully document all steps in the collection process, maintaining copies of correspondence and a log of telephone calls. You'll need to prove that you took every possible action to recover the debt.

Deduction requirements. To be entitled to a tax deduction for writing off an account receivable, you must prove that a receivable existed that had value, that attempts were made to collect and that collection is either partially or completely impossible and the receivable was written off in the year it became worthless—that is, some identifiable event occurred during the year that rendered the debt uncollectible.

In many cases the book write-off and tax deduction will *not* occur in the same year. Consequently, it is very important that accurate records be maintained detailing when deductions have been taken for book and tax purposes so that duplicated or omitted tax deductions do not occur.

Accurate record keeping required. Accounts receivable records should substantiate the existence and value of the receivable. A debt arises from a debtor-creditor relationship based on a valid, enforceable, and unconditional obligation to pay. It must be reasonable to assume that the debt will be paid. Valid debts do not usually arise from voluntary assumption or payment of another's obligation.

Since the taxpayer must prove the debt is worthless, all efforts to collect a debt should be documented including demands made (written or oral), discussions with the debtor, and the reasons for not paying. Failure to collect after a direct confrontation and demand for payment from the debtor is *not* conclusive evidence of worthlessness. Where appropriate, the receivable should be turned over to a collection agency. Again, the agency's efforts to collect should also be properly documented. Legal action may have to be pursued to firmly establish worthlessness, depending on the circumstances.

In general, a tax deduction will not be available if the taxpayer has written off the receivable but is still actively pursuing its collection. The taxpayer must be able to prove that the receivable had value at some point during the year and a later identifiable event during the year deprived it of value. If collection is still being actively pursued, that event probably cannot be proven.

Factors demonstrating worthlessness. In court decisions the following factors have helped establish worthlessness (however, each factor alone may not guarantee a deduction):

Debtor had no assets and had ceased operations

Debtor insolvent and bankruptcy proceedings initiated

Death of sole shareholder of debtor corporation that was already in bad condition

Disappearance of debtor

The following factors have *not* established worthlessness:

Collections are slow or temporarily uncertain because of slowdown in a particular line of business

Debtor's unsatisfactory financial condition rendered collection doubtful

Debtor's actual insolvency, since part of the debt still had value

Debtor's refusal to pay

IRS tough on partial write-offs. Although a debt may not be totally worthless, if a portion is uncollectible that portion may be written off. A partially worthless receivable may be written off in the year it becomes worthless or in a later year as long as it is written off by the year it becomes totally worthless and is not evidenced by a security. The IRS aggressively challenges taxpayers to prove partial worthlessness.

In a court decision, the taxpayer described below was upheld in his claim of partial worthlessness: A debt from a related corporation was 90 percent worthless. The debtor had suffered a disastrous fire in the taxpayer's taxable year and, as of the close of that year, creditors could expect to receive on liquidation only about 10 percent of their claims. It did not matter that the debtor corporation continued in business for about three years thereafter since the taxpayer never recovered the amount charged off.

Partial worthlessness was not shown where, less than four months after the return claiming the bad debt deduction was filed, the taxpayer resumed making sales to the same debtor on open account. There was insufficient evidence that the full amount of the debt could not be collected since the record contained no financial statements such as balance sheets, operating statements, or valuations of the debtor's assets and liabilities. The fact that the lender company's president had tried unsuccessfully for several months to get payment of the debt, had threatened to turn the debt over to a lawyer for collection, and had offered to accept 50 percent payment in settlement was not sufficient to show that the lender company had relinquished its claim.

Personal Tax Planning

Provisions Affecting Individuals

Beginning in 1991, if you are a married individual filing a joint return with income in excess of $82,150 or a single individual with income in excess of $49,300, you will pay tax at a marginal rate of 31 percent. Your capital gains will be taxed at a marginal rate of no more than 28 percent. The alternative minimum tax (AMT) rate has been increased to 24 percent. In addition, if your adjusted gross income (AGI) is in excess of $100,000 your itemized deductions will be reduced. Finally, if your AGI is in excess of $150,000 for joint returns and $100,000 for single taxpayers, you will lose some or all of the tax benefit of your exemptions.

Effective January 1, 1991, up to $125,000 of

wages or self-employment income will be subject to the Medicare hospital insurance tax (1.45 percent for employees and 2.9 percent for self-employed persons). If your wages are in excess of $125,000, your 1991 payroll taxes will be $1,199 more than your 1990 taxes. Self-employed persons will be able to deduct one-half of their self-employment tax in determining AGI.

Limitations on Itemized Deductions

For taxable years beginning after 1990 and before 1996, your otherwise allowable itemized deductions (excluding medical expenses, casualty and theft losses, and investment interest expense) are reduced by 3 percent of the amount by which your AGI, including capital gains, exceeds $100,000. The $100,000 threshold ($50,000 for married individuals filing separate returns) applies to all taxpayers, single or married. This amount will be adjusted for cost-of-living increases. The reduction cannot exceed 80 percent of your itemized deductions (excluding medical expenses, casualty and theft losses, and investment interest expenses). This is effectively a marginal tax rate increase of .93 percent for most individuals.

Example: In 1991, if you have AGI of $300,000 and itemized deductions of $55,000, your itemized deductions are reduced by $6,000 (3 percent of [$300,000 minus $100,000]). Thus, your total itemized deductions for 1991 would be $49,000.

This disallowance of itemized deductions is applied after taking into account any other limitations applicable to those itemized deductions (e.g., the 2 percent floor for miscellaneous itemized deductions). The limitations on itemized deductions do not apply for AMT purposes.

Phase-out of Personal Exemptions

For taxable years beginning after 1990 and before 1996, the deduction for personal exemptions is phased out if AGI exceeds $150,000 for joint returns and $100,000 for single taxpayers. These amounts are indexed for inflation. Each exemption is reduced by 2 percent for each $2,500 (or fraction thereof) by which your AGI exceeds the threshold amount. This is effectively a marginal tax rate increase of .53 percent for each exemption (assuming $2,150 per exemption), until you lose the benefit of all exemptions.

Example: You file a joint return with AGI of $200,000 and four personal exemptions. In this case, 40 percent (i.e., [$200,000 minus $150,000] divided by $2,500 times 2 percent) of each exemption amount is not allowed in computing taxable income. Thus, you will be entitled to four exemptions of $1,290 rather than four exemptions of $2,150.

161

Increase in Alternative Minimum Tax Rate for Individuals

For taxable years beginning after December 31, 1990, the AMT rate for individuals has been increased from 21 percent to 24 percent. You may be subject to AMT if you reduce your regular tax liability by using certain deductions or exclusions. The AMT is imposed only to the extent it exceeds your regular tax liability.

Preference for Contribution of Appreciated Property

The AMT preference for charitable contributions of appreciated property does not apply to tangible personal property for taxable years beginning in 1991.

Disclosure of Social Security Number for Certain Dependents

For taxable years beginning after 1990, if you are claiming an exemption for a one-year-old dependent, you must include that dependent's Social Security number on your tax return. You can obtain a Social Security number by filing Form SS-5 with the Social Security Administration.

Medical Deduction for Cosmetic Surgery

For taxable years beginning after 1990, amounts paid for cosmetic surgery that is not necessary to ameliorate a deformity arising from or directly related to a congenital abnormality, a personal injury resulting from an accident or trauma, or a disfiguring disease, are no longer deductible medical expenses. For example, amounts paid for face lifts or hair transplants generally are not deductible. Similarly, amounts paid for insurance for such surgery are not deductible, and amounts reimbursed by your employer for such surgery are taxable. On the other hand, reconstructive surgery following an accident will continue to be deductible.

Corporate Directors Taxed When Earnings Received

For years beginning after 1990, earnings for services as a corporate director are subject to self-employment tax when paid. For prior years, the tax was imposed in the year the services were performed. Although a corporate director who defers the receipt of such earnings will be taxed when they are received, the earnings will continue to be subject to the Social Security retirement test when earned. Thus, a corporate director still cannot avoid the retirement earnings test by deferring earnings to age seventy or later when the retirement earnings test no longer applies.

Financing a New Car or Boat After Tax Reform

With the deductibility of consumer interest expense being phased out (only 10 percent is deductible for 1990 and the deduction disappears completely for 1991 and later years), prospective buyers of major personal-use items such as a car or boat are wondering what is the best way to finance the purchase. The answer is: There is no single way that is best for every buyer. It depends on a buyer's particular circumstances and the options available. Here are some factors to consider.

For a boat that qualifies as a second residence, interest on any loan that is secured by a recorded security interest in the boat may be fully deductible as qualified residence interest in computing regular income tax liability. A boat may be treated as a residence if it contains sleeping space and toilet and cooking facilities. Compare the interest rates of various financing options. Taxpayers who may be subject to the alternative minimum tax (AMT), however, are not allowed to deduct interest on a boat as residential interest for AMT purposes.

For boats that do not qualify as a second residence and for cars, a promotional interest rate on a loan from the manufacturer's finance subsidiary may be so low that it is the least expensive option—even if the interest is not deductible (subject to the phase-out). Compare after-tax borrowing costs.

Interest on a purchase financed with a home equity loan may be fully deductible, but the closing costs incurred in establishing a home equity line of credit may outweigh the potential tax benefits. Some lenders waive or absorb part of the closing costs but increase their interest rate. Closing costs other than "points," on a qualified home equity loan generally are not deductible; interest may be deductible.

For a borrower who has previously established a home equity line of credit and has already incurred any closing costs, there generally is no additional cost—except interest—for further borrowing. In that event the after-tax cost of additional home equity borrowing may be less expensive than any form of nondeductible borrowing. Compare after-tax interest rates.

A home equity car or boat loan can become due in full upon a sale of the borrower's home. Check with prospective lenders to see how they handle this situation.

Borrowing on an investment account or securing a car or boat loan with investment property will not convert the interest to deductible investment interest (which is subject to certain deduction limitations). For this purpose, the character of the loan and the interest paid on it are determined by the use of the loan proceeds, not by the type of property pledged as security.

A taxpayer who also makes a business or investment expenditure within thirty days before or after receiving the proceeds of a car or boat loan may elect to allocate the loan to the business or investment expenditure to the extent of that expenditure. By doing so, interest on the allocated loan amount would be treated as fully deductible business interest or limited deductibility investment interest, as the case may be.

In the final analysis, a financing decision

should be based on a comparison of the alternative overall costs of the transaction, not just the tax consequences.

Investing in Tax-Exempt Obligations

Beware of losing investment interest deductions. Here is an important point to remember if you are thinking about investing in tax-exempt obligations. Before making an investment you should determine whether it would cause you to lose an investment interest deduction.

A rule against "double-dipping" disallows any deduction for interest on debt to finance the purchase of tax-exempt obligations. The rule may also extend to indirect financing. For example, buying tax-exempt obligations (or shares in a tax-exempt bond fund) for cash while financing the purchase of any other investment property may trigger the disallowance rule. It may not matter whether the tax-exempt obligations are acquired before or after the debt-financed investment property.

Under certain circumstances, indirect financing can also include investment borrowing by a related party or a pass-through entity such as a trust, partnership, or S corporation, while the taxpayer holds tax-exempt obligations—or vice versa.

IRS guidelines state that the purpose of purchasing or carrying tax-exempt obligations will ordinarily not be inferred in the absence of direct evidence (for example, pledging tax-exempt securities as collateral on a loan) where the individual's average investment in tax-exempt obligations during the taxable year does not exceed 2 percent of the individual's investment portfolio (valued at adjusted basis). If tax-exempt obligations do exceed the 2 percent threshold, however, and the taxpayer also owns any debt-financed investment property, the debt will be presumed to relate to the tax-exempt obligations. A taxpayer may rebut the presumption by providing evidence to the contrary; however, the taxpayer has the burden of convincing the IRS. If the presumption is not rebutted, interest is disallowed on the portion of the debt up to the purchase price of the tax-exempt obligations.

As a general rule, if you have outstanding investment indebtedness, you should exercise caution in evaluating your investment in tax-exempt obligations. Similarly, if you own tax-exempt obligations, a decision to incur investment indebtedness should be made with the understanding of the tax consequences.

Land Purchased to Build a Residence

Is interest deductible? IRS regulations clarify that interest on debt to acquire land as a site for the future construction of a residence cannot qualify as deductible residential interest until construction of the residence actually begins. Once construction commences, a taxpayer may treat the property as a principal or second residence for a period of up to twenty-four months, if in fact it will be used as either when it is completed and ready for occupancy. Construction-period interest on amounts borrowed for the land and residence would therefore qualify as deductible residential interest if the loans are secured by the property. If construction is not completed within twenty-four months of the date it commences, the property ceases to qualify as a residence until such time as it is completed and used as the taxpayer's principal or second residence.

But what about interest paid before the start of construction? Rather than treat it as nondeductible personal interest (subject to the four-year disallowance phase-in), a taxpayer might take the position in an appropriate factual situation that preconstruction interest is investment interest. For example, a taxpayer might acquire a parcel of land with the intent of perhaps building a residence or otherwise holding the land for appreciation. At the present time, it is not entirely clear how the IRS will characterize interest on debt-financed investment/personal acquisitions. It is possible that the IRS may adopt a dominant motive test, based on the particular facts and circumstances. Under such a test a taxpayer who buys property intending to commence construction in the near future may have difficulty supporting a claimed dominant investment motive. However, a taxpayer planning to hold the land for a longer period before deciding whether to undertake construction would have a stronger position for treating the interest as investment interest expense.

Saving for a College Education

It now costs an average of more than $50,000 for a family to send a child to a four-year private university and more than $18,000 to send a child to a public university. The Education Department estimates that in 2007 the total cost of attendance will increase to $200,000 for a private university and $60,000 for a public university.

These statistics, cited by a Treasury Department official in testimony before the Senate Finance Committee in 1988, spotlight a major financial dilemma facing parents: how to pay for sending their children to college.

The Finance Committee's purpose in holding the hearing was to explore the feasibility of several proposed tax incentives to help parents save for college expenses. One of those proposals—a special tax break on Series EE savings bonds—became effective January 1, 1990. Interest on these bonds accrues tax free until redemption. This by itself would provide no new tax advantage since Series EE savings bonds have always offered that feature. What is new is that when the bonds are redeemed, the accumulated interest will be exempt from tax if the bond proceeds are used to pay postsecondary educational expenses of the taxpayer or the taxpayer's spouse, children, or other dependents. If the proceeds are not used for this purpose, the interest will be taxable upon redemption.

The exemption from tax on redemption is

phased out for high-income taxpayers. For joint filers, the phase-out begins at $60,000 of modified adjusted gross income (MAGI) and is complete at $90,000 of MAGI. For unmarried individuals, the phase-out range is between $40,000 and $55,000 of MAGI. MAGI generally is adjusted gross income modified by adding back certain exclusions. The phase-out ranges will be indexed for inflation starting in 1991. Married taxpayers who file separate returns are not eligible to claim the exclusion.

For you to qualify for the exclusion, the bonds must be issued either in your name as sole owner or in your name and your spouse's name as co-owners. You also must be at least twenty-four years old before the date the bonds are issued.

To be excludable, interest on qualified bonds must be used to pay qualified educational expenses during the same year the bonds are redeemed. Qualified expenses consist solely of tuition and required fees at eligible educational institutions.

Several limits apply to the exclusion. First, qualified expenses do not include amounts spent for courses involving sports, games, or hobbies unless part of a degree program. Second, if the year's redemption proceeds exceed the year's expenses, the excludable amount is limited proportionately. For example, if the year's expenses add up to only three quarters of the year's redemption proceeds (principal and interest), then only three quarters of the interest portion of those proceeds is excludable for that year.

Residential Interest Deduction

Loan must be secured by residence. Under current law, you can deduct interest on up to $1 million of "acquisition indebtedness"—that is, debt incurred to buy, build, or improve your principal residence or a second residence—provided you satisfy certain conditions. One condition is that the debt must be secured by the residence you are building, buying, or improving. Generally, that means that a recorded mortgage or other appropriate security instrument must be in effect. If a loan secured by your principal residence is spent on improving your second residence, or vice versa, the loan can qualify only as "home equity" indebtedness, which is subject to a $100,000 ceiling.

Note: Unlike acquisition indebtedness, home equity indebtedness does not have to be spent on any particular home or on any home at all. For example, you can use the proceeds of home equity indebtedness to finance the purchase of a car and still qualify for a full deduction as long as the loan is secured by your principal or second residence.

What happens if loan proceeds are spent on a residence but the residence-as-security requirement is not satisfied? As several IRS rulings illustrate, interest payments may be treated as nondeductible personal interest (subject to the personal interest disallowance rule). In one ruling, an individual obtained a bank loan to finance home improvements. However, the loan was secured by a mortgage on a rental building that he owned rather than on his principal or second residence. Accordingly, the IRS ruled that the interest was non-deductible personal interest.

The IRS reached the same result in a divorce settlement in which a wife purchased her husband's interest in their home. She made a cash down payment and gave him her unsecured promissory note for the balance. Citing the statutory requirement that the debt be secured by a principal or second residence, the IRS held that interest on the note would not qualify as deductible residential interest. Similar rulings have been issued to other taxpayers who secured loans to purchase or improve principal residences with savings accounts or an annuity account. Either a principal or second residence must secure the loan or none of the interest is residential interest. The IRS allows no exceptions to the rule.

Does this mean that every home improvement loan should be secured by a mortgage on your home? Not necessarily. There may be valid nontax reasons for avoiding a mortgage even though the interest deduction will be lost. For example, the cost of creating a mortgage or establishing a home equity line of credit may exceed the value of the interest deductions; or the potential adverse legal consequences of placing a mortgage on your home may outweigh the tax benefits.

In other situations, such as a longer-term loan involving the payment of substantial interest, it may be advantageous to secure a home improvement loan with a mortgage to ensure

deductibility of the interest. Your tax adviser can assist you in evaluating the alternatives.

Expenses Incurred in Selling Your Home

A sure sign of spring is the appearance of "For Sale" signs on front lawns. If you are planning to sell your home, you'll probably incur a number of sale-related expenses. How they'll be treated for tax purposes will depend on how the expense is categorized.

Capital improvements. Any improvement to your home, outbuildings, or yard with a useful life of more than one year is a capital improvement. The cost is added to your basis in your home and enters into the determination of gain or loss on the sale. Typical capital improvements made in preparing a home for sale include landscaping, replacing the roof, or installing new wall-to-wall carpeting.

Repairs and cosmetic expenses. As a general rule expenditures that do not rise to the level of capital improvements, such as repairs, maintenance, painting, wallpapering, carpet cleaning, floor refinishing, and other cosmetic activities to improve the appearance of your home, may neither be added to your basis nor deducted as selling expenses. Such expenses are deductible as operating expenses or selling expenses for business, rental, or investment property but not for a personal residence. However, for sellers who buy a replacement home within two years of sale, there is a special rule for expenditures that qualify as "fixing-up" expenses.

Fixing-up expenses. If you sell your principal residence at a gain and replace it within two years before or after the date of sale, the gain is taxable only to the extent that the adjusted sales price of the old residence exceeds the purchase price of the new residence. In computing the adjusted sales price of the old residence you may deduct "fixing-up" expenses. This provision in the gain rollover rule is an exception to the general rule that repairs and other noncapital expenditures are not deductible as selling expenses for personal residences.

To qualify for a fixing-up expense:

The expenditure must be for work performed on the home to assist in its sale.

The work must be performed during the ninety-day period ending on the day the buyer and seller enter into a contract for the sale of the home.

The expense must be paid by the thirtieth day after the date on which the sale closes.

The expense must not be allowable as a deduction in computing taxable income

The expense must not have already been taken into account in computing the amount realized from the sale of the home.

The key point to remember about fixing-up expenses is that they are deductible in computing the adjusted sales price of the old residence only if you buy a replacement residence within two years. In all other cases they are not deductible in computing the gain on the sale of a personal residence.

Selling expenses. Selling expenses are the costs incurred to bring about the sale of your home other than for work done on the home. They are deductible in computing gain on the sale. Typical selling expenses include broker commissions, attorney fees, advertising costs, any points paid by the seller, and the seller's share of closing costs. However, any of these costs that are deducted as moving expenses cannot also be claimed as selling expenses. No double deduction is allowed.

Sale of Property to a Family Member

A sale of property between family members can be subject to much more stringent tax rules than a sale between unrelated parties. Being aware of these rules can help you avoid potential tax traps.

The most common issue that the IRS raises regarding an intrafamily sale is whether the purchaser has paid an arm's-length price. To illustrate the problem, assume that parents own a vacation home that they purchased years ago for $20,000. It's now worth $150,000. They sell it to their son for their cost, $20,000. Although parents may view the transaction as merely a break-even sale, the

IRS would see it as part sale and part gift. Since the sales price is equal to the parents' basis, no gain would be recognized. However, the transfer of the property would be treated as a $130,000 gift (excess of the value of the property over the amount paid by the son). A substantial gift-tax liability could result.

From a planning perspective, two points should be kept in mind about sales prices. First, if you intend an arm's-length sale, document that the property is being sold at its fair market value. Have it appraised or obtain supporting data on comparable sales. Second, if the transaction really is partially a gift, structure it to take advantage of the available planning techniques to avoid gift tax. In the foregoing example, the parents could eliminate any potential gift-tax liability by transferring ownership to their son in stages over a period of several years. If the son is married, the parents could transfer ownership over a shorter period of time by making the gifts to both the son and his wife.

Another trap is that you cannot deduct any loss incurred on a sale to your spouse, brother, sister, ancestor, or lineal descendant. Under certain circumstances, the restriction can also apply to a loss on a sale to an in-law or a spouse's child by a former marriage. However, if the purchaser later resells the property at a gain, the gain will be recognized only to the extent that it exceeds the amount of your nondeductible loss. For example, stock that you purchased for $10,000 has declined in value to $7,000. You sell it to your son for $7,000. The loss is not deductible. Subsequently, the stock increases in value and your son sells it for $15,000. His reportable gain is $5,000 ($15,000 selling price minus the sum of his $7,000 cost and your $3,000 nondeductible loss).

The easiest way to avoid the nondeductibility problem is to avoid selling loss property to any member of the "tainted" class of relatives. However, a prearranged plan to sell to a third party who in turn will sell to the relative is unlikely to avoid the nondeductibility rule, which applies to indirect sales as well as direct sales.

Even selling property at a gain to a "tainted" family member can create a problem in certain situations. If you sell property in an installment sale to a family member who later resells it before the installment obligation is fully paid, the resale may trigger recognition of any deferred installment gain.

With careful planning you can avoid or minimize the adverse impact of all the restrictions on intrafamily property transactions. However, unpleasant surprises can await an uninformed seller.

Tax Benefits Can Reduce Child Care Expenses of Working Parents

Day-care for children can be a major expense for working parents; generally it is a nondeductible personal expenditure. However, for working parents who incur employ-

169

ment-related child care expenses, two special tax provisions can help reduce the net out-of-pocket cost.

Tax credit for dependent care expenses. Certain employment-related day-care expenses for dependent children under thirteen (or older, if physically or mentally incapable of self-care) qualify for a tax credit. For taxpayers with adjusted gross income in excess of $28,000 the credit is 20 percent of up to $2,400 of day-care expenses for one child or up to $4,800 for two or more children. Thus, the maximum credit for taxpayers at that income level is $480 for one child or $960 for two or more children. Eligible expenses are limited to the amount of the taxpayer's earned income. For married couples, eligible expenses cannot exceed the earnings of the lower paid spouse. The cost of sending a child to overnight camp is ineligible for the credit. Payments to a relative (other than a dependent of the taxpayer) can qualify.

Example 1: Bob and Ellen pay Ellen's mother $200 per month to care for three-year-old Bob, Jr., while Ellen and Bob are at work. Both earn more than $2,400 annually. Assuming that Ellen's mother is not their dependent, the payments qualify for the credit.

Exclusion for dependent care assistance plan payments. Many employers offer dependent care reimbursement accounts as part of their fringe benefit plans. Typically, these are funded with salary reduction amounts. A participating employee agrees to have his or her salary reduced by an annual amount determined by the employee. The salary reduction agreement must be entered into before the salary is earned and before the expense is incurred. The reduction amount, which approximates anticipated expenses for the year, is credited to an employer-maintained reimbursement account from which the employee's dependent care expenses are paid or reimbursed. The tax advantage of this arrangement is that an employee can exclude from income up to $5,000 per year of payments from a qualified dependent care assistance plan. By reducing the salary and converting the reduction amount to nontaxable income, qualifying child-care expenses can be paid with untaxed dollars rather than after-tax dollars. In addition, no Social Security taxes are due on the child-care reimbursements. Expenses paid or reimbursed from an employee's reimbursement account are not eligible for the dependent care expense tax credit.

Example 2: If Bob, in example 1, participates in a dependent care assistance plan, he can elect to have his salary reduced by $2,400 and have that amount credited to a reimbursement account. The account would subsequently reimburse him for his child-care payments to Ellen's mother during the year (12 × $200 = $2,400). No credit would be available.

A word of warning. Participating employees should carefully determine the amount to be shifted from salary to a child-care reimbursement account. Any unused amount remaining in an employee's account after the end of the year is forfeited. Cashing out an excess balance is not permitted.

Note: As we go to press, Congress is considering legislation that would phase out the tax benefits of the credit and the exclusion when income reaches a certain level.

Employer-Paid Parking Remains an Attractive Fringe Benefit

As the list of tax-free fringe benefits dwindles with each successive tax act, employer-paid parking remains a popular survivor. It is also one of the very few nontaxable fringes that can be awarded selectively since it is exempt from the antidiscrimination rules that apply to most fringe benefits.

An employee who currently pays for his or her own parking in a downtown business district generally will receive a greater after-tax benefit from nontaxable employer-paid parking than from receiving the same dollar amount as a taxable pay raise. A similar benefit accrues to an employer because the amount paid for employee parking does not constitute wages for purposes of Social Security (FICA) tax.

Employees may exclude from income the value of employer-paid parking whether the employer owns or rents the parking space. The exclusion applies to employer reimbursement of parking expenses paid by an employee as well as direct payments by the employer.

Payments for parking spaces at an employee's residence are not excludable. The location must be on or near the employer's business premises. Cash payments in the nature of a general transportation allowance to an employee are excludable only to the extent that the payment is actually used for parking space rental.

Some employers also use paid parking as an incentive award for employee achievement. For example, a business may rent five parking spaces in a prime location in an adjacent parking garage and award them on a monthly basis to the five highest performing employees.

Travel and Entertainment Expenses

Expenses for travel and entertainment can cause more controversy than any other item on a tax return. Proper record keeping is of critical importance.

Travel expenses incurred while away from home on business are deductible. Examples of these are airline, rail, and bus fares; meals, subject to an 80 percent limit; lodging; taxicabs from airport to hotel; telephone calls; tips; and laundry and pressing of clothing.

Travel expenses must be reasonable and necessary to the conduct of the taxpayer's business. Travel and entertainment expenses generally are scrutinized by the IRS to determine if any part of the costs is truly a personal expense. Lavish or extravagant costs for meals or lodging will not qualify as reasonable. The costs of bringing a spouse on a trip are not deductible unless his or her presence has a bona fide business purpose.

The employee must be "away from home" in order for meals and lodging to be deductible. The employee's cost of meals and lodging while not away from home are not deductible. Note that meals may be deductible as entertainment.

The IRS maintains that a person's home for tax purposes is his or her place of business or employment even though the family residence is located in a different place. If a taxpayer has two or more places of regular employment, the principal place of business is treated as the tax home for the travel expense deduction.

Foreign business travel is deductible but is subject to strict allocation rules if any part of the trip is for personal purposes. No deduction is allowed for expenses allocable to a foreign convention, seminar, or similar meeting unless the meeting is directly related to the taxpayer's trade or business, and it is determined that it is "reasonable" for the meeting to be held outside the United States (including its possessions, Canada, Mexico, and the Trust Territory of the Pacific Islands). Special limitations apply to travel expenses for ocean liners, cruise ships, or other "luxury" water transportation.

Local transportation costs incurred in the actual conduct of a trade or business are deductible even if not incurred away from home. Transportation expenses include cost of travel by air, rail, bus, taxi, and automobile. The cost of commuting between the taxpayer's residence and regular place of business is not deductible. However, the cost of transportation between the taxpayer's residence and a temporary work site (such as a client's office) may be deductible—even if the temporary work site is in the same metropolitan area as the taxpayer's regular place of business.

Meal and entertainment expenses were significantly affected by the Tax Reform Act of 1986. Prior to the 1986 Act, business meal expenses were deductible if the meal took place in an atmosphere conducive to business discussions. Under the 1986 Act, business meals are deductible only if they are directly related to the active conduct of a trade or business or, in the case of a meal directly preceding or following a substantial and bona fide business discussion, "associated with" the active conduct of a trade or business.

Entertainment expenses are subject to the same strict rules as business meals (that is, they must be directly related to or associated with the active conduct of a trade or business). In either case the active conduct of business must be the principal reason for the combined business and entertainment. No deduction is allowed for costs incurred with respect to entertainment facilities such as hunting lodges or fishing camps. An exception is made for dues paid to country clubs; and out-of-pocket food or beverage costs incurred at entertainment facilities are deductible under the general meal and entertainment rules.

The 1986 Tax Reform Act limited the deduction for meals and entertainment to 80 percent of the amount that would otherwise be deductible. This limitation also applies to food and beverage costs incurred while away from home on business.

Taxes, tips, room rentals, and parking fees must be included in total expense before applying the 20 percent reduction. If an employer reimburses an employee for meal or entertainment costs, the employer is subject to the 80 percent limitation. Limited exceptions apply to the 80 percent rule.

Both meal and entertainment costs are subject to strict substantiation and record-keeping requirements. The taxpayer's deduction will be disallowed unless the substantiation requirements are met.

Unless employee business expenses are reimbursed under an "accountable plan," they are deductible from adjusted gross income and are subject to the 2 percent floor on miscellaneous itemized deductions; any reimbursements are included in income. If reimbursed under an accountable plan—generally a plan under which your employer requires you to substantiate your expenses and to return any amounts in excess of your actual expenses—the IRS says you should neither include the reimbursement in income nor deduct the expense on your return.

Personal Estate Taxation

Estate Planning

Entrepreneurs or owners of closely held businesses should give estate planning as much consideration as income tax planning. But all too often these business owners neglect to address the issue early enough and thoroughly enough to develop workable plans.

Estate planning embraces a number of areas including the following:

Successor management. Often much of the value of a closely held company depends on the owner—his or her knowledge, ideas, drive, imagination, and contacts. Thus, owners must consider who is best suited to succeed them in both short- and long-term situations. Family members or other key people are the most likely candidates. But if they will be unavailable, it's time to develop an executive compensation strategy to attract and retain potential successors. Bonuses, qualified pension plans, stock option plans, and phantom stock plans are among the possible elements of such a strategy.

Sale of the business. In connection with estate planning, owners of closely held companies may want to consider selling their businesses. Whether you sell to relatives, employees, or a third party will determine what price you get and the terms of the agreement. The main thing to remember is that it takes a long time to sell an interest in a closely held company. You'll need to start the process long before you may want to retire.

Leveraged buyouts (LBOs) and employee stock ownership plans (ESOPs). These are two means by which an owner can sell a company to family members or key employees. In an LBO, relatives or employees make a down payment for the company, borrow the remaining money needed, and then repay the loan with the operating profit from the business. In an ESOP, employees create a trust that borrows from a bank to buy the company. The company makes tax-deductible contributions to the ESOP, which in turn repays the bank loan. An ESOP provides very significant potential tax advantages to both the seller and the employees.

Lifetime gifts to family members. Giving gifts to your children during your lifetime is one way to extract some of the value from your estate before your death, thus reducing estate taxes. Gifts of real property or securities will be taxed based on their value at the time you gave them away, not on their appreciated value upon your death.

Building a second estate. If the closely held business is a significant part of the estate, the owner may want to look for ways to take money out of the business and diversify his or her holdings. In many cases you don't want the

estate's beneficiaries to be entirely dependent on what happens to the business.

Liquidity of the estate. Once the owner determines the value of the estate, he or she must plan to create enough liquidity to pay federal and state estate taxes along with debts and funeral expenses, administration expenses, and cash bequests. If the closely held business is a significant part of the estate, the IRS does allow you to pay estate taxes over a fifteen-year period.

Section 2036(c) Estate-Freeze Provisions Replaced with Revised Gift Valuation Rules

The controversial estate-freeze rules known as section 2036(c) were repealed retroactively and replaced with a set of modified transfer tax valuation rules, as stated in the Omnibus Budget Reconciliation Act of 1990.

"The estate freeze rules were originally adopted in 1987 to prevent taxpayers from making gifts that removed future appreciation from their estates without giving up control over the estates," says Deborah Walker, KPMG Peat Marwick Washington National Tax Practice partner, who testified at congressional hearings in favor of the repeal on behalf of the AICPA. "However, the rules were severely criticized because they were overly broad and impeded the transfer of family businesses."

Unlike the former estate-freeze rules—

which taxed future appreciation by including previously transferred property in the transferor's gross estate—the new provisions impose new valuation rules to determine the transfer tax liability at the time of the transfer for certain property. The new rules use existing principles for valuation of the property. However, if a transfer involves a residual interest, it is valued by subtracting that interest from the total value of the property before the transfer. The rules focus on the valuation of the retained interest; they do not apply to publicly traded property.

The rules are generally effective for transfers and agreements entered into or substantially modified after October 8, 1990. Some of their applications are explained below.

Valuation of retained interest. A retained liquidation, put, call, or conversion right of a corporation or partnership interest is valued at zero, unless the right must be exercised at a specific time and amount. A retained distribution right, other than a periodic payment determined at a fixed rate, is valued at zero if the transferor and family members own at least 50 percent (by vote or value) of the stock of the corporation, own at least 50 percent of the capital or profits interest in a partnership, or are general partners in a limited partnership. An irrevocable election can be made to treat a retained corporate or partnership distribution right as if it were payable in amounts and at the times specified in the election. Treasury regulations will provide for appropriate transfer tax

adjustments to prevent the double taxation of rights.

To prevent taxpayers from undervaluing a transferred interest, minimum valuation rules apply to certain equity interests. "The new rules generally apply when nonpreferred ownership interests are transferred to members of your family and you retain preferred interests," notes Walker. "The rules do not apply, however, when preferred interests are transferred to younger-generation family members and nonpreferred interests are retained, commonly referred to as a reverse freeze. However, it may be possible to effectively freeze the value of common stock by creating new classes of preferred stock that depress the value of the common stock."

Transfers in trust. When transfers (other than transfers of a personal residence) are made in trust, a retained income interest is valued at zero unless the retained interest is a right to receive fixed payments or a fixed percentage of the trust's property, payable at least annually.

A joint purchase of property is treated as an acquisition of the entire property by the holder of the term interest, followed by a transfer of the remainder interest. As a result, the purchaser of a term interest is treated as making a gift of the entire property, less the amount of any consideration paid by the purchaser of the remainder.

"This provision reduces, but may not eliminate, the tax benefits of using a grantor-retained interest trust (GRIT)," says Walker. "Although the new provision may impose a high initial transfer tax cost, it may be possible to shift value to junior family members tax free to the extent the transferred asset appreciates or produces more income than market rates."

Buy-sell agreements. The value of property generally is determined without regard to any option, agreement, or other right to acquire or use the property at less than fair market value. In addition, the terms of the buy-sell agreement must be negotiated at arm's length. These requirements apply to any restriction included in a partnership or shareholder's agreement, articles of incorporation, or corporate bylaws, or implicit in the capital structure of a partnership.

Lapsing restrictions. The value of property is determined without regard to any restrictions, other than a restriction that by its terms will never lapse. In valuing the property in the estate, any right held by the decedent with respect to property includible in the gross estate that effectively lapses on the death of the decedent will be deemed exercisable by the estate. In addition, the lapse of a voting or liquidation right in a family-controlled corporation or partnership results in a transfer by gift or an inclusion in the gross estate.

Enforcement. To help the IRS enforce these rules, the gift tax statute of limitations will not expire on an undisclosed or inadequately dis-

closed transfer, regardless of whether a gift tax return was filed for other transfers the year in which the transfer occurred.

"The passage of these rules provide certainty where none has existed in recent years," says Walker. "While valuations will still be important and may be an arguable point, the taxation of transfers of remainder interests or common stock while retaining preferred stock is dictated by the new statutory provisions. Now is the ideal time to review your estate planning and determine if this new certainty makes it appropriate to make lifetime transfers."

OBRA 1990: Income Tax Rates for Trusts and Estates

To discourage the use of multiple trust arrangements, for taxable years beginning after December 31, 1990, the tax rates for trusts and estates have been compressed. Income up to $3,450 is taxed at 15 percent, while earnings in excess of that amount up to $10,350 are taxed at 28 percent. The 31 percent tax bracket applies to all income in excess of $10,350. The maximum tax on net capital gains is 28 percent. The rate for alternative minimum tax for trusts is increased to 24 percent. The itemized deduction limitation does not apply to trusts and estates.

Technical Corrections to Qualified Domestic Trust Provisions

The unlimited estate tax marital deduction generally is not allowed for the value of property passing to a noncitizen spouse. However, the deduction is allowed if property that otherwise qualifies passes to a qualified domestic trust (QDT) and a special election is made. No QDT election may be made on a return filed more than one year after the due date of the return (including extensions). However, this period ends no sooner than six months after the date of enactment. In addition, a reformation to meet the QDT requirements may be commenced any time prior to six months after the date of enactment, notwithstanding the prior filing of an estate tax return.

Observation. This change provides time for an estate to reform a marital trust to qualify for and to elect an unlimited marital deduction under the QDT exception.

8

Real Estate

Like-Kind Exchanges

Imagine selling an asset like real estate that has soared in value over the years without being taxed on the gain. "Impossible," you say. Not really. By employing a little-known transaction called the *like-kind exchange,* owners can avoid the taxes on property dispositions.

It works this way: Assume small-business owners Smith and Jones bought separate parcels of land a decade ago for $100,000 each. Today their holdings are worth $1 million and $1.1 million respectively. Because Smith prefers Jones's location and vice versa, they decide to swap. Were they to sell to each other,

Smith would be liable for a tax on $900,000 of gain and Jones on $1 million. But by exchanging the properties rather than selling them, a tax is levied only on the cash receipts paid for the properties. In this case, if Smith exchanges his land plus $100,000 for Jones's land, Jones would recognize a gain of only $100,000. Because Smith received land only, he would have no taxable gain.

The rules governing like-kind exchanges hold that no gain or loss will be recognized on the exchange of property held for productive use in a trade or business, or for investment, if such property is exchanged for property of a like kind to be held for productive use in a trade or business or for investment. As the name implies, like-kind exchanges are limited to swaps of similar types of property; real estate for real estate, trucks for trucks, machines for machines. But the assets need not be identical and therein lies the motive for many trades.

Assume that CEO Green owns a warehouse that is no longer useful to her business. Instead she needs additional office space. Rather than selling the warehouse, recognizing a gain on the property, and then purchasing an office building with after-tax dollars, she can seek to exchange the property with CEO Brown, who is up to his ears in offices but desperately in need of a warehouse. In this way both Green and Brown can apply the full, untaxed value of their properties to acquire the space they need.

Like-kind exchanges can also include raw land for developed real estate, urban properties for suburban facilities, and a computer used in a trade or business for a printer to be used in the trade or business. Interestingly, both parties to a deal need not own property at the outset in order to make an exchange. If Green owns an appreciated building lot in Rhode Island but prefers to construct a new warehouse in Colorado, she can arrange for a purchaser of her Rhode Island property to buy a comparable piece of land in Colorado and then swap. If both properties are equal in price (or close to it), the exchange will be subject to little or no tax. The technique could save Green a substantial sum of money.

But there are limits to the use of like-kind exchanges. You can't cross categories, swapping real estate for machinery or business equipment for pickup trucks. What's more, the tax-free rules don't apply to exchanges of inventory, stocks, bonds, notes, securities, or partnership interests.

Like-kind exchanges must be carefully structured. Most important, the new property must be received within 180 days after the taxpayer transfers his or her property or by the due date of his or her income tax return, whichever is sooner. Also, the new property must be identified in the exchange contract within forty-five days after the taxpayer transfers the property.

Consider these new provisions concerning like-kind exchanges:

U.S. real estate cannot be exchanged for foreign real estate. By definition, these properties are no longer "like-kind."

If there is an exchange of property between family members or between certain related businesses and the property is disposed of within two years, there will be a tax on the gain.

The Treasury has published proposed regulations that provide additional rules for exchanges of personal property and create a series of "safe harbors" for like-kind exchanges. Exchanges that fall outside the safe harbors will probably be closely scrutinized. Qualified accountants and tax attorneys can help you properly structure like-kind exchanges.

How to Cut Your Property Taxes

When it comes to business property taxes, do you know what you're paying? Are you footing your fair share or shouldering another company's burden as well? If you can't say for sure, you're not alone. Confused by property taxes, many businesses pay their bills and hope for the best. Quite often they end up enriching the tax man at their own expense.

Here are four reasons why you may be overpaying your property taxes and what you can do about it:

A common source of confusion stems from the so-called *equalization rate*. This refers to the percentage of full market value on which property assessments are based. In a jurisdiction using 50 percent equalization rate, properties would be assessed at half their market value; therefore, a factory worth $4 million would be assessed at $2 million. Here's where the confusion comes in: You see the $2 million assessment on your tax bill and feel confident that you're being taxed fairly because the factory is worth at least that amount. But with a 50 percent equalization rate, the factory is actually assessed at $4 million. If that's above the property's value, you're being overtaxed. The point here is that you'll want both an independent appraisal of the property's value and an explanation of the local equalization rate. With this ammunition in hand, you may be able to win a tax reduction.

Mistakes and carelessness can add dollars to your tax bill. Perhaps the assessor figured the wrong dimensions for a store's footage. The retailer believed his tax bill was out of line and he asked consultants to look into the matter. Their findings confirmed his suspicions: In calculating the store's square footage, the assessor included a substantial section of space that belonged to the shopping center, not the merchant. This innocent mistake inflated the store's assessment by 25 percent.

Changes in a property's status such as the destruction or demolition of a back office or a warehouse are not always reflected in the assessor's records. As a result, the assessment fails to take into account the property's reduced value. Companies can correct this by informing tax authorities of any material changes in their facilities.

CEOs often overlook technical adjustments that can reduce their properties' tax assessment. Assume, for example, that a retail store suffers a sharp decline in sales when competitors open shop in a spanking new mall a mile away. By proving that competition has cut deeply into revenues the retailer may qualify for a reduced assessment based on "economic hardship." Also, when part of a facility is no longer useful to a business because it is either excess or abandoned space, the property may qualify for a reduced assessment based on "functional obsolescence." In either case, taxes may drop.

Property tax consultants can assist in this process. Some charge hourly fees; others work on a contingent fee basis, based on a percentage of the refund if one is claimed. Ask your lawyers or accountants for the names of reputable consultants.

Managing Real Estate Assets to Control Costs

"A company's corporate real estate is among its most valuable assets, but most U.S. firms make the mistake of treating it as overhead rather than as an investment of significant proportion," according to Peat Marwick senior manager Michael K. Plummer in Atlanta.

"Rising property values in the 1980s have resulted in U.S. companies controlling as much as $2.5 trillion in commercial and industrial real estate assets," says Plummer. "These assets typically account for 25 percent of a company's total book value but may represent as much as 50 percent of its total market value." Clearly, no company of any size can afford *not* to identify and control the costs—and the potential risks—associated with its real estate assets. Indeed, such an effort should be a priority for all businesspeople.

Studies support strategic management. The concept of strategic real estate asset management developed as property values grew during the last ten years, and it is only beginning to take hold. The National Association of Corporate Real Estate Executives (NACORE) sponsored two significant studies of U.S. corporations' attitudes toward the management of corporate real estate assets. The first study was conducted by Harvard University in 1981, the second by the Massachusetts Institute of Technology in 1987. Their findings are relevant for companies of all sizes.

"Attitudes toward real estate asset management improved very little, if at all, in the six years between the two studies," notes Plummer. "In fact, one of the most significant conclusions of both studies is that large numbers of corporate real estate managers do not maintain adequate information on their real estate assets." One in four does not maintain a current, consolidated record of all owned and leased properties. One in four is uncertain of the market value of the organization's real estate, and one in three is uncertain of the acquisition costs, information necessary to obtain accurate property tax assessments, and adequate insurance coverage.

Developing a real estate inventory. A properly designed real estate inventory is a principal device for the appraisal of a company's resources, strengths, and weaknesses. It assists in protecting the company's assets by enabling senior management to identify operations or properties that need attention. Information as basic as who is responsible for maintenance and repair—the owner, the tenant, or the property manager—as well as a record of these activities should be included in an inventory.

Real estate inventorying generally focuses on the dollar value and utility of real estate, providing estimates of fair market value for owned properties and comparable rent figures for leased properties. The inventory provides information about book value, property tax values and payments, and cash investments as well as debt and equity positions. Such a record helps prevent potential losses resulting from selling property below market value or making inappropriate investment decisions as a result of inaccurate information.

Management should periodically review and update its real estate inventory. Property values may have changed as a result of capital improvements, market conditions, or neighborhood shifts, all of which must be reflected in property-tax assessments and business insurance coverage.

9

Managing Your Technology

Computerizing Your Accounting Systems

Your company may be able to keep track of all necessary information manually or with outside processing services, but as you grow computerization becomes more practical to maintain efficiency. Most companies begin by installing a relatively low-cost microcomputer system, which is versatile and can be used for word processing, database management, spreadsheets, and general accounting—thus paying for itself in many areas.

Far too many companies practice what is known as shoebox accounting. Whenever taxes, government reports, or requests for fi-

nancial information from banks or investors are needed, they call in a bookkeeper or accountant to organize and analyze the data. Clearly, this is not a wise method. In addition to the strain on employees to drop everything and get the job done, this practice doesn't allow you to do tax planning, cash management, or other types of financial management that can save both time and money in the long run. Setting up your accounting system can occur in the following two phases—the first designed for the start-up and the second put into place as you grow.

Phase I: tracking payables, receivables, inventory, and payroll. During Phase I you need a simple, manual system for keeping track of cash flow. Generally, this comprises a checkbook register accounting system supplemented by accounts payable, accounts receivable, inventory cards, and payroll records. You'll probably require a part-time bookkeeper in Phase I. This could be your receptionist or secretary, but be sure that he or she is trained in setting up and keeping the books. Accounting is not always intuitive: consider having your bookkeeper take community college courses in accounting. You'll also need an operations manager (one of the necessary members of your initial management team) to handle inventory, order processing, and other production-oriented tasks.

Phase II. Cash management and computerization. You'll know when you're ready for Phase II—beefing up your systems—in the first month that you can't get the information you need on cash flow, order processing, or some other area. At this point you need a full-time accounting person. In Phase I you probably got by with a simple checkbook register accounting system. Now, however, you're ready for a more complete journal and ledger system that will result in a formal monthly statement of your financial position.

No matter what phase you're in, a good accounting system not only makes your internal operations run more smoothly, but it also shows outsiders (such as venture capitalists, bankers, or other investors) that you operate a viable, professionally managed company.

As you develop into a Phase II company, two important issues arise: cash management and computerization. Cash management allows you to conserve cash in order to enhance profitability. Computerization is often the most efficient way to manage all the areas of the company that influence your cash position such as accounts receivable, accounts payable, and inventory.

Computer-based information systems. Your internal systems are the "bloodline" of your company. When properly set up and managed, these systems can provide you with up-to-the-minute reports on your operations and finances as well as with the structure for a comprehensive management controls system that complies with legal requirements and sound business practices.

What does it cost you to produce your product? What sales level do you need to achieve to break even? What are your fixed and variable costs? How many days' supply of inventory do you have on hand? How many active customers do you have and how many are repeat customers? These are but a few of the questions you need to be able to answer to manage your business. Efficient and flexible administrative systems will provide you with this information on a timely and reliable basis and also help you to uncover potential problems before they materialize.

Unfortunately, many companies make the fundamental mistake of assuming that they are "too small" to worry about systems or that they "can't afford" a trained bookkeeper, controller, or operations person to manage these systems. This is shortsighted thinking and very expensive in the long run. The cost to you of not starting on day one with an integrated approach to administration and management controls will be far greater than if you do. Every time you don't know the answer to a customer's inquiry on the status of his or her order, your banker's request for an aged accounts receivable list, or an employee's question on the number of sick days he or she has accrued, you're losing time, goodwill and ultimately, money.

Accounting and other systems. You need a system that will give you an up-to-date picture of your current cash situation, inventory, and order processing in order to measure the financial status of your business. Good staffing, computerization, systems maintenance, and policies and procedures are equally important.

Reporting requirements. In addition to the administrative requirements for starting and maintaining a business, many types of business records, licenses, tax registrations, and personnel records are required by various federal, state, and/or local laws.

It is beyond the scope of this book to give you every detail on setting up and maintaining your internal systems. Rather, we intend to give you an understanding of the reasoning behind each component of a comprehensive administrative and management controls sys-

tem and why these components are so vital to your company's success.

Systems planning in a high-growth environment. As a growing company, you will have some special needs for systems. Among them are the following:

Flexibility. It is important to stay ahead of your information needs by adopting systems that can adapt as your company grows and changes.

Of course, you can't always be sure what your ongoing needs will be, but just as you would with sales projections or cash-flow projections, you can develop some well-thought-out projections about your systems needs. Talk with your outside professionals and other CEOs about their experiences.

Be sure that your initial systems are flexible and allow for growth. For example, you may purchase a phone system with a capability for more lines than you now need to allow for growth.

Ease of implementation. Your personnel will often be extremely hard-pressed for time. It seems to be almost a law that in many companies administrative duties are the first to be neglected when a crunch is on to get a product rolling and out to market. Therefore, avoid extremely complicated or unwieldy systems in favor of ones that save time and are easy to learn and maintain. For example, don't implement a complex custom database that only your computer people can understand. Rather, try to work with a packaged program that others can readily be trained to use.

Simplicity. Try to keep your systems simple and streamlined. You may think that you absolutely must have an accounts payable program that sorts invoices by date received (versus the invoiced date); but keep in mind the 80/20 rule. If the software meets 80 percent of your needs, how important is the other 20 percent? The point is that you have to examine the trade-offs between the "perfect" system and one that does the job.

Consistency. Integration of system capabilities is an important issue. If, for example, you know that eventually you want to track customer records from the time they are leads through their subsequent order processing, invoicing, and on-going customer support, you'll need to be sure that all these databases are compatible. Therefore, before you implement any systems sit down with your key people in each area of the business, compare information needs, and plan. You'll often find logical data needs that you never dreamed existed as well as ways to simplify and streamline your data systems.

Clear definition. In scores of interviews with growing companies, one issue invariably stands out. When asked what they disliked most about their jobs, virtually every employee responded, "lack of organization." They specifically cited lack of clear, written policies and procedures and disorganized in-ternal systems such as order tracking and inventory. Overwhelmingly they wanted more structure and controls to help them do more jobs efficiently.

With these general requirements in mind, let us now turn to a more detailed look at individual components of computerized systems.

Selecting and Implementing Microcomputer Systems

The importance of timely and reliable accounting information cannot be overemphasized. Maintaining a competitive edge means providing better service, containing costs, making better pricing decisions, tracking customer demand and balancing inventories, and controlling cash flow. Manual accounting systems are good for certain jobs, but have difficulty handling large volumes of data in a hurry. Microcomputers have emerged as powerful tools for accumulating and analyzing information needed when important decisions must be made. With their use, meaningful information can be assembled from today's data and used as a basis for the decision making of tomorrow.

Before considering the benefits of computer processing, it must be made clear that the computer should not be considered the total or only tool to be used in solving business problems, but it can be an aid in achieving business objectives. The microcomputer is an effective tool for streamlining operations; it is not a miracle worker.

Also, the selection and implementation of a practical and workable system for your business is not a trivial task. The process should be well thought out and should follow a well-designed plan. You must start with a clear definition of your requirements and continue through system selection, purchasing, and implementation.

Before purchasing a microcomputer and related software, you should answer the following questions:

Is the system flexible enough to expand as your business expands? For example, will a chart of accounts allowing only 100 accounts be enough for you in the future? You may not need cost and profit center reports now, but will you need them when your business doubles in size?

Is the system integrated, eliminating reentry of data? If you enter payroll information, does it automatically transfer to your general ledger?

Is the software powerful enough? Is the processing fast enough when you have hundreds of items to enter and balance? Can you get reports generated in a reasonable amount of time? *Note:* Power and speed are often functions of the computer and its operating system, not just the software.

Is the system easy to learn and use? Is the documentation complete and clear? Is it geared for the first-time or more advanced computer user? Are there "help" prompts on the screen?

What other software is available (such as database management, word processing, spreadsheets, and graphics)? Is there compatibility between systems—can you transfer files directly between word processing and databases?

Are software and hardware both available from the same vendor? Installation and support are often simplified if you have to deal with only one firm.

Who will install the system? Is the software self-loading or will you require assistance from the vendor? If assistance is required, is it included in the base price?

What type of support is offered and what are the charges for it? Is there a toll-free number for support? Is support free, are you billed by the minute, or do you need to purchase a support contract?

Is the software vendor a stable, well-managed firm? Will it be in business when you need it to provide ongoing support?

Does the company provide updates on a regular basis? How are these charged? Do you pay an ongoing maintenance fee or a one-time fee when updates are available?

Are the vendor's other customers happy? Request user references and check them.

One of the things you need to remember is that people who run computer systems may understand the accounting principles, data flow, and systems operations but often have no experience in setting up a system. You, therefore, may need to hire an experienced consultant to ensure smooth installation.

Assuming you have hired and trained staff and implemented an accounting system, you are well on the way toward an efficient, profit-oriented operation. However, there is one more area you must address—that of system maintenance.

System maintenance. Always be alert to signs of system overload—on both the equipment and operating personnel. If you are constantly two weeks behind on logging in new orders, you haven't acted soon enough. Rather, you should set acceptable targets and continually monitor them. Thus, if your target on logging in orders is two working days but you're constantly slipping to three, it's time to consider adjusting your system.

Procedures for system maintenance should be documented, preferably in a manual. Each system component needs an accountable manager in charge. For example, your operations manager may be responsible for order processing and inventory and the sales manager for the customer database. System maintenance must include procedures for computer backups, periodic tests of system accuracy, and training of new employees.

Microcomputer accounting system overview. Deciding to replace all or part of your manual accounting system with a microcomputer accounting system is just the first step in a process that must be well planned and carefully carried out. With the large variety of sophisticated software available, it could be very difficult to find a software package that is right for most of your needs. Proper software selection can save you the time and money you would need for custom programming or modification of packaged software. The hardware purchase will be principally determined by the software package selected. The basic steps in the process are as follows:

Define your requirements. The selection of hardware and software should be based on the current and future needs of your organization. A planning horizon of five years is recommended.

Determine which software packages most closely meet your needs. The software should allow for growth and change without being too difficult to use initially. Here again, remember the 80/20 rule—if 80 percent of your needs are covered, how important is the remaining 20 percent?

Implementing the system. Having the best hardware and software does not guarantee the success of a system. The system you choose must become an integral part of the infrastructure of your business. The implementation of that system will require the involvement of everyone in your organization.

A microcomputer-based accounting system can be a valuable tool, allowing you to access timely information when making critical decisions. As with any other tool, its value depends upon how well you understand how to use it. Therefore, following a structured approach in selecting and implementing the system is critical in assuring the success of that system.

Which software is right for you? To find the best software for you, first take a close look at your business. Don't forget to consider the impact of future growth plans. Be sure to document your requirements so that you can check the features of the software against the requirements you have listed.

List all the activities and functions that you consider could benefit from computerization either now or in the foreseeable future (such as general ledger, accounts receivable, inventory, and sales analysis).

Consider each activity in turn and document the existing system and related procedures: identify specific problem areas; measure transaction and storage volumes, both present and future (for instance, over the next five years); and decide what you will require from a computer package in the form of reports, historical data, and budgets.

Include any other activities that may be of benefit to you, for example, financial modeling and word processing.

For each function to be performed by the computer, assign a high, medium, or low priority as follows: High priority items are essential. They are the primary motivation for seeking a computer solution. Medium priority items are desirable but not essential. Alternative methods of dealing with the problem would be acceptable, at least initially. Low priority would be assigned to the remaining items.

Once this is done, assign a priority level to the areas to be computerized. For example, accounts receivable, order entry, inventory, and accounts payable.

Financial considerations. In addition to the one-time cost of hardware and purchase price of software, the following ongoing costs should be considered:

Hardware costs. Monthly maintenance costs; consumable costs, for example, disks and ribbons; upgrade costs, for example, memory increment, additional terminals, and further storage

Software costs. Purchase price of additional individual application software packages; documentation costs; staff training costs; and implementation and support costs

Other costs. Space; procedures manuals; special furniture; and forms (such as invoices and checks)

Once your objectives and requirements have been carefully defined and the decision has been made to computerize some or all of your business activities, you will be ready to proceed to the evaluation and selection of software.

Software selection. The crucial element in the successful implementation of any computer system is the user's recognition of the important role that application software plays in the buying decision. A first-time user, when evaluating any computer system, should be primarily concerned with the quality and features of the application software, that is, the business programs within each system (accounts receivable, inventory control, and so forth). In this regard, one of the most important decisions to be made in the process of automating an accounting system is whether or not to use a software package. Ask yourself: Do the features of the software translate to benefits for my company's operations? Will using this software help the problem areas and make my operation more efficient?

Consultants who are familiar with available packages and your business can help evaluate them against your specific needs and can be helpful in your search.

Packaged software. In most cases, packaged software will offer an acceptable trade-off between functionality and those business requirements that must be satisfied. Which software comes closest to meeting your needs? Compare the software characteristics in terms of ability to meet essential requirements, ease of installation and use, quality of documenta-

tion and support, ability to accommodate growth in transaction volumes, and so forth.

A qualified consultant will be able to assist in software selection and hardware configuration. The consultant can also act as "interpreter" in discussions with dealers.

Key steps. The key steps in implementing a computer system include the following:

Assign a responsible management-level person to coordinate implementation activities.

Install the equipment.

Perform operational trials and learn the software.

Develop the chart of accounts and other coding structures to give required analyses and reports.

Define management and other reports.

Develop links with other systems.

Set up computer files and convert from the old system.

Develop procedures and controls to assure system integrity and security.

Train the user and operator and run the new system parallel to the old one.

Implementing the system. Reliable equipment, well-designed software and, even clear, understandable operating instructions do not necessarily guarantee successful implementation of a computer system. In many cases, the introduction of a computer system either has been a failure or has led to major difficulties, resulting in both delay and disillusionment. Implementing a new computer system requires a great deal of management attention and commitment.

The success of computer system implementation, like other important projects affecting your business, requires the commitment and involvement of management. There must be effective communication among everyone concerned with the project from top management to supervisors to computer operators to the users.

Protecting Your Software

Computer Viruses

Viruses can infect even the least sophisticated microcomputer systems, with potentially dangerous and costly results. Don't make the mistake of thinking your system is immune. Knowing how to avoid or alleviate the effects of a virus could ultimately save your company both time and money.

A virus is a small bit of code developed by often unknown "hackers" who attach it to software that is then legitimately loaded onto a computer's hard disk. To develop a virus requires substantial programming expertise; depending on the intention of its creator, that small bit of code can range from an innocuous message that flashes across the screen to a very destructive chain reaction. A virus can spread throughout a system and begin doing irreparable damage before operators are even aware of its presence.

Viruses rarely enter a system by way of packaged software. They are usually picked up off a file or program acquired from a public bulletin board. (Public access bulletin boards should not be confused with those operated by many software firms for their dealers' and customers' use. These bulletin boards offer shortcuts and general information to help users get the most out of their systems. Some are equipped with downloadable program correctives that can save a user a great deal of time.)

Public bulletin boards offer a variety of useful programs or files including utility programs such as hard-drive reorganizers and games and other bells and whistles. Many reputable, well-intentioned programmers place clever and helpful programs or files on public bulletin boards for the benefit of other users. Other less honorable individuals create viruses and attach them to the public programs, which are freely and frequently downloaded onto private systems. Bulletin board operators are clearly aware of this problem and many are taking extra precautions to avoid it.

In most cases computer viruses are nothing more than pranks and probably won't do real harm. In some cases, however, they are as insidious as their name indicates. They can spread from that handy little utility file you downloaded to almost every piece of software on your system or even your network. What they do varies with their creator's intent. Some just fill memory with garbage data and drag the performance of your system almost to a dead stop. Others can eat away at data or program files and eventually destroy the system.

One preventive measure is simply to forbid any employee to download files from a public-access bulletin board. However, this action may be more drastic than is necessary. Choosing carefully among the enormous range of available public bulletin boards and databases is probably a better answer.

If you choose to access a public database, download its files initially onto diskettes only. Never load them onto your hard drive or operating disk until you've run them through a virus detection program. Preventive and curative software packages are available for both Macintosh and PC-based systems. Many are offered by your computer or software dealer free of charge. These devices will detect the presence of a virus on a file and warn the user before the virus is activated. They are limited by their specific orientation to known viruses. Other software devices can eradicate the virus from your system. In most cases the combination of prevention and cure programs can safeguard your computer's health.

The best defense is still a good offense. Back up all work regularly. Keep an accurate log of what software was loaded, when it was loaded, and who loaded it. Maintain reliable and accessible storage for your original software diskettes. The companies that maintain public bulletin boards are spending large sums of money to prevent viruses. Software firms with bulletin boards are restricting access and read/write privileges. Nonetheless, business owners and systems operators must remain the first line of defense.

Protecting Computer Data: Is Your System as Secure as It Could Be?

Most businesses will never be threatened by a serious computer virus infection, but many will be plagued by more common threats to computer security such as theft, fire, or breach of confidentiality.

These problems have serious repercussions. About 43 percent of all businesses that lose their computerized data to theft or fire go out of business within six months, according to a recent *American Office Dealer* study. You can replace the hardware, but you can't always replace the data, especially valuable business records such as accounts payable and receivable.

Security exposures on business computers have grown from a theoretical threat to a very real problem during the past two years. As a result, computer protection products have become big business. Products are now available to manage passwords, restrict access to programs and data, encrypt files, manage dial-in phone lines, automate computer audits, manage program libraries, and prevent or expunge computer viruses. Before buying one or several products, consider the following questions.

What are you trying to protect? "Your first step in selecting a security system is to define carefully what information should be secured and how secure that information should be," says R. Bradley Jude, a manager in Peat Marwick's Atlanta office who is responsible for technical services consulting. "Begin by reviewing all computer applications to determine which contain data or capabilities that should be restricted. Understand what you are trying to protect the data from—disclosure, modification, or accidental loss."

Jude also recommends that companies define up to five levels of access to their mainframe computers such as the following (accompanied by sample access requirements):

Noncritical (any valid user with password)

Internal use (access limited to specific users)

Critical (access limited to specific users and logged to an audit trail)

Restricted (access logged and limited to specific users and terminals)

Registered (access logged and limited to specific terminals, users, and time periods)

Don't assign a complex system of passwords and then tape a copy to the side of the terminal—this happens a lot more often than you might think. An ideal password protection scheme allows no one other than the user access to a particular password. However, in most personal computer (PC) and minicomputer environments, the password protection scheme also allows access to a security administrator who keeps a copy of all passwords and their access rights, preferably in a fireproof safe.

How careful have you been in selecting a vendor? The major vendors of security products can be relied on to provide products free of any "back doors," or gaps in protection. In addition, you may require custom security within your applications programs. "Take at least the same care in selecting a logical access security system vendor as you would a physical security guard," says Jude.

Is compliance enforced and are employees security conscious? Whenever possible, the security system should force the user to comply with corporate policies. "For example, if computer passwords are to be changed every thirty days, the logical access system should force the user to make this change, not simply permit it," emphasizes Jude. "In addition, employees should be regularly educated in corporate security policy and they should understand their role in enforcing the policy. Take every opportunity to remind employees of this responsibility. One approach I've found effective is to ask employees to acknowledge their responsibilities in signed statements."

Will a third party review the implementation? Even the most complex access security systems depend on proper implementation controls. The people installing the system may be too close to the technology to adequately assess the project's success.

"One company I work with installed a sophisticated dial-back modem that, after entry of a password, would dial the user back at a prearranged telephone number," says Jude. "When we were asked to review the system we found that standard telephone lines were being used instead of special secure lines. In a matter of minutes we were able to dial directly into the computer, completely bypassing the new security system."

Are you making use of the PC security you already have? Every PC system includes certain basic security systems. Perhaps the most common is the "write protect" notch on a diskette. Covering this notch with a small piece of tape will prevent any accidental attempt to write on the diskette or to erase its data.

Users of DOS systems can set "read only" and "hidden" file attributes to protect particular data. The "read only" attribute keeps a file from being modified or erased. It should be used on programs and permanent data files to prevent accidental destruction. The "hidden" attribute prevents the file from being seen on most file displays, but the file can be accessed by those who know its name. Entire subdirectories may be hidden from the casual observer.

Although a determined hacker can easily circumvent these basic techniques, they provide simple safeguards against accidental damage to PC programs and data without the expense of a PC security system.

Remember also that backup procedures are the basis of any computer security system. Critical and continually updated files and databases must be backed up daily, depending on the application. The backup disks or tapes should be stored in a fireproof safe and at least once a month a copy should be made and stored off site.

Telecommunications and Office Equipment

Your Telephone System

A telecommunication system is critical to your success: It is your link with the outside world—your suppliers and your customers.

Choosing a good telcom system is increasingly complicated since the divestiture of AT&T and the subsequent rash of many new companies and technologies on the market. Many companies leave the selection to the bookkeeper or secretary. In a word, *don't.* The importance of this decision merits the involvement of you and your key employees, as we'll see.

Selecting a Telcom System

These basic steps will help you to evaluate and select a suitable telcom system:

Designate a person to be in charge of the evaluation. Choose someone who can understand both the technical and cost aspects of the system. That person also needs to be able to evaluate the current and future communications needs of each department in the company.

Perform an analysis of both your current and future telcom needs. Most Bell companies (and some others) will perform an analysis for you at no charge. All departments should be surveyed and asked these questions:

How many incoming lines do you need for customer service, for sales, for executive offices, and for production?

How many outgoing lines do you need for outbound telemarketing and sales, market research, and customer support?

Are there peak periods for different types of communications? For example, are inbound customer service calls heaviest on Monday morning? Are outbound telemarketing calls heaviest on Tuesday, Wednesday, and Thursday afternoons?

Do you need any "800" numbers, perhaps for customer service or inbound telemarketing?

Do you need codes for accounting purposes or to control access?

Do all or only some phones require hold buttons, intercoms, or conference call capability?

Do you need credit card capability for calls made away from the office?

Will you require an off-site telephone answering service? If so, during what hours? Is a telephone answering machine with remote call-in capability a better alternative?

Do any of your personnel require "beepers"? What hours and locations are required?

Do any personnel require automobile "cellular" phones? What range is required?

Since cost and range of services can vary from company to company, try to evaluate as many vendors as you can for both long-distance services and telcom equipment. Equipment must be reliable and easily maintained. Look at system expansion capability. Look for quality. Unfortunately, many of the less expensive long-distance carriers often give poor line quality. Look for connectibility.

Note: Service is very important. Be sure that your vendor can provide quick, effective turnaround. Frequent and/or extensive telcom downtime can destroy sales and customer satisfaction quicker than almost anything else.

Be sure to ask for references from both the equipment vendor and the long-distance carrier, and then take the time to carefully check them.

Your telcom system as well as other equipment—like computers, photocopiers, and typewriters—need to be kept in good working order. Thus, their maintenance is an integral part of your facilities plan.

Five Steps to Buying Your Next Telephone System

For many businesses, "deregulation" of telephone services is just another word for "confusion." With hundreds of companies now competing in what was once Ma Bell's exclusive domain, phone users are forced to choose among a dizzying array of carriers and equipment vendors. Just who to pick for what can leave you baffled.

But there is a way to simplify the process, basing the choice of telephone systems on a thorough review of the options. The idea is to break down the search to five interrelated steps that take the business from identification of its telephone needs to the selection of an appropriate vendor to service them.

The step-by-step approach helps you to resist the first sales pitch you hear, basing the decision on a more thoughtful approach. Going through the exercise prompts management to look inward first, gauging the company's communications needs. Only then does it look outward to the inventory of available hardware and systems. This way each step in the process reinforces the other.

Consider this five-step approach:

Define your needs. Before contacting a single vendor, create a blueprint for the ideal telecommunications system. Consider qualitative and quantitative factors: How can the new system enhance the company's business operations and how many phones and lines are needed to handle the work load?

In this stage it's a good idea to distribute questionnaires to your customers asking them to tell about their pet peeves in dealing with (or being frustrated by) your telephone system and soliciting their ideas for making improvements. Ask employees, vendors, and professional advisers (your lawyer, CPA, and others) to do the same. This helps to create a system that functions effectively in practice as well as in theory and that pleases those whose goodwill is important to you.

Prepare a request for proposal (RFP). This document translates the company's telecommunications needs into language that vendors can understand. It provides the raw data—including system size and required features—that vendors need to design an appropriate system and to bid on its sale and installation. Because vendors deal in a technical jargon, it is wise to work with a consultant in preparing the RFP.

Prescreen vendors. Ask trade groups, business associates, or consultants for the names of those telephone companies specializing in systems for your business or industry. Send the RFP to this select group, limiting submissions to a maximum of five vendors. Sending proposals to dozens of companies only complicates the selection process.

Create a selection matrix. In reviewing vendor bids, assign point values to each of the competitive features, service provisions, warranties, and prices. Base the final selection on that vendor with the highest point total.

Review the vendor's contract. Be certain that you have at least a one-year warranty. Also, negotiate for a nonperformance clause. This obligates the vendor to reimburse you for business losses suffered from his failure to service the system properly. If the vendor resists, make it clear that you will look elsewhere for your telecommunications needs.

Telephone consultants can work with you through all or part of the selection process. Most charge hourly fees from $100 to $250. To avoid potential conflicts of interest, make certain the consultant does not earn commissions on recommended equipment.

Seven Ways to Cut Your Phone Bills

Whoever said talk is cheap never owned a telephone. In spite of a plethora of discount long-distance services, most companies are finding their phone bills going only one way: up. Added together, the cost of calls, phones, and related services take its toll on the bottom line.

But there is a way to reverse this upward spiral. By tracking down billing errors, eliminating waste, and shopping for low-cost options, management can control what in many cases has become a runaway expense.

Check into your company's calling patterns. Recent bills will reveal who in the company is making calls and where those calls are going. Look for strange or excessive use and investigate further.

Make certain that telephone charges reflect your actual inventory of leased equipment. In many cases telephone companies remove phones from a company's premises but fail to delete the charges from its bills. When a production employee moved from an office to a warehouse job, for example, his phone changed from a desk to a wall unit. Although the phone company switched the equipment properly, both the desk and wall units remained on the bill.

Companies with telephone systems acquired some years ago on a lease-purchase plan may find that the underlying interest rates are far in excess of more attractive deals available today. Buying out the system and refinancing it with a bank loan can yield substantial savings in monthly carrying costs.

Explore alternatives to current systems. Sometimes current solutions to your telecommunications needs are the most costly. In a typical case, a CEO moving his business to a new site in the same town asked to retain his old phone number. To accommodate him, the phone company provided "foreign exchange service," meaning the system was hard-wired from one exchange to the other, a procedure that carries a substantial monthly service charge. But when a consultant reviewed the company's bills, he found that the same objective could be achieved with "call forwarding," a low-cost option that switches calls from one number to another electronically. The change saved the company $1,100 a month.

Determine if you have more telephone lines than you need. As a business grows, lines are often added to meet a projected calling demand that never materializes. Using traffic studies, which measure telephone usage during maximum periods, consultants can recommend the ideal number of lines for your business. Have the phone company remove those lines that prove to be excessive.

Take advantage of local-use package rates. Although the carriers rarely volunteer this information, most have flat-rate plans that allow for unlimited dialing in the company's immediate vicinity. Many businesses will save by switching from measured service—where a charge is levied for each call—to these bulk-rate plans.

Monitor telephone bills for evidence of calls to area code 900. Most are money-wasting abuse calls to such numbers as dial-a-joke, sports scores, and the like. Showing that you are aware of these calls and that you will penalize employees who make them, quickly halts this activity.

Ask all suppliers if they have toll-free 800 numbers. Give these numbers to em-

ployees and insist that they use them. This simple step can save hundreds or thousands of dollars a year.

Maintaining Office Equipment

All new equipment has at least one thing in common: It will get old and likely break down. Although you can't prevent that occurrence, with good preventive maintenance you can minimize the occurrence of breakdowns. Companies may be inclined to skimp on maintenance because "we don't have the time now" or "we don't have the money." However, the loss in asset value and additional downtime makes this a poor strategy.

To keep the value of your equipment high and your business running reliably, you need two types of maintenance:

Internal maintenance. Each piece of equipment needs an internal "key operator" who is responsible for routine cleaning, basic repairs not requiring outside service, training people on equipment operation, ordering supplies, and generally watching over the machine and troubleshooting any problems. Copiers and typewriters are the most common examples, but you should also include computers, production machinery, and other types of equipment.

You may have one person assigned to maintain a group of or all machines in the company, or several individuals assigned to maintain individual machines. Either way, these equipment maintenance tasks should be part of these employees' official, written job descriptions. A lot should be kept on each machine to detail any work done, by whom, and the date. Key operators are usually trained in basic maintenance at no charge by the vendor. More advanced knowledge can be obtained through formal classes and seminars offered by either the vendor or an independent firm.

Outside maintenance service. Some equipment will require an outside maintenance contract (for example, if a lease agreement requires it or the equipment is too complicated to repair in-house). Other equipment (such as a fully owned typewriter or copier) may not require a service contract, but it makes good business sense to purchase one. Generally, "as-needed" service is more expensive and slower to get than service under a regular service contract. On items such as typewriters and copiers, you almost always come out ahead on a service contract.

With some equipment you'll need to take a calculated risk to determine whether to purchase a maintenance contract. Ask yourself the following:

How often do we use the equipment?

Are employees able to perform most maintenance tasks?

Do we know a reliable vendor who will service at a reasonable time and cost on an as-needed basis?

What is the value of the equipment versus the cost of a maintenance contract?

Do we have a backup machine?

Many vendors have different levels of service contracts. Thus, if you use a machine daily and can't afford for it to be down, you may want to pay more for a "four-hour guaranteed service with a swap-out if required" or similar type of contract. If you're not as tied to the machine, you may want to pay only for "service within three days and swap-out at a nominal extra charge" or similar type of contract.

If you're dealing with a new vendor or type of equipment, ask for references from other users and check them—ideally *before* you've purchased or leased that particular equipment! This will tell you how often on average the equipment is down, what type of maintenance it requires, and the quality of service from the maintenance company.

Selecting a Maintenance Firm

There are two types of equipment maintenance firms:

Equipment manufacturers or vendors. (For example, Apple, IBM, Xerox, or the local computer dealer.) Many of these are "authorized dealers," which means that they can perform warranty work and get brand name parts more easily. Repair staffs have received approved training by the manufacturer.

Independents. Many "ex-IBMers" or "ex-Xeroxers" have gone into business for themselves. They tend to offer competitive rates. If you have several different brands of typewriters or office copiers, you may find an independent repair firm that can competently service them all at a volume discount. Potential drawbacks to using independents are the following:

Their staffs may be smaller, meaning longer response time to calls.

Their original training may become obsolete as sophisticated new machines enter the marketplace. When checking references for independents, be sure to ask what specific machines they have maintained.

The old adage "an ounce of prevention is worth a pound of cure" is especially relevant to plant and equipment decisions. If your equipment constantly malfunctions due to poor maintenance or your phone system is so overloaded that your customers can't get through or you sustain a loss through fire or theft but don't have adequate insurance, you are severely crippling your operational efficiency. Be prepared and willing to invest in preventive maintenance of your plant and equipment. They are among your most precious assets and are well worth the cost of keeping them operating efficiently.

10

The World Marketplace: Global Expansion Opportunities

In less than a year the world has seen unprecedented regional and global economic and political change. Three major trading communities have evolved: the EC (European community), North America—including the United States, Canada, and Mexico—and the Pacific Rim, dominated by Japan. Just as the United States is developing its trade policy, U.S. companies doing business or considering doing business outside the country need to develop business strategies for coping with the rapidly changing international scene. What follows is a discussion of some of the opportunities that are developing.

EC 1992

The economic unification of the European community formally takes effect in 1992, with the major initiatives to be fully implemented by January 1, 1993. However, the single market is very much a reality now. If economic integration works for the European community—and it will—it can work for other clusters of market economies.

The EC single market will comprise the twelve nations of the European community that operate without any business borders. Those nations are Belgium, Denmark, France, Germany, Italy, Luxembourg, the Netherlands, United Kingdom, Greece, Ireland, Portugal, and Spain.

The 1992 program will result in a single market with a gross national product exceeding $4 trillion. It will initially be made up of 320 million consumers bound by a single set of regulations and directives. This market will no longer be fragmented and divided by investment and financing limitations, border controls, differing technical standards, and divergent value-added tax rates and excise duties. In 1989, the United States exported $87 billion to the EC and imported $85 billion from it, resulting in a $2 billion trade surplus.

Historically, the EC has been a difficult market to penetrate for most small to midsize middle market American companies. The individual countries not only have different languages and cultures, but also:

Different customs, tariffs, and duties

Different border restrictions

Different technical and product standards

Different methods of distribution

Different currencies

Different business laws and regulations

Small or midsize U.S. companies have had extreme difficulty in dealing effectively with all these variables. Major U.S. companies recognized that these differences could present enormous problems to any firm that wanted to do business in more than one EC country. To deal with these problems, the big companies set up separate distribution or manufacturing operations in each major country or market of choice.

However, this alternative is not a viable one for smaller companies. Most U.S. exporters target niche markets, choosing one or two markets or countries in the case of Europe.

Now all of this is changing. A uniform set of standards makes trading with the EC not much different than trading with other states or with Canada. The elimination of the technical, physical, and fiscal barriers is expected to provide a very significant boost to the overall EC economy. Estimates of savings of companies based in the EC range from $190 billion to $280 billion annually. When the provisions are fully implemented, these savings will boost the EC's gross national product by at least 5 percent. This by itself is the equivalent of two to three years of satisfactory growth in a healthy economy.

The EC will be the largest single global market, providing economies of scale far beyond what any of the individual nations could offer. With that comes tremendous new opportunities for U.S. middle market companies to sell their products to this large market. It also presents them with some new problems.

Many nationally focused European firms are actively attempting to expand their operations within the EC and at the same time develop strategies that will make them more effective as global competitors with American and Japanese companies. They intend to come to the United States and compete directly with major

U.S. companies. Their midsize counterparts are likely to follow.

The leaders of the EC member states are feeling pressure from their business constituencies, which may push them to make transitional and protectionist decisions. We should have no illusions that 1992 is going to be smooth sailing, either for the member states or for foreign companies doing business within the EC.

The single European market *is* inevitable. The changes that are taking place could affect your business at any time. That means U.S. companies need to prepare now to seize the opportunities and meet the challenges of participating in this expanded market while maintaining their market share at home.

Eastern and Central Europe

Recent developments in Central and Eastern Europe have no parallel in history since the fall of the Roman Empire in the fifth century. Most people from the sections of the globe that we traditionally refer to as the "free world" are euphoric about the changes that *appear* to be taking place.

The dissolution of the Soviet Empire; a withdrawal from the occupied territories and perhaps a retreat within Russia's ancient borders; the liberation of Eastern and Central Europe; and a move toward the reintegration of a greater Europe—all were unimaginable not so many years ago.

In Western thinking, the countries of eastern and central Europe seem to be homogeneous—but of course they are not. The five main countries traditionally included Czechoslovakia, the former German Democratic Republic, Hungary, Poland, and Romania. The population is approximately 116 million, plus 280 million in the USSR. This compares with 360 million in North America, 325 million in the EC, and 200 million in the Pacific Rim (excluding Indonesia and China). The age distribution is similar to that of the United States, with 60 percent under the age of forty.

There are now many opportunities developing in the East where there once were only barriers. One barrier that seemed insurmountable was the wall between the two Germanies. Today, Germany has reunified. What started as a rolling snowball is turning into an avalanche. As a result, the former East Germans are the first to actually feel the benefit of a free market economy. The ex–East Germans, like the Soviets, had a high consumer savings rate—because no consumer products have been available for them to purchase. When currency exchange was complete, the average East German had the equivalent of U.S. $2,000.

The former East Germans also had the most productive of the Eastern and Central European economies as well as the highest standard of living. However, when the two countries reunited, the east German productivity level was one third that of the west German. What's more, the west Germans estimated that up to one third of the outdated east German plants and factories would fail within a year. In addition, the potential exists for the development of double-digit unemployment.

In spite of these adversities, the citizens of what was formerly East Germany are relatively lucky. They enjoy tremendous national commitment and support from their economically powerful and stable western counterparts. The USSR and the other Eastern and Central European countries won't have comparable economic investors or support. They will be competing among themselves as well as with every underdeveloped country around the world for every dollar of foreign investment and aid.

The countries of Eastern and Central Europe are widely diverse. However, they face similar, substantial problems in creating market-based economies. The state-run systems have precluded the development of a work ethic, which will remain a problem for many years to come. Additionally, most business is conducted in English in the EC while in Eastern Europe, German is the primary business language. American companies will need to work hard to overcome cultural and language barriers.

One problem for Americans is that EC investors will have the competitive advantage in business activities in Eastern and Central Europe. What's more, in the short term— which means five years—EC companies will be placing their own managers in Eastern and Central European companies to get them up

and running. Likewise, American companies will need to install their own staffs in any sites they may choose in Eastern or Central Europe. Large U.S. companies with EC subsidiaries will be able to position themselves in Eastern and Central Europe, perhaps as easily as EC-based companies. Those that are able to do so will certainly have a much greater advantage than American middle market companies that have no EC presence.

However, before the Eastern and Central Europeans can become consumers they must build structures to support market economies. This means building a major infrastructure of transportation, communications, and manufacturing capabilities, as well as addressing the overwhelming problems of environmental decline and pollution control. Western manufacturers of components for these industries will have significant opportunities to sell their products to Western companies investing in Eastern and Central Europe.

Japan and ASEAN

Inevitably, the future development of the Asia/ Pacific region will be affected by conditions in the United States and the EC. Increasing activities among the countries that make up ASEAN, the Association of Southeast Asian Nations, is also significant. These countries include Brunei, Indonesia, Malaysia, the Philippines, Singapore, and Thailand. Their economic interests are competitive as well as interdependent with the newly industrialized countries of the Pacific Rim—the so-called NICs, which include Hong Kong, South Korea, Taiwan, and also Singapore.

The ASEAN countries are particularly concerned about maintaining foreign investment in their countries while the world looks to the EC and Eastern and Central Europe. Most of the Asia/Pacific countries are heavily export-oriented, but they are beginning to recognize that the United States and Western Europe will not support further imbalanced trade with them. Japan and Taiwan, in particular, have adopted trade policies that encourage the import of U.S. products to balance their large U.S. export surpluses.

Many different opinions exist on how to resolve the U.S./Japan trade imbalance, but statistics show there is clearly a problem that needs to be resolved. In 1989, the United States exported $45 billion in goods to Japan and imported $94 billion in goods, leaving a Japanese trade deficit of $49 billion.

According to the U.S. Commerce Department, the Japanese trade imbalance has failed to respond to market-oriented adjustment mechanisms, contrasting to our experiences in other markets. Between 1987 and 1989, the U.S. trade deficit with the world shrank 29 percent, while the deficit with Japan declined by only 13 percent.

With U.S. imports from Japan still more than twice the level of U.S. exports, export growth must expand at a rate more than twice import growth just to hold the deficit constant. Despite export growth three times as large as import growth, the trade deficit with Japan shrank by only $2.6 billion in 1989.

In July 1989, President Bush and then–Prime Minister Uno launched the Structural Impediments Initiative "to identify and solve structural problems in both countries that stand as impediments to trade and balance of payments adjustment, with the goal of contributing to the reduction of payment imbalances." Suffice to say that these are major economic and social issues that won't be resolved overnight. However, in recent years the U.S. and Japan have reached trade agreements covering supercomputers, satellites, telecommunications, and wood products.

The U.S. Commerce Department is working hard to assist U.S. companies trading with Japan, having identified a number of "best prospects" for the Japanese market including high technologies, consumer goods such as home and office furniture and sporting equipment, health care products and technologies, and construction and transportation equipment. The Commerce Department district offices can offer more details.

China

A different turn of events took place in China in 1989. Three years ago the United States viewed the People's Republic of China as potentially the next great investment and trading opportunity for the world. Now, after the tragedy of Tiananmen Square, we see it as a country that has drawn a curtain around itself once again. Potential investors have drawn back—unsure of the future social, political, and economic course of events in that country. China may not change its infrastructure and it may continue to be isolationist for the balance of our lifetimes. Or, it could totally surprise us with tumultuous change, not unlike what is happening in Eastern Europe and the USSR.

Canada and the Free Trade Agreement

Companies that are not actively taking advantage of opportunities in Canada should realize that they are ignoring some very significant opportunities.

On January 1, 1989, the United States and Canada formed what is currently the world's largest free trading area—substantially freeing up trade in goods and services as well as investment between the two countries. The Free Trade Agreement removes, in some cases gradually over the next five to ten years, tariffs on all goods by 1998. It opens up $500 million annually in Canadian government contracts to U.S. companies and liberalizes trade in certain services including telecommunica-

tions, tourism, and architectural and financial services. It assures open investment policies, creates a more stable and predictable business environment, and streamlines border-crossing procedures. U.S. goods will be more competitive in Canada since third-country imports will not benefit under the FTA.

Originally, Canadians were concerned that this agreement could cause significant economic displacement for Canadian business. However, after the first year of implementation, both countries are so pleased with the results that many of the provisions of the FTA are now being accelerated. This will continue until the provisions are completely implemented.

Canada is the single largest market for U.S. products: The United States exported $77 billion in goods to Canada in 1989, which adds up to 70 percent of their total imports. Canada is by far the largest consumer of American products—and it has less than 10 percent of the population of the United States. Per capita, Canada buys almost ten times as many U.S. products as any other country. Major American exports include computers and telecommunications equipment, precious metals, motor vehicle engine parts and other vehicle parts, and electronic tubes and semiconductors.

Canada's geographic proximity, common language, the similarity between U.S. and Canadian distribution practices, and currency exchange stability make Canada the ideal first foreign market for new U.S. exporters. Plus, in general, the Canadians are keen on doing business with the United States.

"Middle market companies that want to develop a niche in the export marketplace would do well to consider opportunities now available in Canada because of the FTA," says John O'-Brien, a partner in Peat Marwick's Buffalo office. "Canada and the United States are already each other's largest trading partner, with total bilateral trade in goods and services exceeding $166 billion in 1987 alone. Now that the FTA has eliminated most barriers to trade Canada is the ideal starting place for U.S. companies that want to begin exporting their products or services."

Seventy-five percent of all trade between Canada and the United States was tariff-free before the FTA. The agreement calls for tariffs to be phased out on the remaining 25 percent of export business over the next ten years. Specifically:

The FTA immediately abolished tariffs on computers and computer equipment, furs and fur garments, fresh-frozen fish, animal feed, skis and skates, and whiskey. All goods must be of either American or Canadian origin.

Duties on certain other products were immediately reduced by 20 percent, with additional 20 percent reductions to be made each January 1 until 1993. These products include machinery, paint, furniture, paper and paper products, printed matter, hardwood, plywood, petroleum, and certain auto parts.

Tariffs on all other goods dropped by 10 percent and will decrease by 10 percent each year through January 1, 1998. This category includes beef, clothing and textiles, appliances, most processed foods, plastics, tires, footwear, drugs, and cosmetics.

The U.S. Department of Commerce maintains that as a result of these changes businesses and consumers on both sides of the border will benefit from economic growth, increased trade and investment, greater energy security, more jobs, lower prices, and increased global competitiveness.

"Companies will find that the FTA makes their products more price competitive," says Doug Murphy, a tax partner in Peat Marwick's Buffalo office. "American imports to Canada will be less expensive to the customer than imports from other countries." Canadian competitors will be a new factor in the American marketplace as well, a development that middle market companies should begin to consider.

The FTA will also enhance services trade since simpler border-crossing procedures will facilitate the entry of U.S. business professionals into Canada. Future Canadian laws and regulations affecting trade and investment by U.S. service providers will be nondiscriminatory. Moreover, the FTA covers a range of service sectors, including finance, insurance, health care facilities management, hotel and motel management, training, real estate, computers, advertising, and promotion.

Mexico

Opportunities are also developing with Mexico, another neighbor that middle market companies should not overlook. The Salinas administration is working hard to improve the Mexican economy and it is very open to improving relations with the United States. In fact, formal talks are beginning on a free trade agreement with Mexico, which might develop into something similar to the agreement we have with Canada.

Two years after a reduction of tariffs and the removal of most barriers to trade, Mexico remains a strong market for U.S. exporters. In fact, Mexico is now the United States's third largest trading partner after Canada and Japan. A growing economy and a favorable exchange rate combined with trade liberalization have created a great demand in Mexico for U.S.-made products.

U.S. exports to Mexico grew by 21 percent in 1989, to almost $27 billion. Two-way trading totalled $52.2 billion in 1989, nearly a 20 percent increase over the previous year.

The Mexican market is strong for all types of intermediate and capital goods as well as raw materials. This reflects the growth in investment in Mexico, which is the result of lower interest rates and increased internal demand. The recently concluded debt agreement will free even more capital for investment. Likewise, the tax treaty currently under discussion with the United States will no doubt boost the Mexican economy.

How to Get Started

Remember that whether or not you decide to expand overseas, you cannot simply ignore these international developments. To continue to be successful, you need to find out *how* world events are going to affect your business—because they *definitely* will. Even if you decide against going overseas, at least you'll be making an informed decision.

There are innumerable resources that will help you identify the most appropriate market for your product or service. The U.S. Department of Commerce (DOC) is focusing its trade efforts on small and midsize companies, especially through its International Trade Administration (ITA). Two of the ITA's units, the Office of International Economic Policy and the U.S. and Foreign Commercial Service (US&FCS) offer extensive services to U.S. firms that are interested in exporting.

The DOC maintains extensive up-to-date marketing data on thousands of individual products and markets and can provide this information for more than two hundred countries. The country desk officers of the Office of International Economic Policy can provide this marketing and other export-related information for companies that are interested in exporting.

The US&FCS has hundreds of trade professionals located in foreign markets who are dedicated to helping U.S. companies export successfully. The Department of Commerce professionals are positioned to observe first-hand the latest business, political, and government developments in local markets. They offer their services to help U.S. companies export goods and services to their markets. The overseas commercial officers can analyze local markets or conduct customized in-country studies of specific product competition. They also can help identify buyers and sales representatives and even take individual U.S. products on country-specific trade missions or catalog or video shows. Contact your district DOC office for guidance.

When investigating a foreign market, you'll need to ask yourself some of the same questions you'd ask if you were investigating a new domestic market:

Who can use the product/service and for how long?

How will the product/service be transported and distributed to these potential customers?

What are the costs of freight, packaging, and storage?

What media and personnel are available for advertising, sales promotion, publicity, and selling?

What demands will an export operation place on the company's personnel and other resources?

Must the product be modified (in terms of its quality standards, technical specifications, alternative uses, and/or price) to suit the needs of a new market?

Does serving this new market fit with the company's goals for growth and development as expressed in its business plan?

Once you've identified an appropriate foreign market, start by clearly defining your objectives for that market. Is your goal to have your company's name recognized in country X? Perhaps you are interested solely in increasing revenues, in which case you may be willing to license or distribute through other companies. Do you want to increase sales through exports or also establish a direct presence through sales, servicing, or manufacturing? What are your sales objectives for the foreign market in terms of value or market share? As part of your research you should seek to gain a better understanding of competitors' activities and strategies in the chosen market, including detailed information on distribution methods, sales agents, and joint ventures.

In general, you can choose among the three alternative strategies described below to increase your company's presence in a foreign market. You can tailor each strategy to meet your own goals and objectives as well as financial resources. You may decide to use a combination of these strategies or to progress from one scenario to another as the foreign market becomes more important to your revenues.

Selling Directly to the Foreign Market

In selling directly, the company continues to manufacture its product wholly within the United States for export. Most companies find it useful or necessary to use the services of qualified agents, representatives, or distributors with hands-on local expertise in the foreign market.

Exporting allows a company to retain total control over manufacturing, quality, and the proprietary process and manufacturing know-how that can be critical to your success. In addition, this option requires the minimum amount of additional investment capital.

As for disadvantages, the most important point to consider is that success in the foreign market may be dependent on the quality and capabilities of the agents you choose and the support, through technical training and financial resources, you provide. As in your domestic markets, sales expertise is crucial in a foreign market.

An alternative is to set up an agreement with a distributor in the foreign market who is currently distributing products that are complementary to yours. If necessary, such a distributor may also be able to assume responsibility for a certain amount of maintenance and servicing.

Joint Ventures and Co-Ventures

A joint venture or co-venture is a form of partnership between an American firm and a foreign counterpart in the host country, each with a common commercial objective. Each partner in the venture makes a significant contribution to the venture in the form of money, technical skill, and knowledge or inroads into local markets.

The key to a successful joint venture is to clearly define the company's objectives and identify a partner that will offer complementary capabilities. A joint venture may enable you to expand your knowledge and resources in a foreign market and spread the risk and establish a distribution network through your foreign partners. Further advantage is gained through the potential to use host-country export enhancement or financing facilities, as well as various forms of tax incentives.

The greatest potential disadvantage to a joint venture arrangement is that in many countries the foreign partner cannot exceed a 49 percent interest in the venture, which might threaten your managerial control of the venture and result in inferior product quality or other hazards. In practice, however, agreements can be arranged that overcome these pitfalls.

Joint ventures can be very flexible and companies may not need to invest in new facilities. For example, a venture could be structured that allowed the partners to cooperate on production and marketing using existing facilities or resources, with less emphasis on new equity. As an alternative, you may wish to consider licensing certain technologies or know-how to the partner. You may also need to consider the possibility of marketing the partner's products in the United States.

Establishing a Wholly-Owned Branch or Subsidiary Operation

This strategy requires the most substantial investment of money and senior management's time. However, with 100 percent ownership, you would also be assured of maintaining total control of the operations. Clearly, the issues involved in establishing a manufacturing or sales/servicing subsidiary are complex, including choice of location, tax treatment, financing, and, above all, financial risk.

In most cases manufacturers enter a foreign market first through export sales, progress to some type of joint venture that allows greater exposure and marketing potential, and proceed over time to establish a subsidiary operation to either complement or replace existing arrangements. You may want to consider whether a wholly-owned subsidiary is a long-term goal and, if so, how to structure arrangements that would facilitate this objective.

The Middle Market Response to Changes in the European Economies

Increased demand for American products and services overseas as well as concern about continued competitiveness at home offers small and midsize companies innumerable opportunities to begin or expand their international operations in the EC and in Central and Eastern Europe.

Middle market companies—defined by Peat Marwick as companies in the high technology, manufacturing, merchandising, and service business industries with revenues of less than $100 million—are the focus of a variety of public and private efforts encouraging American businesspeople to enter foreign markets.

Thus far, their response has been mixed, according to Charles M. Ludolph, director of the U.S. Department of Commerce Office of European Community Affairs. "A bumper sticker I saw recently provides middle market companies with a motto for the 1990s: 'Think Globally, Act Locally,'" says Ludolph. "That motto should serve as a call to action because, in general, after two years of hoopla and literally hundreds of conferences, we still find that small and medium-sized companies are neglecting to develop strategies for 1992.

"At the same time," he adds, "we've seen some extremely interesting developments, among them an effort by the National Association of Wholesalers and Distributors to develop joint ventures with European concerns, thus exporting U.S. distribution techniques, which are uniquely suited to a continental market. With yet another means of distribution in place for middle market companies, their goods should follow."

Global does not necessarily mean big, notes Peat Marwick's Francine Lamoriello, a manager in the international trade group. "Improvements in communications technology make it easy for truly small firms to spread across frontiers," she says. "They no longer need vast bureaucracies to export as they have quick and relatively cheap access to information about overseas markets."

All in all, operating internationally makes good business sense for middle market companies. "In the international arena, these companies' relatively small size is more advantageous than problematic," says Gary L. Keefe, national director of Peat Marwick's middle market services. "They often can be more flexible and alter their operations more quickly than larger organizations. Easier entry and more uniform standards in the EC will be tremendously beneficial to them. In addition, they'll be able to take advantage of opportunities for joint ventures and other alliances because as in the United States, most companies in Europe are in the middle market."

Survey Shows Developing Interest

A Peat Marwick survey of U.S. manufacturing and high technology middle market execu-tives in 1989 revealed that 63 percent of those middle market companies were conducting business in the EC. These middle market businesspeople are fairly evenly divided among those who are currently making plans for the single market (31 percent), those who are considering the impact of 1992 but have yet to do anything (35 percent), and those who are doing nothing (34 percent).

Middle market respondents who are making plans for the EC market rate (1) marketing products more broadly (61 percent), (2) creating joint ventures (57 percent), and (3) changing their distribution arrangements (44 percent) as important business strategies for responding to 1992. These companies plan to make such changes because they want major growth in the EC (53 percent) and expect to benefit internally from a single market (45 percent), not just because they believe their competitors are preparing actively for 1992 (30 percent).

Among those actively planning for 1992 and developments in Eastern Europe is Nancy Matthews, international sales manager for Georgia-based Computone, part of the World-Wide Technology Group, a computer hardware manufacturer. "We're looking forward to our business growing dramatically as a result of 1992 and subsequent developments in Eastern Europe," says Matthews, whose company currently ships one third of its products to Western Europe, where it has marketing and technical support.

"I expect our foreign sales to grow by as much as 50 percent in the next two years," says Matthews. "After recent trips to Europe I was amazed to realize that the Eastern Europeans are so well educated in the uses of sophisticated technology. Our distributors are opening offices in Berlin, Moscow, Yugoslavia, and Hungary, and we know there will be a market for our product."

Taking the Plunge

Despite public and private encouragement and assistance, middle market companies in general remain hampered by preconceived concerns about the complexities of the international arena and their capacity to enter it. In addition, S corporations may be dissuaded by what amount to export tax disincentives, which Peat Marwick Washington National Tax partner, John Raedel, believes should be of more concern to Congress than they are at present.

"The foreign sales corporation (FSC) and the interest-charge domestic international sales corporation (IC DISC) enable exporters to reduce the federal corporation tax rate on export profits, which in turn also provides permanent cash flow benefits," notes Raedel, who heads Peat Marwick's Export Shepherding program. "However, these incentives are not available to companies organized as S corporations—entities in which earnings are not taxed at the corporate level but are passed along to shareholders and taxed only at the individual rate. Since middle market companies are often closely held firms organized as S corporations, the tax law puts them at a disadvantage."

Tax laws aside, other companies simply believe they belong on the home front—at least for now. "Many fast-growing midsize companies have such strong opportunities for growth in their domestic markets they don't have the incentive to go overseas," says Peat Marwick international practice senior manager Stan Garrison. "As with any expansion into new markets, the timing has to be right."

Bob Carr, president of Atlanta-based Executive Adventures, agrees. "It's important for a company to evolve to the point where expansion makes sense," says Carr, whose company offers management development training designed to build teamwork in corporate organizations.

"Years ago a European businessman told me we should expand our operations in Europe, but the time wasn't right until recently," he says. "You don't want to lose your U.S. base of operations by moving too fast." A recent participant in a friendship tour to Soviet Georgia, Carr emphasizes that 1992 and the opening of markets in the Eastern bloc offers his company considerable new opportunities. He is making plans to open a European operation in the near future.

Peat Marwick partner James J. Tuchi understands the importance of timing; but, like Ludolph at the Commerce Department, Tuchi is concerned about whether too many middle market companies will end up waiting too long and lose their window of opportunity. "To some degree, middle market businesspeople in the United States continue to look at 1992 as a European problem," he says. "It should be perceived as a tremendous opportunity as well as a threat since EC products will eventually be priced more competitively in this country."

Indeed, a big consideration for middle market companies is how foreign competitors will affect their domestic businesses. The 1989 survey revealed that a majority of these companies would be "called to action" if EC companies were to become a more competitive force in the United States. Ludolph believes this will happen sooner rather than later, fearing for companies that fail to develop a European strategy.

"We're already operating in a global market and there's going to be a lot more competition in the United States in the years to come," he notes. "Middle market companies that rely on their U.S. market as a private preserve will be caught unaware by the inevitable influx of European competitors. We're already seeing midsize French and Italian manufacturers and distributors seeking to diversify in the United States. It offers them a lucrative, open market. Small and medium-size companies need both offensive and defensive strategies to cope with these developments."

Dallas Peat Marwick partner Jette Campbell finds that midsize companies tend to think 1992 doesn't affect them—until they run into an unexpected roadblock. "One of our clients is a semiconductor manufacturer with three major customers," says Campbell. "Ten to 15 percent of its sales are overseas, primarily in the EC, which is the company's fastest growing market. A purchasing agent recently told the company its products now must have 40 percent local content. Realizing the difficulty of complying with such a directive, management immediately saw the potentially adverse effects of 1992 and asked for our assistance. We're now helping them understand that local content is measured at the product level—not at the component or subassembly level—to enable them to negotiate more effectively with the purchasing agent. EC 1992 got one company's attention—which is how we often get involved."

Peat Marwick's mergers and acquisitions network is also busy dealing with middle market companies interested in allying with others overseas. "Deals done by smaller companies don't get much press, but we're seeing an increased interest among these companies in alliances and joint ventures with foreign companies," says Peat Marwick's M&A codirector Herb Adler. "Middle market companies are cautious in this area, but their caution is warranted. A joint venture is like an acquisition, except that you must try to anticipate the consequences of the deal breaking down. Companies need to look very carefully for alliances that fit their own objectives, and they must consider how to protect themselves if these arrangements don't work out."

On the other side of the coin, European midsize companies are continuing to look for partners or purchasers that will enable them to survive in the single European market. "Our figures show strong growth in middle market transactions, especially EC companies buying cross-borders within the EC," says Lamoriello. "All of this is being triggered as companies streamline and prepare for 1992."

What guarantees success for the middle market business owner overseas? "EC 1992 and the developments in Central and Eastern Europe cannot be ignored," says Keefe. "Middle market companies need to learn how these developments are going to affect their businesses, so that if they ultimately decide against expanding transcontinentally they will be making informed decisions."

Maquiladoras

Middle market manufacturers have been among the significant number of domestic and international companies that have established assembly operations in Mexico in recent years. These facilities are part of the Mexican *maquiladora* (twin-plant or in-bond assembly) industry, a government-sponsored program that is an attractive alternative to the distant locations manufacturers have otherwise used to secure the benefits of low-cost labor.

The Mexican government designed the *maquiladora* program to eliminate traditional barriers to doing business in Mexico. Under a series of laws intended to encourage foreign investment in local assembly plants, the government permits 100 percent foreign ownership and duty-free importation of raw materials, components, machinery, and equipment as long as the end-product is exported. Mexico's proximity to the United States, permitting easier supervision and reduced inventory costs, provides American firms access to offshore manufacturing in one of the world's premier cost-competitive labor centers.

The products manufactured in *maquiladora* plants include integrated circuits, wiring assemblies, automotive and computer harnesses, disk drives and floppy disks, radio and television components, multilayer ceramic capacitors, precision instruments, pacemakers, and hearing aids. Apparel and other textile products are also assembled in these plants.

Second only to petroleum as a generator of foreign currency in Mexico, the *maquiladora* industry currently employs 450,000 workers in more than 1,800 plants. Moreover, the Mexican government estimates that the industry indirectly supports another 750,000 people. The number of *maquiladora* plants has increased by a minimum annual rate of between 10 percent and 14 percent, so that by the year 2000 the Mexican government estimates that the industry will employ three times as many people as it does today. Assembly wages including full benefits currently average U.S. $1.10 per hour.

In the program's early years, production sharing in Mexico was principally used by the large multinational corporations including General Electric, RCA, Ford, Philips Petroleum, and General Motors. As the global economy has spurred international competitiveness, however, middle market manufacturers have become major participants.

Foreign Credit Insurance

If you've always eyed the export market with a mix of envy and fear—aware of its potential but wary of its risks—you may want to take a second look. A little-known service backed by the federal government can help you boost the rewards and reduce the risk exposure of export sales. It works by insuring export receivables against commercial and political losses.

Available through the Foreign Credit Insurance Association (FCIA), a private agency operating in association with the Export-Import Bank, the service helps U.S. companies compete more effectively in foreign markets. The FCIA offers four different types of policies for small businesses.

New-to-export policies. Designed for companies first getting their feet wet in foreign markets or with limited experience in exporting, new-to-export policies combine insurance with administrative assistance in conducting export sales. Available to fledgling exporters with average export credit sales of less than $750,000 during the past two years, these policies cover receivables for 95 percent of commercial losses (due to the customer's bankruptcy, insolvency, or default) and 100 percent of political losses due to the customer's inability to pay because of war, insurrection, or dollar inconvertibility.

"This policy takes the risk out of long-distance credit and collections," says Carl Nederman, vice president of FCIA. "In each case the FCIA reviews the creditworthiness of the foreign buyer before a sale is made. Once we approve the extension of credit, an endorsement is made on the exporter's policy showing the full extent of his coverage on the transaction. In effect, the policyholder gains from our years of experience in exporting."

Rates for new-to-export coverage vary with the customer's classification (private companies are the highest risk, government agencies are the lowest) and the terms of the sale (the longer the payment schedule, the greater the cost of coverage). Premiums for the highest-risk transactions are $1.88 per $100 of gross invoice value, but this rate can drop to $0.80 per $100 for the lowest-risk sales.

New-to-export policies are good until a company's annual export credit sales exceed $1 million; then it must convert to another type of coverage.

Umbrella policies. These gather a group of exporters under the umbrella of a single policy administered by a third party, generally a state agency or trade association, which assumes all of the clerical responsibilities associated with the coverage. The administrator prepares credit statements, files shipment reports, and pays the premiums. The exporter has no discretion in granting credit.

Premiums are the same as for new-to-export policies, but administrators will sometimes add a service charge. Umbrella policies are available to companies with average export credit sales of $2 million or less over the most recent two years.

Multibuyer export credit insurance policies. These policies can give experienced exporters substantial discretion in making credit decisions. The coverage is written with deductibles that must be satisfied before the insurance proceeds are paid. Premiums average $0.75 per $100 of invoice value.

Short-term single-buyer policies. These are designed for those cases when an exporter wishes to insure a single-buyer relationship rather than a series of export customers. The policy—which carries a minimum premium—covers credit terms for up to one year.

"Our policies can be used as marketing tools," Nederman adds. "That's because with this policy you have the ability to extend credit terms. For example, assume a U.S. exporter sells widgets to an English customer on thirty-day terms. When the customer complains that he can get ninety days from a German supplier—and will switch unless the American can match it—the U.S. exporter can use the comfort provided by the insurance policy to extend his terms to ninety days or longer if he wants. In this case the insurance helps him to increase his market share."

There is another significant advantage for FCIA-insured companies who use their accounts receivable for loan collateral. Foreign receivables are normally excluded from a company's collateral base, reducing the amount that it may borrow against the accounts receivable. Most lenders, however, will advance funds on accounts receivable that are covered under Foreign Credit Insurance.

For more information on the Foreign Credit Insurance Association, write to the association at 40 Rector Street, New York, N.Y. 10006, or call 212-306-5000.

Export Controls

A high-technology company or other middle market business seeking to enter the export marketplace may find that its particular product or commodity is subject to specific export controls imposed by the U.S. Department of Commerce. The Export Administration Act of 1979 calls for these controls to apply in the following situations:

"Where the exports would make a significant contribution to the military potential of any other country [that] would prove detrimental to the United States"

"Where necessary to further the foreign policy of the United States"

"Where necessary to protect the domestic economy from the excessive drain of scarce materials and to reduce the serious inflationary impact of foreign demand"

All commodities and technologies exported from the United States require an export license. There are two principal categories of export licenses—general licenses and validated licenses. An exporter must first determine which category of license applies to his or her product. Within each category of license there are various specific types of licenses, depending on the product, the destination, the end-use, and other circumstances.

Products that are not strategically significant may qualify for a general license. A general license does not involve application processing or approval from any licensing authority. The exporter simply notes the applicable general license in item 21 of the "Shippers Export Declaration." There are currently more than fifteen general licenses (for example, GDEST, G-CoCom, GTE, GTW, and so on).

Validated licenses are required for all exports for which a general license is not authorized. These licenses are in the form of a document issued by the responsible licensing authority, and must be obtained prior to shipment. There are four types of validated licenses. The Individual Validated License, or IVL, is available for the exportation of a specific quantity and value of commodities within a specified time period. Multiple shipments of unspecified quantities of commodities may be made under the terms of one of the remaining three validated license types, known collectively as "bulk" licenses. These licenses are all alternatives to the IVL and may benefit the

client depending on the circumstances: The Project License, which is generally applicable to exports in support of a specific project abroad; the Distribution License, which allows unrestricted quantities of commodities to be shipped to multiple preapproved consignees; and the Service Supply License, which allows shipments of replacement parts for previously exported items.

The Distribution License represents a significant logistical advantage for the frequent exporter; without it, the exporter must submit a separate application for an Individual Validated License for each shipment. However, the Distribution License application and approval process is difficult for both the applicant and the government issuer; therefore, a company cannot qualify unless it can show that it expects to export in substantial volume.

The Distribution License is a privilege that places a high degree of responsibility on participating exporters. It subjects holders to periodic reviews by the Department of Commerce and requires them to monitor their own systems as well as to review the internal control procedures of their foreign consignees. Failure of a holder or its foreign consignees to maintain a high standard of compliance may result in loss of the license or, in extreme cases, loss of all export privileges.

When reviewing an application for a Distribution License, the Department of Commerce's Bureau of Export Administration will consider such factors as:

Will the Distribution License replace at least twenty-five Individual Validated Licenses in its first year of operation? Commerce officials will not go to the trouble of issuing a Distribution License unless doing so will very likely result in measurable time savings.

Does the applicant have at least three foreign consignees who will receive shipments under the license?

Has the applicant adopted an internal control plan as required in the regulations?

The latter requirement calls for the license holder to implement a thirteen-point internal control plan for ensuring compliance with export regulations. Elements include record-keeping requirements; education and training requirements; a system of screening for unauthorized consignees; a system for assuring compliance with nuclear end-use restrictions; and an internal audit system to verify each foreign consignee's compliance with its own ten-point control plan, which it is required to implement.

For many prospective licensees, the foreign consignee audit requirement is the most daunting aspect of compliance. When the license holder owns or has an interest in its foreign consignees, auditing those consignees and ensuring their compliance is usually manageable; but such is often not the case when the consignee is an unrelated entity.

Duty Drawback

American companies that export their products overseas may have refunds coming from the federal government in the form of "duty drawback" benefits. The U.S. Customs Service estimates that many millions of drawback dollars go unclaimed each year due in part to exporters' lack of awareness of the program.

Customs regulations provide that 99 percent of the duty paid on imported merchandise may be refunded to the exporter when the merchandise is exported either in the same condition as imported or after it is incorporated into other merchandise.

These cash refunds are available to exporters in a broad range of industries including the high-technology, apparel, chemicals, boating, and fresh and prepared foods industries. In addition, the refunds are available to exporters even if they were not the importers of the articles being exported.

The drawback regulations are quite technical, but their most important provisions are summarized as follows:

First-time claimants may be entitled to refunds on exports shipped up to three years prior to the date of the claim. This provides the claimant with three years' worth of duty drawback opportunity, which even for relatively small companies may be worth the effort to make the claim.

The exporter is not required to be the importer of the duty-paid merchandise. The regulations assume that the duty paid by the importer is passed through to any purchaser of the merchandise. Therefore, if an exporter purchased imported, duty-paid merchandise that he or she subsequently exported, the duty drawback benefit accrues to that exporter.

Under the rules governing "substitution drawback," an exporter may claim drawback funds on exported merchandise that does not, in fact, contain imported merchandise. For example, assume that a computer manufacturer purchases a particular component from both domestic and foreign sources and that the domestic and foreign components are interchangeable in the manufacturing process. Exports of finished computers containing these components may entitle the exporter to a drawback of the duty paid on the imported components, even if the exported computers actually contain only domestic components.

Under the accelerated payment plan administered by Customs, duty drawback claims are usually paid in three weeks or less. To participate in the accelerated payment plan, the claimant is required to post a bond with Customs in the amount of the claim. All claims are finalized after the claimant is paid and are subject to audit by Customs's regulatory audit division.

Duty drawback may not provide sufficient incentive for some companies to enter export markets, but for companies already exporting duty-paid merchandise, drawback opportunities can reduce the cost of doing business.

Index

221